# After National Democracy
# Rights, Law and Power in America
# and the New Europe

Edited by

LARS TRÄGÅRDH

OÑATI INTERNATIONAL SERIES IN LAW AND SOCIETY

A SERIES PUBLISHED FOR THE OÑATI INSTITUTE
FOR THE SOCIOLOGY OF LAW

·H A R T·
PUBLISHING

OXFORD AND PORTLAND OREGON
2004

Published in North America (US and Canada) by
Hart Publishing
c/o International Specialized Book Services
5804 NE Hassalo Street
Portland, Oregon
97213-3644
USA

Hart Publishing is a specialist legal publisher based in Oxford, England.
To order further copies of this book or to request a list of other
publications please write to:

Hart Publishing, Salters Boatyard, Folly Bridge,
Abingdon Rd, Oxford, OX1 4LB
Telephone: +44 (0) 1865 245533 Fax: +44 (0) 1865 794882
email: mail@hartpub.co.uk
WEBSITE: http//:www.hartpub.co.uk

British Library Cataloguing in Publication Data
Data Available

ISBN 1-84113-328-0 (hardback)
1-84113-329-9 (paperback)

Typeset by Olympus Infotech Pvt Ltd, India, in Sabon 10/12pt
Printed and bound in Great Britain by
TJ International, Padstow, Cornwall

# Preface and Acknowledgements

This book originated in the workshop 'After National Democracy: Rights, Law and Power in America and the New Europe' that took place at the Oñati International Institute for the Sociology of Law, in Oñati, Spain on 31 May to 2 June 2000. The author would like to thank the Oñati Institute for not only making the workshop possible but also turning it into such a pleasant experience. We all enjoyed tremendously both the beautiful surroundings and the attentive service that the Institute bestowed upon us. In particular I would like to thank Malen Gordoa and Bill Felstiner, who at various points provided assistance and advice, both before and during the workshop and afterwards as I began the arduous process of turning the workshop papers into the present anthology. I would also like to acknowledge the contributions made by Jeff Friedman and Roland Anrup, both of whom participated as enthusiastic commentators on the papers that were presented, adding a great deal to the richness of the discussion at Oñati and the subsequent revisions as we all returned home. Additionally, I especially would like to mention the crucial role played by Tony Sebok. He not only presented a paper at the workshop, but he has during the entire process been a constant source of inspiration, advice, and feedback. Although he, in the end, was not in a position to contribute a chapter to the present book, his ideas and creative spirit are nonetheless amply expressed in the volume, especially in the chapter written by Michael Delli Carpini and myself. Furthermore, Michael and I would also like to thank Sasha Soreff, whose keen intelligence and extraordinary analytical skills ensured that her research assistance went well beyond what could have reasonably been expected. Finally, I would like to add a note of thanks to Bengt Sandin for providing a peaceful yet intellectually stimulating environment during the crucial weeks when the final editing of the book manuscript was undertaken.

# Contents

# List of Contributors

**Richard Bellamy** is Professor of Government at the University of Essex and Academic Director of the ECPR. His recent publications include *Liberalism and Pluralism: Towards a Politics of Compromise* (Routledge, 1999), *Rethinking Liberalism* (Continuum, 2000) and, as co-editor, *Citizenship and Governance in the EU* (Continuum, 2001) and *The Cambridge History of Twentieth Century Political Thought* (CUP, 2003).

**Warren Breckman** is an Associate Professor of Modern European Intellectual History at the University of Pennsylvania. He is the author of *Marx, the Young Hegelians & the Origins of Radical Social Theory: Dethroning the Self* as well as numerous articles on nineteenth and twentieth-century intellectual history and political theory. He is currently writing a book titled *Adventures of the Symbolic: French Postmarxism and Democratic Theory*.

**Dario Castiglione** is Senior Lecturer in Political Theory at the University of Exeter. His main research interests are in the history and theory of political thought, European constitutionalism, and ideas of civil society. Recent publications include co-edited volumes on *The History of Political Thought in National Context* (CUP, 2001), and *The Culture of Toleration in Diverse Societies* (MUP, 2003).

**Michael X. Delli Carpini** is Dean of the Annenberg School for Communication at the University of Pennsylvania. His research explores the role of the citizen in American politics, with particular emphasis on the impact of the mass media on public opinion, political knowledge and political participation. He is author of *Stability and Change in American Politics: The Coming of Age of the Generation of the 1960s* (New York University Press, 1986) and *What Americans Know About Politics and Why It Matters* (Yale University Press, 1996), as well as numerous articles, essays and edited volumes on political communications, public opinion and political socialisation.

**Lisa Hilbink** is Assistant Professor in the Department of Political Science at the University of Minnesota. Her research interests lie at the intersection of comparative politics, public law, and political theory. She has been a Fulbright scholar in Chile and a post-doctoral fellow in the Society of Fellows in the Liberal Arts at Princeton University. She is currently completing a book manuscript on the political role of the judiciary in Chile from 1964 to 2000, and is beginning a new project on 'Judges for Democracy' organisations in Europe and Latin America.

**Lars Trägårdh** is a Visiting Scholar at the Institute for the Study of Europe at Columbia University, New York. He is currently directing a research project concerning state/civil society relations in Sweden through the Sköndal Institute in Stockholm. His most recent publications include (as editor with Nina Witoszek) *Culture and Crisis: The Case of Germany and Sweden* (Berghahn Books, 2002) and 'Sweden and the EU: Welfare State Nationalism and the Spectre of "Europe"' in Lene Hansen and Ole Waever (eds), *European Integration and National Identity: The Challenge of the Nordic States* (Routledge 2002).

**Juliet Williams** holds a joint appointment as an Assistant Professor in the Law and Society Program and the Women's Studies Program at the University of California, Santa Barbara. Her research has focused primarily on state regulation of sex, gender, and sexuality in American law and society. She has published articles in numerous scholarly journals, including *Critical Review, Women and Politics,* and *PS: Politics and Political Science,* and she is the co-editor of *Public Affairs: Politics in the Age of Sex Scandals* (Duke University Press, forthcoming).

**Daniel Wincott** is a Senior Lecturer in Political Science and International Studies at the University of Birmingham, having previously worked at the Universities of Leicester and Warwick. His research focuses on European integration and comparative public policy. He has published numerous articles in journals including the *European Law Journal, Government and Opposition, International Political Science Review, Journal of Common Market Studies, Journal of European Public Policy, Political Quarterly, Political Studies* and *Public Administration.*

# 1

## *Introduction*

### LARS TRÄGÅRDH

THE SEPTEMBER 2003 referendum in Sweden, in which the introduction of the Euro was rejected, is but one in a series of votes that has signaled a gap between an EU enthusiastic elite and a nationally minded and EU sceptic 'people'. Indeed, the recent Convention on the Future of Europe is, as Richard Bellamy and Dario Castiglione point out in their contribution to this volume 'the culmination of a decade long concern with the EU's legitimacy', starting with the Treaty of Maastricht and the ensuing problems in getting the treaty approved at the national level. However, the legitimacy crisis of the EU cannot simply be understood in terms of the constitutional deficiencies of the EU. Rather, the EU, far from being the root cause of the crisis, is itself at heart a sometimes principled, sometimes *ad hoc*, sometimes inchoate expression of, and response to, trends that for a long time have undermined and challenged the ruling paradigm of what we call 'national democracy'. More specifically, this challenge to national democracy is occurring at several levels: political context, ideological currents, polity identity, and regime structure. In terms of context we are dealing with a shift towards a transnational market society, in terms of ideology we are in the throes of both a new kind of individualism and of identity politics, in terms of polity we no longer have an even remotely homogeneous nation or people, and in terms of regime, the formerly hegemonic form — parliamentary democracy — is no longer sufficiently responsive to the new demands coming from a new polity operating in a new political and economic context.

In this book we will attempt to understand from a variety of perspectives what these trends are, and to consider the normative and constitutional stakes as the EU embarks on what at times appears as a make it or break it attempt at addressing and mastering the legitimacy crisis by replacing a set of agreements grown piecemeal through a process of intergovernmental negotiation to a more coherent, democratic, and federal constitution proper.

But first, let us briefly consider the broad secular trends that inform both the current crisis and the attempts at response through constitution making. One obvious starting point is the phenomenon commonly referred to — often rather abstractly — as 'globalization'. While globalisation is hardly a new phenomenon, it is still the case that during the high age of nation-statism, stretching from the nineteenth through the twentieth centuries, national democracy at least temporarily served to contain the perceived threat of a globalisatised market society by strengthening the power of the state and giving primacy to politics over economics. However, the end of the fascist and communist challenges to the Western way of combining free market capitalism with liberal democracy paradoxically has served to expose the radical tension that exists between politics — the imperatives of national democracy and social solidarity–and economics — the logic of the transnational market and the ethos of individualistic, economic man — that had been largely covered over during the Cold War struggle against Communism. Today, as a result, it has become commonplace to speak of increasing challenges to the nation-state itself. The 'imagined community' of the nation, which served as the affective basis for the post-French Revolution social contract, as well as its modern institutional counter-part, the welfare state, are now, many observers argue, under critical duress as states lose control over what once was referred to as the 'national economies'.

So dramatic are the processes under way perceived to be that they have led otherwise prudent political scientists to turn to the idiom of 'postmodernity', meaning in the context of international relations theory first and foremost 'post-sovereignty'. Thus John Ruggie has argued that what he sees as 'the unbundling of territoriality' — ie the incipient decoupling of sovereignty and (nation) state — constitutes 'nothing less than the emergence of the first truly postmodern international form' (Ruggie 1993, 171ff). Similarly, Saskia Sassen notes that in the process of globalisation the notion of a 'national economy' has come to be replaced with that of a 'global economy'. As a consequence, she argues that while sovereignty and territory very much 'remain key features of the international system', they have been 'reconstituted and partly displaced on to other institutional areas outside the state'. Thus, she concludes, 'sovereignty has been decentered and territory partly de-nationalised' (Sassen 1995, 34). From our point of view, this undermining of national sovereignty over the economy has the crucial consequence of narrowing the field within which national politics matter. Without the power of purse, the national governments, and the citizens who elect the parliaments from which such governments issue, play a less important role than before. Power shifts from national political institutions, such as the parliaments, to international economic organisations, such as the World Bank, the IMF, or the World Trade Organisation; economic policy is decoupled from national politics, and politics as such is consequently devalued and in the place of national political communities we see the rise of a global market society.

In the case of Europe this process can be thought of more narrowly as 'Europeanization', and as located more precisely within the concrete institutional framework of the EU. Indeed, whereas it has become commonplace to either bemoan or celebrate the decline of the nation-state and the rise of the global 'network society', as Manuel Castells put it in his influential three volume enterprise, or the de-centered 'Empire', as Michael Hardt and Antonio Negri called it in their equally commented upon book, 'it has also been noted that Europe represents a special case' (Castells 2000; Hardt and Negri 2000). According to Ole Wæver, a leading student of the travails of the 'New Europe', Western Europe is probably the part of the world that currently exhibits 'the most advanced case of border fluidity and transgression of sovereignty' (Wæver 1995, 1). That is, while at the global level the processes are chiefly economical, particularly since the remaining superpower — the United States — steadfastly and jealously is guarding its national sovereignty, in Europe the process also involves the political and politico-legal structures. While the EU started as an attempt at constructing a European wide market society (without deeply engaging in how such a construction would challenge national democracy), it is today openly concerned with itself as a democratic political regime.[1] Thus it is not simply that the European nation-states are losing control over their (formerly) national economies; they are also actively involved in setting up a common constitutional regime that even if it cannot (yet) be described as a true federation along the lines of the US, it is also clearly more than a mere inter-governmental organisation, such as the UN.

The move towards constitutionalisation must, as we have argued, be understood as an attempt at reasserting the power of politics in relation to the market, as a way of addressing the increasing concern over the 'democratic deficit'. However, in widening the ambition in this manner, this effort opens up the question of legitimacy, that is, of how well the regime 'fits' the polity, and how well it responds to the demands and concerns of 'the people'. And here it must be noted that 'the people' must be understood both as *demos* and as *ethnos*. Thus resistance to the EU has been associated not only with left-wing opposition to an EU viewed as lacking in democratic institutions, but also with the rise of right-wing, neo-nationalist parties hostile to the EU-project for xenophobic reasons. Indeed, as the Swedish referendum rejecting the Euro indicated, it is often impossible to de-couple the (positive) democratic and (odious) nationalist sentiments that often are fused in what is perceived as an unholy alliance against the European Project. This is particularly alarming since the very idea of a constitutional convention at the European level suggest that this attempt at redressing the balance between politics and the market indeed involves the emergence of a

---

[1] To be fair, the EU project from the outset had a normative and political side, most often cast in terms of the peace argument, grounded in the experience of the two world wars and formulated as a desire to create conditions that ensured that there 'never was to be a war again in Europe'. However, as important as this is, in practice the EU before the Maastricht Treaty can primarily be understood in terms of a project devoted to economic integration.

'United States of Europe', by necessity created at further expense of national sovereignty and thus of national democracy and social solidarity at the national level. The construction of such a large democratic political regime — indeed, even larger than the Unites States of America — implies less, not more, space for the kind of substantive democracy that has been associated with the smaller and relatively homogenous nation-states of Old Europe.

Here it should be recalled that the European welfare state was from the very outset a profoundly national project, based on a social contract that ultimately rested on the social imaginary of the nation. The nation thus served as the affective basis for an order that asked from individuals that they pay taxes and make other sacrifices in the name of national community, in return for a plethora of social rights such as health care, schooling, pensions, etc.[2] The EU polity, on the other hand, consists of a much more diverse population, and the corresponding political regime, while including voting for a representative body, is today and is likely to remain radically different from traditional European parliamentary and majoritarian democracy. Furthermore, the population that is not simply more diverse but also made up of individuals who are less inclined to accept the primacy of the social and national good over the pursuit of individual happiness and minority interests.

This is the second aspect of the secular trend that is providing the context for both the crisis of national democracy and the constitutionalisation of the EU, namely the rise of the modern individual, with his and her insistence on a right to pursue a chosen individual life-style with a maximum of freedom from constraints imposed by collective traditions and institutions in general and the state in particular. In fact, modern individualism is the other side of the same general secular trend that we just discussed under the heading of globalisation, for it is through the market society that the modern individual emerges, and it is the ethos of economic and political liberalism that gives primacy to the individual in both political and economic terms. The global market society thus at the one and the same time threatens the power and legitimacy of the nation-state and emancipates, after a fashion, the individual. At the same time the individuals who thus resist the uniform identity of the imagined community of the nation do not necessarily choose the path of atomised individualism, but paradoxically express resistance to narrow national identity by embracing alternate forms of group identity based on gender, sexuality, ethnicity and other forms of identity. The result is

---

[2] The darker side of this order was a practice of normalising or excluding 'the other', both 'foreigners' and those deemed as socially abnormal and in some cases genetically defective. The work by Michel Foucault might be seen as one extended meditation on this normalising mission. On the matter of the politics of genetic normalisation, it is noteworthy that the welfare state par excellence, Sweden, is also the country where eugenics, including the forced sterilisation of (primarily) women who were deemed to be genetically or socially unfit, gained particular force outside of Nazi Germany.

the rise of identity politics, the assertion of minority and group rights. Since a political system based on the idea of a national and majoritarian democracy does not easily accommodate demands for the protection of minority rights, it is not surprising that many minorities view the old nation-state and its political regime with suspicion. A similar logic pertains with respect to a third crucial secular trend associated with both globalisation at large and European integration in particular, namely, increased migration within Europe, on the one hand, and increased immigration from outside Europe, on the other. Indeed, the fundamental dogma of laissez-faire economics involves the free movement of people (as well as of goods and capital). While this is an idea that has hardly been realised in full, there has been enough immigration, legal and illegal, to create a substantial diversification of the populations in most European countries, creating minorities that are likely to resist for the foreseeable future the integration into the old national community.

While both the US and the EU are subject to the same broad secular trends, there are important differences that can be put to productive use in a comparative analysis. To put it starkly and perhaps controversially; the trends we have identified can be thought of loosely in terms of the Americanisation of Europe. If we consider the EU as it is, not to mention the proposed new constitution, what we see ahead is the construction of a regime that looks less like a traditional European national democracy and more like an American-style procedural republic, one that involves less of majoritarian democracry and more emphasis on strong individual and minority rights, constitutionally embedded separation and limitation of powers, a strong and autonomous judiciary, and a federal system that provides extensive powers to local communities and member nations according to the ethos of the subsidiarity principle. If this is the case, then we may also want to ask if perhaps the Europeans can learn, positively and negatively, from the American experience.

In the chapters that follow, the themes briefly introduced above will receive more sustained attention. In the first chapter Richard Bellamy and Dario Castiglione focus on the future of the EU and take as their point of departure the question of how to address the lack of legitimacy that the EU enjoys among the peoples and citizens of Europe. Taking note of the highly complex character of the postmodern European polity, with its multiple identities and overlapping sovereignties that have rendered the old nineteenth century ideal of the homogenous and sovereign nation-state obsolete as a normative model for the members states, not to mention the EU itself, they cast their essay as an attempt at rethinking from the point of view of normative theory the kind of regime that this new type of polity requires to govern itself with legitimacy. Critiquing those who either ignore normative and regime considerations or the de facto peculiar character of the Euro-polity, they call for an open-ended democratic process that involves dialogues among the multiple European constituencies, and which is sensitive to the fact that the EU is what they call a 'poly-centred polity possessing a multi-level regime'. Rather than imposing a radically new constitutional regime, they advocate a more subtle reform process primarily aimed at improving the ability of the EUs main institutions to check and balance each other and granting citizens opportunity structures for direct input into the legislative process. Bellamy and Castiglione are sceptical when it comes to rights and court-based adversarial politics, seeking instead inspiration in the neo-Roman tradition, which gives priority to dialogue, compromise, and reciprocal accommodation.

Lars Trägårdh and Michael Delli Carpini, by contrast, shift the focus instead to consider the possibilities as well as the pitfalls of a juridified political regime. At heart their essay is a comparative account of the inter-twining of law and politics in the US and Europe, in which they first seek to lay bare the roots of what they call the 'anti-juridical tradition' in Europe, and then move on to conversely understand the emergence of the 'rights revolution' and 'adversarial legalism' in the US. They contend that the juridified American political regime must be understood in the context of American liberalism, that litigation, just as voting and market transactions, constitute activities where private vice and self-interest produce, in an efficient and (to the state) inexpensive way, public virtue and goods. Thus law-suits by private citizens are seen to curb asocial behaviour on the part of other citizens as well as large corporations and the institutions of the state. It also serves as a decentralised, non-statist, privatised substitute for European-style social welfare structures, such as universal health care, and the state's regulation of corporations. The courts, they argue, should be viewed as political arenas located at the border zone between the state and civil society. They end their essay by considering the normative implications of a juridified political system for power negotiations in a socially complex society such as the US and the emerging 'New Europe', with particular reference to social vs. individual rights, state-civil society relations, and competing concepts and practices of citizenship.

Next Daniel Wincott first provides a historical account of the emergence of the EU as a 'community of law', and then considers this emergent law-based, regulatory polity from the point of view of the European political left, which traditionally has been suspicious, if not openly hostile to the power of the judiciary insofar as it encroached on the legitimate power of democratic assemblies. With respect to the historical development, Wincott echoes Juliet Williams, whose chapter will be discussed below, in emphasising how complex and messy it was in contradistinction to the standard 'first generation' accounts that tend to view the European Court of Justice as committed from the outset to a programme of defending an essential and unchanging body of rights and concepts of law. Looking at the emergence of what he calls the 'regulatory state' from a normative standpoint, Wincott also considers the prospects for leftist politics in this new context. While noting the danger of majoritarian welfare states squashing individual and minority rights, he none the less remains equivocal on the potential of turning to a rights-based, leftist politics, seeing problems in a US-style politics in which the victim, as Pierre Rosenvallon has argued, has overtaken the citizen as the central figure in the politics of distributive justice.

Juliet Williams and Lisa Hilbink focus on the American experience. Williams raises the issue of 'pre-settlement', ie, the conception of the Constitution as a fixed system of legally entrenched rights (of states and individuals) and limits (of the power of the federal and state governments). She contrasts this idealised view of how the American political system was constructed by the Founding Fathers with a rather different account, one that emphasised that it was in fact a much longer historical and dynamic process through which limits on government arose in the course of political struggles. She suggests that her analysis might be helpful to Europeans who are currently engaged in thinking about and plotting a new constitution for the EU. While the idea of pre-settlement is a powerful lure to those who seek an escape from the chaos of ordinary politics, Williams shows that in the American system while the idea of pre-settlement is common the dominant practice is far more dynamic and open-ended. Thus, she concludes, Europeans may well be better off studying what Americans have done than what they (or at least some of them) say that they have done.

Lisa Hilbink begins her chapter by noting the stark traditional difference when it comes to the relationship between law and politics in Europe and the US. In Europe, she argues, judges were trained to become civil servants whose role it was to apply but not to create, adapt, or reject law. A strict separation between law and politics was adhered to, with the law-making role reserved for the democratically elected parliaments. Given that in more recent times developments have occurred that indicate a move in Europe towards a US- style political system, the aim of her chapter is to consider the role of the American judiciary in practice as well as in theory from the point of view of citizen empowerment. She warns that neither should the Europeans underestimate the potential benefits of transgressing the traditional separation of law and politics, nor should they harbour illusions about judges doing the work of vigilant citizens and the deliberative democratic process typical of parliaments. Her analysis thus suggests that a proper understanding of the American political regime must go beyond an analysis of the constitutional structure and also consider the sociological dimension, the translation of political theory into political practices, as well as the broader political culture underpinning and sustaining those practices.

In his chapter, Warren Breckman fastens upon the North American debate pitting the 'proceduralist' and 'republican' conceptions of politics against each other, a debate that has its counterpart in Europe as well, where the putative national substantive democracies, with their emphasis on the primacy of national interest, social rights, and majority rule, are contrasted with the EU as a procedural regime, wedded to the principle of the free market, individual rights, and the primacy of law. Breckman's chapter constitutes a critique of this distinction, which, he argues, restricts our understanding of democracy. Building on the works by Cornelius Castoriades and Claude Lefort, Breckman argues that the notion that democracy can be reduced to a set of procedures while substantive concerns are privatised is an illusion that obscures the fact that democracy at the core is not a 'particular set of institutions', but rather an 'open, indeterminate, and unmasterable process' of self-questioning, whose ultimate value is what Castoriadis calls 'autonomy'. This ideal of the autonomous individual, it would seem, bring Castoriadis (and Breckman) close to the civic republican citizen ideal, for this is an individual who seeks not merely to indulge in the pursuit of private happiness in the liberal market place, but rather to promote the substantive values of society. Breckman symptomatically ends his essay by discussing what he sees as the fundamental crisis of democracy, which he relates to the hegemony of capitalist globalisation, with political apathy and privatisation in its wake, on the one hand, and to the crisis of the very value of autonomy that Castoriadis champions, on the other.

By juxtaposing Breckman's analysis to those that celebrate the rights revolution, we can identify a fundamental paradox. The liberal, atomised market society tends to emancipate the individual from the shackles of community — be it national or more localised — by promoting an atomised legal person, equipped with juridically embedded rights, but at the price of alienating him or her from both the values and experience of community. It then becomes unclear what the meaning of democracy and citizenship will be. If substantial democracy is wholly replaced by the procedural republic, on what basis and for what purpose will the procedures be created?

## REFERENCES

Castells, Manuel. 2000, *The Information Age*, 3 vols, Oxford: Blackwell.

Hardt, Michael and Antonio Negri. 2000. *Empire* Cambridge, Mass: Harvard University Press.

Ruggie, John. 1993, 'Territoriality and Beyond: Problematizing Modernity in International Relations'. *International Organization*, 47, 1.

Sassen, Saskia. 1995, 'On Governing the Global Economy', draft of the 1995 Leonard Hastings Schoff Memorial Lectures. Later published as part of *Losing Control? Sovereignty in an Age of Globalization* New York: Columbia University Press, 1996.

Wæver, Ole. 'Identity, Integration and Security: Solving the Sovereignty Puzzle in EU Studies' in *Journal of International Affairs*, 48, 2.

# 2

# Normative Theory and the EU: Legitimising the Euro-Polity and its Regime[1]

## RICHARD BELLAMY AND DARIO CASTIGLIONE

T HE RECENT CONVENTION on the Future of Europe is the culmination of a decade long concern with the EU's legitimacy. The Treaty of Maastricht, and the difficulties experienced in getting it ratified in subsequent referenda, raised fundamental questions about the ultimate goals and methods of European integration, while the crisis of the Santer Commission added concerns over the propriety of the institutional mechanisms employed to govern it. With the introduction of the Euro and the prospect of Enlargement these worries have grown. The resulting need to publicly legitimise the EU has prevented the main political actors adopting a purely pragmatic approach, in which the EU's development is simply the incremental result of *ad hoc* calculations of national advantage. To a lesser or greater degree, European politicians and peoples can no longer avoid strategic-oriented action or normative argument concerning the purpose, underlying values, future shape and desirable structures of what Jacques Delors once called '*un object politique non-identifié*'. Academics, too, have begun to discover that the integration process depends not only on functional efficiency or its furtherance of national economic or defence interests, but also on people's ideals and perceptions. Consequently, explanation and justification have proved less easily distinguishable than earlier positivistic and behaviouralist models assumed.

This essay seeks to clarify certain implications of the resulting normative turn in European studies.[2] Jean Monnet thought the Community would

[1] Research for this chapter was supported by an ESRC Grant L213 25 2022 on 'Strategies of Civic Inclusion in Pan-European Civil Society', and benefited from involvement in FP3 EURCIT Network and FP5 RDT CIDEL Research Consortium financed by the European Commission. Earlier versions have been presented at seminars in Oñati, Florence, Edinburgh, Belfast and Montreal. We are grateful for the comments of Lars Tragardh, Peter Wagner, Neil Walker, Philippe Schmitter, Lynn Dobson, Alex Warleigh, Antje Weiner, Daniel Weinstock and Wayne Norman, amongst others, on these occasions, and for the suggestions of the publisher's referees.
[2] This chapter develops the argument of Bellamy and Castiglione (2000a) and is a revised version of Bellamy and Castiglione (2003). We are grateful for comments on those earlier papers, especially Shaw (1999); Shaw (2000a) 22–5; and Chryssochoou (2000) 123–44;

operate as a 'public utility state' and this broadly economic and utilitarian focus has been shared by many analysts of Europe.[3] More recently, however, there have been attempts by both academics and politicians to supplement and even modify the EU's market orientation through reference to the ideals of liberal democracy and proposals for a written constitution, a Charter of Rights and the strengthening of the European parliament (Pinder 1990, 284; Habermas 1999, 46–59). However, once we take seriously the normative content of people's demands and beliefs, treating them as judgements and not merely as preferences, then legitimacy cannot be either reduced to performance *per se* or conceived in purely ideal terms (Beetham and Lord 1998; Bellamy and Warleigh 1998). People disagree not only over what goods ought to be produced, but also about which institutions should produce them, when, how and for whom. Concepts of rights and justice are also disputed, likewise leading to debates over which institutions have the authority to decide certain issues, in what ways, for which people and so on. Because the EU results from and stimulates a dispersal of sovereign power and a multiplication of political identities, disputes within the Union over both the good and the right are highly complex. Our claim shall be that this complexity is reflected in the EU's character as a polycentric 'polity' possessing a multilevel governance 'regime'. Though the efficiency and equity of this system could undoubtedly be improved, departures from such admittedly complicated and messy structures towards either a purely interest-based liberal intergovernmentalism or an idealistic federalism will weaken rather than strengthen legitimacy. The EU's evolution as both a 'polity' and 'regime' has been an on-going process of multiple negotiations over the normative issues raised by integration (Wallace 1985, 453–72;

---

Chryssochoou (2001), ch 6. The literature involving the normative analysis of the EU is now growing apace. By and large the lawyers promoted this turn, perhaps because law — especially constitutional law — is explicitly a normative order. Any list will necessarily exclude important work, so the following is meant to be illustrative rather than exhaustive: De Witte (1991); Habermas (1992); MacCormick (1995); Wincott (1995a); Walker (1996); De Búrca (1996); Curtin (1997); Craig (1997); MacCormick (1997); Shaw (1998); Shaw (1999); Shaw (2000b); Shaw (2000c); Weiler (1999); Bankowski and Scott (2000). More recently, however, there has been a growing body of work that has built on collaboration between political theory and political science. See especially the following edited collections: Lehning and Weale (1997); Føllesdal and Koslowski (1997); Nentwich and Weale (1998); and Eriksen and Fossum (2000). See too Beetham and Lord (1998); Wiener (1998); Chryssochoou (1998); and Schmitter (2000). In contributions to some of these volumes and in collaborative volumes of our own, we have attempted a similar mix that also draws on the legal literature — notably, Bellamy, Bufacchi and Castiglione (1995); Bellamy and Castiglione (1996); Bellamy (1996); and Bellamy and Warleigh (2001). See too Bellamy and Castiglione (1997b); Bellamy and Castiglione (2000b); and Bellamy and Warleigh (1998). For a recent overview, see Friese and Wagner (2002).

[3] This has been particularly true of the functionalist and (in a different way) the liberal intergovernmentalist approaches discussed in section two.

Wallace 1996; Elgström and Jönsson 2000 684–704). Legitimacy will be enhanced only by constitutional and democratic mechanisms that foster rather than restrict such dialogues.

We begin in section one with an analysis of legitimacy. We argue it possesses an internal and an external dimension, the one linked to the values of the political actors, not least the European peoples, the other to the principles we employ to evaluate a political system and assess its effects for outsiders as well as insiders. Both dimensions apply to two distinct aspects of any political set up — its justification as a 'polity', where collective decisions can be made about particular issues, and the acceptability of the prevailing 'regime', or form of governance, whereby those decisions get taken. We claim these four elements of legitimacy are related and interact with each other. The internal and external legitimacy of a 'polity' is shaped by and shapes the internal and external legitimacy of the 'regime' that governs it. By contrast to many accounts (Beetham and Lord 1998), performance figures as an aspect of both 'polity' and 'regime' legitimacy rather than being treated as an independent factor.

The next two sections deepen this analysis by examining respectively the normative weaknesses of many accounts of the 'polity' building process and of proposals for improving the EU's 'regime'. We shall contend that the EU (and increasingly the member states too) suffer from a four-fold legitimacy deficit that involves, on the one hand, defining and legitimising what the EU *qua* 'polity' is and is for, and on the other, devising a legitimate 'regime' that corresponds to the Union's structure and does not overstep the degree of allegiance people are prepared to give it. Yet, many theories of European integration exclude normative and 'regime' considerations from their accounts of the 'polity'-building process, whilst certain theoretical (but also empirical) analysts of EU institutions and policy-making propose normative 'regimes' that fail to address the *sui generis* characteristics of the Euro-'polity'. Moreover, in both cases the role played by what we refer to as the internal dimensions of legitimacy are ignored. Section two explores the weaknesses of theories of the EU 'polity' that bracket the issues of its 'regime' and internal acceptance by European citizens. Section three reverses this perspective. It criticises attempts to devise 'regimes' for the EU that ignore the character of its 'polity' and the complex ways its citizens identify with both the Union and each other. We shall argue that the process of unification has reconfigured both sovereignty and identity within Europe, altering in the process the internal and external legitimacy of the 'polity' aspect of the member states and the EU. Internally, the interests of the member states and their peoples cannot be taken as givens, because ideals and allegiances are being partly shaped by the EU. Externally, major modifications are also being introduced to the governance structures within which they operate. Function, territory and civic identity have begun to pull apart, so that the nineteenth century construct of the homogenous, sovereign nation-state no longer provides an adequate model 'polity' for the member states let alone the EU. As a result, the standard normative vocabulary of rights, citizenship and representation has to be rethought in ways suited to the multiple civic identities and levels of governance that characterise the EU. In sum, a novel type of 'polity' requires a new form of 'regime' to govern it.

## 1.    THE DIMENSIONS OF LEGITIMACY

The growing appreciation of normative considerations in European Union studies follows from the discovery that the strategic and evaluative aspects of politics matter: political actors are not simply motivated by short term calculations of interests, whilst the political arrangements within which they operate have to be more than a convenient *modus vivendi* (Jachtenfuchs, Diez and Jung 1998, 409–45). As we noted, both aspects were raised by the questioning of the EU's legitimacy following Maastricht and its difficult passage through national legislatures and referenda. For very different reasons, both Federalist orientated Europhiles and nationalistic Eurosceptics have questioned the 'polity' and 'regime' aspects of the EU. For the one, the EU 'polity' is too narrowly defined and its 'regime' too complex and dominated by élite bargaining. They wish the EU to encompass ever more tasks, to strengthen a pan-European democracy by such measures as giving more power to a European Parliament, and to put in place a constitutional structure committed to common values (eg Duff 1994, 147–65). For the other, the EU has become too much like a 'polity', encompassing too many issues that are more appropriately dealt with domestically. To the extent they seek a constitutionalisation of the EU 'regime', it is to limit its political powers and reassert those of the people within their member states (eg Barry 1994, 10–27).

The legitimacy issue has become increasingly prominent as the implications of monetary union, enlargement and co-operation in defence have been thought through (De Búrca 1996). Legitimacy can be defined as the normatively conditioned and voluntary acceptance by the rule of the government of their rulers. It involves both an internal and an external dimension, both of which apply not only to the type of 'regime' but also to the 'polity' itself. The *internal* dimension reflects the ways people within any organisation, including a state, relate to each other and to the institutions governing their lives. Such internal legitimacy arises from a fit with socially accepted norms, customs and beliefs, and formalised processes of authorisation through relatively direct or, more usually, various indirect forms of consent. The *external* dimension reflects a supposedly objective as opposed to subjective point of view, such as might be adopted from the outside (though not necessarily so). It stems from the justification of these institutions' rationale and their congruence with certain formal and substantive norms, such as legality and human rights respectively.

The legitimacy of a 'polity' concerns the *subjects* and *sphere* of politics. The first term refers to how citizens are defined, the second to the ways the policy areas and geographical boundaries where political power is exercised are demarcated. Internally, the *subjects* who make and have to obey collective decisions must recognise each other as equal citizens and acknowledge the designated decision-making body as rightfully holding sway over a given *sphere* of their lives, be that *sphere* territorially or functionally defined. Such recognition is both contingently conditioned by such factors as language, culture, historical accident and geography, and more deliberately agreed to by various forms of tacit, express or hypothetical consent, from referenda and oaths of allegiance to military service or mere residence. Externally, a 'polity' must meet certain formal and substantive criteria, such as are found in international law, both to obtain the recognition of other states or those who are excluded from citizenship, and to achieve the minimal standards of economic viability and justice for those on its territory, regardless of citizenship, to be morally obliged to support it.

The legitimacy of a 'regime' concerns the *styles* and *scope* of politics. The *styles* of politics refer to the manner in which institutions work — the electoral system, the relationship of the judiciary to the legislature and so forth. Internally, such legitimacy involves a mixture of conformity with traditional practices and expectations, such as surrounds the attachment of many British people to the monarchy, and a more active willingness to participate in some degree in making the institutions work, even if that is only by voting in an election or paying taxes. Externally, the *styles* of politics must possess the rational-legal characteristics associated with the rule of law if they are not to be so chaotic as to be unworkable and offer protection against various kinds of oppression and injustice, and uphold those rights implied by democracy, though these are more contentious. Only then will citizens feel securer supporting rather than opposing their rulers. Finally, the *scope* of politics refers to how far power can be exercised within its given *sphere* — for example, whether there can be economic intervention or merely regulation. Internally, legitimising a given *scope* for politics will once again be a matter of political culture and deliberative debate. Externally, legitimacy involves some division of the public and the private. In this respect, a constitution often tends to offer a distinctive *internal* conception of what are assumed to be the *external* characteristics of any legitimate regime.

| LEGITIMACY | POLITY<br>*sphere* and *subjects* | REGIME<br>*scope* and *styles* |
| --- | --- | --- |
| **Internal**<br>a) **socially accepted norms** | Political identification amongst 'subjects' and between them and a particular power centre as having authority within a given 'sphere' (be it territorial, functional or both) | Institutions recognise ideals, interests and identities of governed |
| **Internal**<br>b) **authorisation by**<br>    **(usually indirect) consent** | As in plebiscites and referenda over such issues as secession | Collective decisions seen as authoritative because involve mutual recognition |
| **External**<br>a) **formal — established**<br>    **rules** | *De jure* compatible with international law | Legality — a regular system of governance/not arbitrary |
| **External**<br>b) **substantive — freedom,**<br>    **justice,**<br>    efficiency/benefits | Viable, existence does not entail oppression of insiders or outsiders. | Not oppressive, unjust or incompetent |

*Fig 1    The Dimensions of Legitimacy*

Figure 1 offers a diagrammatic representation of the above schema of the dimensions of legitimacy.

Three important observations are necessary at this juncture. First, though analytically distinguishable, the resulting four aspects of legitimacy identified in the matrix are all interrelated. None on its own is more basic than the others or sufficient to make a political system or organisation legitimate. Each has knock on effects for the others, with the character of one having implications for the configuration of the rest. For example, recent studies have noted how high levels of support for certain external 'regime' criteria, such as the principles of democracy, can lead citizens to an internal dissatisfaction with the character of the actual 'regime'. Thus, in Britain the politically dissatisfied are more likely to favour constitutional changes such as reform of the House of Lords (Dalton 1999, 75–6). However, these *external* criteria are in themselves too abstract to determine precisely what kind of 'regime' should be in place. There is a certain variation between different constitutional traditions on matters such as how 'freedom of speech' might be balanced against 'the right to privacy'. These differences reflect the *internal* legitimacy embodied in the political culture of the country concerned. Meanwhile, a 'regime' may satisfy standard external criteria of democratic acceptability but lack internal 'polity' legitimacy amongst the populace. Yet, if the *sphere* and *subjects* of politics appear inappropriate, then the *styles* and *scope* may ultimately come to be questioned both externally and internally without significant adjustment. For example, those Scottish Nationalists who dispute the legitimacy of the United Kingdom do not deny so much that the British political system meets standard democratic criteria as that it is not their democracy. However, this questioning of the UK's 'polity' legitimacy has nonetheless generated demands to adapt its 'regime' by incorporating devolution and possibly electoral reform. In Northern Ireland, Canada and Belgium, a similar dynamic has led to calls for minority group rights and various forms of power sharing at the executive and other levels of government. At the same time, the internal probing of the external dimensions of legitimacy are themselves to some degree externally constrained. Proposals for secession, for instance, standardly must ensure not only that the resulting new 'polity' would be economically viable and secure but also the former parent state. Additionally, they should take account of the preferences of substantial minorities who favour staying with the parent state or a degree of autonomy of their own, and so on. Such considerations may in their turn constrain the type of 'regime' the new 'polity' could legitimately adopt. Indeed, in many cases 'polity' legitimacy will depend on 'regime' legitimacy. Arguably, this has been the case in Northern Ireland, where greater regional autonomy has been made possible by a degree of executive power sharing.

Secondly, these four aspects of legitimacy are constantly evolving as people's interests and ideals change and social and economic life is transformed by technological and other innovations. For example, a greater awareness of environmental issues, itself linked to enhanced international interconnectedness in economic production and consumption, has resulted in changed perceptions of the shape of the 'polity' and of types of 'regime'. Thus, the *sphere* and *subjects* of politics in policy areas such as climate change has come to be seen as global. That has involved envisaging a new *scope* and *style* for politics, requiring novel forms of regulation by international agreements and agencies. Such changed perceptions have operated both at the élite level, albeit for the most part cautiously and conservatively, and more radically at the popular level, with the growth of transnational environmental movements.

Finally, performance as such does not appear within this scheme, except as a minimal external requirement of viability. Two reasons motivate this omission. One reason is that the impact of policy outputs generally, and economic performance in particular, may affect the allegiance of citizens to incumbent politicians but plays a minor role in shaping their confidence in a given 'polity' and 'regime' (McAllister 1999, 201–3). The legitimacy of these depends on more deep-rooted cultural values. Consequently, established democracies can retain support during quite extended periods of economic failure if both 'polity' and 'regime' have internal and external legitimacy, though citizens may severely criticise the government or even politicians in general. The other reason is that the four dimensions shape what counts as *legitimate* performance. No body values productivity *per se*. Rather, they want more of some things and less of others. Moreover, certain ways of producing a good may result in various bads, such as unemployment or pollution, while different goods can sometimes be in competition. So any increase in good A will have costs as well as benefits, including harmful or beneficial effects for goods B, C and so on. Thus, performance is an evaluative concept. Many of the norms shaping people's notion of *good* or *legitimate* performance stem from the cultural values underpinning both the 'polity' and 'regime'. These, either implicitly or explicitly — often via some constitutional norm — constrain what gets produced and how. Debate over performance usually remains within these norms. However, occasionally it challenges them, requiring that both 'polity' and 'regime' be rethought in certain respects. For example, during the Thatcher period in Britain, government policy gradually moved from suggesting that, within the existing rules, Conservatives could run the economy better than Labour, to seeking to change the social democratic character of the British state. The result was that of taking some *spheres* and *subjects* out of politics, while altering both its *scope* and *styles* through far reaching privatisation programmes.

These observations have important implications for how we think about the legitimacy of the EU. Most politicians and citizens within the EU agree that the external dimensions of 'polity' and 'regime' legitimacy fall within a liberal democratic spectrum ranging from the social democratic to the moderate libertarian. However, this broad consensus does not in itself generate any particular allegiance to the EU.[4] For it is compatible with considerable disagreement over the internal dimensions of the EU. A liberal democrat could just as plausibly argue that these values would either be best defended at the level of the nation-state, with some minimal interstate co-operation for humanitarian purposes, or that they pointed to a cosmopolitan form of governance, as that they required extensive European integration. These disagreements over which *spheres* should be covered by the EU, and hence the degree to which the citizens of member states should be its *subjects*, have important implications for the *styles* and *scope* of the EU's political

---

[4] Habermas has argued that rights *per se* can provide the focus of a 'constitutional patriotism' for the EU (Habermas, 1998, 118, 225–6). But an abstract agreement on the appropriate external criteria any 'polity' or 'regime' should meet, will not tell you which 'polity' they ought to be realised in, or even the best form of 'regime' to do so. Both of these involve internal forms of legitimation that Habermas either ignores or simply assumes match his argument. For an explicit critique of Habermas' position, see Bellamy (2000a, 99–103).

and legal system. For example, the sort of 'regime' required to legitimately govern an essentially intergovernmental free trade zone will not be as extensive as that needed for a federal state, demanding considerably less in the way of democratic control. At the same time, though, the creation of a European 'regime' of any type has implications for the development of the EU 'polity' — constraining it in some respects while sustaining and fostering it in others, many of which are hard to predict. A limited 'regime' will restrict the policy areas into which the EU can extend. Thus, Fritz Scharpf has suggested that because the EU's inadequate democratic arrangements prevent it offering the 'in-put legitimacy' of 'government by the people', it can only engage in those public policies where the 'out-put legitimacy' needed to ensure 'government for the people' is sufficient (Scharpf 1999, 2, 6, 23, 203). Yet it should be noted that this thesis cannot be viewed simply as a purely 'external' form of performance legitimacy, as some — notably Giandomenico Majone — come close to arguing (eg Majone 1996, 284, 287; Majone 1998). For without the elements of 'internal' legitimation needed to define even those performance standards required for the EU to be deemed an 'efficient' facilitator and regulator of transnational trade, then it is doubtful whether purely 'external' out-put legitimacy could justify more than the threshold levels involved for humanitarian aid.

Even a restricted 'regime', however, will allow and encourage debates about the nature of the 'polity' to occur, with demands for greater democratic accountability, for example, fuelling the evolution of the EU into new policy areas. Therefore, there is an element of truth in both the Eurosceptic argument that 'regime' change in the EU must remain in step with the low levels of 'polity' allegiance it receives compared to member states, and the Europhile counter-argument that if the EU's 'regime' was strengthened, people would look more favourably on the construction of a more extensive European 'polity'. What both sides of the debate miss are the mutual interactions of 'polity' and 'regime', explored in the remainder of this chapter.

## 2.  THE NORMATIVE AND 'REGIME' DIMENSIONS OF THE EUROPEAN 'POLITY'

Despite their important differences, the hitherto dominant theories of European integration, namely neo-functionalism and liberal intergovernmentalism, share a common aspiration to provide scientific explanations that minimise the independent role of both the EU's 'regime' and normative ideals. Both focus on the EU's 'polity' legitimacy, regarding its 'regime' legitimacy as a secondary matter that is achieved largely indirectly. Both also adopt a predominantly instrumental and purely performance-based view of the development of the EU 'polity'. This perspective equates the internal aspect of the EU's 'polity' legitimacy with its success in securing the goods of peace and prosperity. Because these goods are basic to the ideals of a majority of the European peoples, no additional internal normative justification is assumed to be necessary. Since most people have an interest in maximising them, how far integration should proceed becomes largely a matter of cost-benefit analysis. External legitimacy is either transferred to the EU, or indirectly guaranteed, as a result of integration being promoted in accordance with international law by states that are themselves recognised as externally legitimate. Moreover, the terms of this external legitimacy are believed to be the same for all states and for the EU.

Thus, for neo-functionalists such as Haas: 'the public is … concerned with income, price stability, better working conditions, cleaner air, more recreational facilities … [and] does not greatly care whether these are provided by national government or by Brussels (1958, 79–80). That such policies were increasingly co-ordinated at a European rather than a domestic level was the product not of idealism so much as the interconnected nature of modern economies. Such economic integration was predicted to prove self-sustaining. Because the different parts of the economy are linked, an economic spillover effect was expected whereby increasing integration in one area would lead to it proceeding elsewhere. The removal of constraints on the free movement of capital, services and labour would generate in turn an increasing number of common regulations, the need for a single currency and so on. In its turn, economic spillover would encourage and be accompanied by political spillover. Supranational organisations would arise to oversee the ever more integrated economy and themselves produce a self-reinforcing range of institutions. Because the cost-benefit calculations of integration are complex within a modern interconnected economy, the lead had inevitably to come from élites and technocrats. Indeed, they often operated by stealth to avoid the possible irrational prejudices and faulty instrumental reasoning of their electorates. However, it was expected that the 'loyalties and expectations' of all economic and political actors would gradually shift to where the action was — at the centre (Haas 1958).

On the neo-functionalist account, 'polity' construction creates its own 'regime' and internally legitimating norms. Moreover, these norms are treated as mere properties of the economic system that facilitate its healthy functioning. Satisfying standard 'external' aspects of legitimacy are assumed to bring the 'internal' aspects in their wake, with little interaction between the two. People will identify with the EU 'polity' and accept its institutions so long as integration provides certain desired goods and the means for controlling their supply without damaging productive efficiency, infringing international law or inflicting injustice. As we saw, this position presupposes a consensus on what goods people want and an indifference to who delivers them, how and amongst whom they are distributed. However, such agreement has not been obtained in practice. Indeed, it is precisely because people disagree about the *sphere* and *subjects* of a 'polity', that it needs a 'regime' where such issues can be raised and internal legitimacy generated. Moreover, as we also noted in the previous section, these debates can have knock on effects for the type of external legitimation that are applied. If the EU begins either to act externally as a 'polity' when people internally regard it as an international organisation, or *vice versa*, that will produce both an internal and an external legitimation crisis.

To some degree, it was the first scenario that undermined the neo-functionalist account when De Gaulle refused to contemplate an expansion of the Parliament's powers in agricultural policy (the Empty Chair crisis of 1965). Liberal intergovernmental approaches see themselves as filling the explanatory gap left by the failure of the economic and especially the political spillover mechanisms to work as smoothly as neo-functionalists had supposed. In his influential account of this thesis, Andrew Moravcsik proposes a tripartite argument whereby national governments first define an ordering of preferences in response to the domestic pressures of societal groups, second bargain amongst themselves to realise these interests, and third choose appropriate institutions to realise them (1993, 481; 1999, 20, 473). In this approach, the 'regime' and internal normative aspects of legitimacy are exogenous to the process of EU 'polity' building. They belong to the domestic realm, with national political institutions aggregating the interests of the population and so setting the agenda for their representatives. Though the theory does not specify the content of national government preferences, he also identifies the crucial factors as economic interests and the need to co-ordinate them given the economic interdependence of member states (Moravcsik 1999, 473–5). Moreover, all interests are assumed to be pursued economically. The EU's chief purpose is to resolve collective action problems within a globalising economic environment. European agreements bind states to uphold common policies that reduce negative externalities whilst allowing them to recoup some of the benefits generated by positive externalities (Moravcsik 1993, 509–10; 1999, 35). Since all groups within a state will not benefit from such action, the profile of domestic preferences provides the 'bargaining space' within which inter-state negotiations take place (Moravcsik 1993, 497; 1999, 36–8, 475–7). States have to weigh up the costs of negotiating and losing some freedom of action in the future against the benefits of integration. The chief gains of creating a settled European organisation rather than proceeding by *ad hoc* agreements are efficiency and stability, not least the removal of prisoner dilemmas and free-riding (Moravcsik 1993, 512–4; 1999, 73–7, 485–9). However, the EU's 'polity' structures and its governing 'regime' remain firmly intergovernmental, albeit of a highly developed kind.

As with neofunctionalism, liberal intergovernmentalism sees normative legitimation as resting on largely invariable external standards. If the member states are recognised as legitimate and their agreements are compatible with international law and norms, then the EU must be legitimate. Provided its quasi-'regime' satisfies external criteria of legality and justice, it too is legitimate. However, the more the EU does resemble a 'polity' with a 'regime' of its own, the more problematic this scenario becomes. Rightly or wrongly, most of the electorates of all member states believe significant powers have been ceded to EU institutions and either wish them returned to domestic control or desire a strengthening of European controls. In other words, there is a mismatch between what they perceive as the changed external standing of the EU and its member states, on the one hand, and the forms of internal legitimacy they now receive, on the other. They believe the *sphere* and *subjects* of the EU are changing without either adequate authorisation or sufficient popular identification to allow the establishment of a 'regime' with sufficient *scope* and the requisite *styles* to offer accountable and effective governance.[5]

Although liberal intergovernmentalism appears to fill gaps left by neofunctionalism, the neofunctionalist spillover mechanism offers a theoretical source of internal legitimation that, at least in principle, would overcome problems in its position (Waever 1995, 389–431; Diez 1999, 360). For even if we accept the EU is primarily intergovernmental in both 'polity' and 'regime' terms, it is doubtful liberal intergovernmentalism can avoid assuming the emergence of certain internal European norms and a related 'regime' to structure the bargaining of state actors (Wallace 1990, 215) Moravcsik himself concedes that geopolitical factors, that were generally more ideational than objective, mattered 'where the costs and benefits of co-operation were uncertain, balanced, or weak', predominating in issues — such as foreign policy co-ordination or purely institutional matters, such as the role of the European parliament — with no immediate economic impact (Moravcsik 1999, 477). He also acknowledges that such factors were often connected to prestigious national leaders and could influence core national preferences (Moravcsik 1999, 478). However, he contends these were secondary to the commercial motivations to co-operate in various areas within an increasingly global and interconnected economy (Moravcsik 1999, 6–7, 473–77). Where such motivations were not present, integration rarely advanced. By and large, Moravcsik sees states as being pushed by key economic interest groups eager to co-operate for mutual interest. He makes light of the likelihood of different state actors adopting different bargaining strategies and claims that the pay-offs and the rules of the game were clear to and agreed by all, that all saw themselves as involved in a supergame

---

[5] As noted, countries differ widely in their views of the EU. But although 51% of European citizens in the most recent poll expressed support for the Union, only four member states (Spain, Portugal, Luxembourg and Ireland) recorded a majority satisfied with the way democracy works in the EU. By contrast, over 50% in all but one member state (Italy) were satisfied with national democracy. (Figures from Eurobarometer Report 52, April 2000 (based on research October–November 1999).

rather than a series of one-shot games, and that all concurred on the economic focus of the arrangements (Moravcsik 1999, 60–2). If true — and it is beyond the scope of this chapter to test these empirical claims — then the decisions surrounding the choice for Europe were fortuitously free of the dilemmas of collective action to which one might otherwise have suspected them to be prone. After all, international politics is replete with examples, from the failure to tackle global warming to the arms race, where states have been tempted by free riding or have got caught in games of chicken in ways that prevent them co-operating in mutually beneficial ways (Hollis and Smith 1990, 137–41).

Even if European ideals and institutions were not necessary to bring about European integration, they have been products of it. The focus on making choices and decisions misses the way the subsequent behaviour of the main political actors is shaped by the on-going processes of implementing them. As a number of commentators have noted (eg Wincott 1995b, 597–609), the liberal intergovernmentalist position has difficulty accounting for the way the European Parliament and especially the European Court of Justice have developed an authority of their own which is to some degree independent of, constrains and moulds the decision-making of the member states (eg Vink 2001, 875–96). In many respects, these developments provide a stable context for bargaining to take place, which, for well known reasons, rational actors may be unable to provide for themselves (Wallace 1990, 225; Diez 1999 361–3). They offer not only rules for the game, as historical institutionalist accounts argue (eg Pierson 1996, 123–64), but also, as constructivists have indicated (Christiansen, Jorgensen and Wiener 1999, 528–44), roles for the actors involved, even if they do not determine their actions anywhere near as strongly as certain accounts suggest. Put another way, European law and institutions help create normative expectations that fill the gaps in the various actors' rational expectations of each other. Indeed, institutional arrangements may even lock them into policies they come to find undesirable, such as continuing surpluses arising from the Common Agricultural Policy (CAP) (Sharpf 1988, 239–78). Moravcsik partly grants some of these claims, but argues that most of these institutional restraints and their consequences — including the apparently undesirable ones — were intended in order to commit all future governments to particular policies (Moravcsik 1999, 491–4). This thesis may hold for the medium term but there are limits to how far-sighted one can be in the long term. Consider the creative and ultimately incoherent ways in which some American legal scholars refer back to the 'intentions' of the founders to justify their interpretations of the American constitution (eg Bork 1990).[6] Any attempts by future European lawyers or politicians to take this tack

---

[6] For a critique, see Sunstein (1993), ch 4.

would similarly be doomed to fail. For good or ill, EU law and institutions such as the Parliament and Commission have a dynamic of their own, albeit it is one still strongly constrained by intergovernmental decision-making.

In contrasting ways, neo-functionalists and liberal intergovernmentalists seek to bracket the question of the EU's 'polity' legitimacy from that of its 'regime'. Respectively, they see the latter either as a product of 'polity' formation or as its pre-condition (ie as a mechanism for national preference formation within the member states). Likewise, they separate internal legitimation from external legitimacy and assume the former to be non-normative in nature because people simply wish to maximise peace and prosperity. However, these attempts to partition normative issues ultimately fail. Debates over how far the extension of the EU's powers is either necessary or desirable have accompanied the whole course of European integration. These divisions occur within most member state populations and even many governments. They involve not only technicalities but also different ideological and ethical stances concerning the proper *sphere*, *subjects* and *scope* of EU politics, the *style* of accountability available and so on (Diez 1999). Contrary to the neofunctionalist position, these differences have meant that the 'spill-over' from economic gains into enhanced internal legitimacy has been partial and patchy. Moreover, the fragility of the economic benefits and their contested nature has also produced some questioning of the EU's external legitimacy. Contrary to the liberal intergovernmentalist position, the normative as well as economic character of these disagreements renders them hard to aggregate, making a stable 'national' position that a government might represent hard to achieve. These kinds of dispute will only be resolved when purely instrumental reasoning gives way to moral argument and the belief that a certain course of action is right. Here norms are not mere rationalisations of material interests, they structure them. Mass normative opinions are not only operative in shaping the policies of élites towards Europe within the member states,[7] both formal and informal channels have also developed at the EU level whereby citizens can express such divergent opinions in ways that by-pass national executives — most notably the European Parliament, but also via subnational or transnational lobbying organisations of various kinds (Imig and Tarrow 2000). In addition, such bodies as the ECJ allow citizens to invoke European norms against national ones (eg *Cowan v Le Trésor public*; *Konstantinidis v Stadt Altensteig*). Meanwhile, and for the present most influentially, deliberation between élites within European settings establishes patterns of socialisation whereby agreements result not from bargains but persuasive argumentation as to the merits of a given policy (Checkel 1999, 83–114). In other words, a European 'regime' has begun to emerge which offers a rival source of EU

---

[7] For a study of how such issues structured German policy towards EMU, see Merlingen (2001).

'polity' development and external and internal legitimation to the member states.

At a mainly descriptive level, multi-level governance analysts of the EU have traced this intertwining of the various dimensions of 'polity' and 'regime' within the EU, noting that authority is now shared (and contested) between national executives and actors operating above and below the state, such as the EP and the regions respectively (Marks, Hooghe and Blank 1996, 341–2). Moreover, these multiple levels coalesce in different ways according to policy area. No one set of institutions is ultimately responsible for all competences, whilst the membership and character of these institutions varies. For example, foreign, monetary and social policies require different types of agreement between different sets and sorts of actors concerning different *spheres* and *subjects*. To cite a notorious case, Britain is a full member of the EU yet secured an opt-out from stage three of EMU and the Amsterdam Protocol (Art 73Q) on 'freedom, justice and security', and until 1998 was exempt from the commitment to a common social policy. Different kinds of institutional arrangement govern these areas and the relationships between them are obscure to say the least. Thus, the Commission can promote binding accords between management and labour in areas such as health and safety that give these private non-state bodies a quasi-legislative power that can pre-empt both Community and Member State action (Arts 117 and 118). The Western European Union is the EU's putative defence arm and as such 'an integral part of the development of the European Union' (Art J4), but only 10 of the 15 belong to it. As a result, the EU is polycentric as well as multi-levelled (Schmitter 2000, 15–19). Put another way, there are multiple polities involving multiple 'regimes'. There are considerable overlaps between them but also certain tensions.

Multi-level governance rejects the liberal intergovernmentalist separation of domestic and international politics.[8] Though 'states are an integral and powerful part of the EU', these analysts note 'they no longer provide the sole interface between the supranational and the subnational arenas, and they share, rather than monopolise, control over many activities that take place in their respective territories' (Marks, Hooghe and Blank 1996, 346–7). Thus, the Commission cannot be seen simply as an agent of the states (Marks, Hooghe and Blank 1996, 358, 361). Not only is it able to

---

[8] It should be noted that similar considerations also work against attempts to distinguish different levels of analysis within EU decision-making, from historic decisions about the nature of the EU system to sub-systemic policy-shaping (Peterson 1995). Because the four dimensions of *subjects*, *sphere*, *scope* and *style* are related, with a continous interaction between European and member state considerations amongst the relevant actors, super-systemic issues will be raised in ordinary policy-making and policy issues arise in historic decisions on the nature of the system. Differences of emphasis may of course exist, but they will not be clear-cut (a point, to be fair, that Peterson partly concedes at p 85).

exploit tensions amongst the states, but it also has various informational and agenda setting advantages that give it a certain autonomy of action over often divided and temporary government officials and politicians. Likewise, the EP's growing power of co-decision have further limited the competence of both states and Commission, rendering the making of EU legislation a 'complex balancing act' amongst the main EU institutions (Marks, Hooghe and Blank 1996, 364). The existence of these distinctive sites of power to the state also means that non-state actors at subnational and transnational level can appeal to them when governments fail to respond to their needs. Capital and labour have long employed such tactics. However, other groups have also availed themselves of Union political structures. Indeed, it is now estimated that some 20 per cent of European groups are 'public interest' organisations covering the whole issue and ideological spectrum (Greenwood 1997).

Pressure by trans- and subnational groups, on the one hand, and the development of multiple levels of governance that cut across states either above or below, on the other, tend to reinforce each other. The latter facilitates the emergence of the former, who demand in their turn enhanced powers for the latter, even if this process has so far occurred unevenly and in fits and starts (Jeffrey 2000, 1–25). Moreover, these institutions not only provide rules and norms that constrain purely calculative and self-interested economic behaviour, but also offer a forum within which values and ideals as well as interests can be deliberated (Stone-Sweet and Sandholtz 1997, 305; Christiansen, Jorgensen, and Wiener 1999, 541–2; Checkel 2001). However, the complexity of a multi-level system can increase the possibilities for inefficient and inequitable decision-making. Some commentators propose the best way of overcoming this situation is to provide the EU with a written constitution and more transparent and democratic decision-making.[9] At this point, therefore, we need to reverse our perspective and ask how far the *sui generis* nature of the EU's 'polity' structure places normative constraints on the type of 'regime' it might adopt.

### 3.  THE NORMATIVE AND 'POLITY' DIMENSIONS OF THE EUROPEAN 'REGIME'

The last section argued that the EU's 'regime' played an important role in shaping the EU 'polity', especially by offering various channels for its internal legitimation through discussion of which *spheres* and *subjects* should fall within its domain. This section argues that the character of the EU 'polity' shapes in its turn the character of the EU's 'regime'. Our argument

---

[9] Most influentially Habermas (2001).

starts from the, admittedly contentious, assumption that the multi-level account of the Euro-'polity' described above is roughly correct. Thus, we assume sovereignty to be partially dispersed between different policy *spheres* involving different *subjects*, for which different sorts of 'regime' might be appropriate. We also believe this situation to be fluid, and the dispersal of sovereign power to be partly horizontal as well as vertical (See Ruggie 1993, 172). The EU is very different, therefore, to a standard, albeit somewhat idealised, conception of a federal nation-state. Within this arrangement, there is a strong political allegiance to the boundaries of the 'polity' and the competences of the sub-units are relatively clear. Broad agreement exists over the complexion of the *subjects* and *spheres*, and hence who can decide what and where. The 'regime' distributes power vertically and hierarchically from the top down. Meanwhile, a shared political culture provides a rough consensus on the appropriate *styles* and *scope* of politics. In other words, the particular complexion of the 'polity' and 'regime' possess widespread 'internal' legitimation as an appropriate embodiment of the abstract liberal democratic values that offer the main sources of 'external' legitimacy. As a result, the 'regimes' of such states can combine a formal or informal constitution and tradition of judicial review that sets out the basic principles of the public culture, and a majoritarian system of democracy that operates within this constitutional framework. By contrast, the EU's 'internal' legitimacy is decidedly thin. Most people believe it to be useful without feeling deeply attached to it. There are profound disagreements about its respective competences *vis-à-vis* the member states and how the two relate to each other. Consequently its *spheres* and *subjects* are uncertain, and there is no shared 'political culture' as to the *styles* and *scope* of EU politics. This circumstance places certain constraints on the sort of constitution likely to be suitable for the EU and the political mechanisms appropriate for resolving its 'democratic deficit'.

Constitutions are often assumed to normatively constitute both a 'polity' and its 'regime' by providing them with the external legitimacy offered by universal principles such as human rights (Dworkin 1995, 2–11). However, as we have noted, such lists of rights are too abstract to offer in themselves much guidance as to how a regime should be organised. People reasonably differ over the justification of rights, their interpretation in particular contexts and the balance to be achieved between them (Waldron 1999; Bellamy 1999, ch 7). Not only philosophers and judges but also ordinary people disagree about such matters as whether pornography or racist opinions are entitled to protection under a right to freedom of speech, and the extent to which different forms of speech can or do infringe other rights, such as privacy and non-discrimination. The view one takes on these sorts of issues implies a certain conception of the good society: of the ways we should recognise and show concern and respect for others. Consequently, rights also require internal legitimation of both their 'polity' and 'regime' aspects

(Bellamy 2001). In fact, constitutions differ in the ways they balance rights because they offer internal interpretations of external legitimacy requirements that reflect national political and legal traditions. They reflect the *styles* and *scope* of politics adopted by certain *subjects* within a given *sphere*. When no congruence between sovereignty and identity obtains, then constitutions will lack internal 'polity' legitimacy because they cannot express the normative consensus of an already existing 'people'. As a result, debates about the content and interpretation of constitutions, and the different *styles* and *scopes* these give to politics, will have a far greater tendency than within settled polities to shade into debates over the appropriate *sphere* and *subjects* within which a particular constitutional system can operate. For example, differences over the *scope* of monetary policy have produced in the EU context differences over its *sphere* and *subjects* too, with those outside EMU aspiring to a different configuration of the EU 'polity' to those within it.

In this situation, constitutions can no longer operate as the apex of a normative hierarchy in which they frame and offer the basis for democracy, as is the case in the standard federal model referred to above. Instead, they become co-equal as part of a horizontal as opposed to a vertical division of powers. Legitimation of either a 'polity'-based demand, such as for greater regional autonomy, or of a 'regime'-based demand, like affirmative action, cannot be grounded in appeals to constitutional rights or popular sovereignty alone. Rather, the arguments invoke both: namely, that the character of a particular group of people warrants a certain understanding of their rights — including where and how they are implemented. These debates about constitutional rights are in practice, if not necessarily in principle, open-ended and ongoing. The judgements involved in applying abstract rights to concrete circumstances are inconclusive, and the ideals, interests and identities of those involved are constantly evolving as their situation and relations to each other change. Instead of a consensus that sets the terms of debate, therefore, constitutions have to be seen as part of a continuous series of dialogues and compromises as different groups seek to accommodate the views of others.

Jim Tully has noted how even within established polities, multiculturalism and a renascent multinationalism have produced just such a dialogical turn in understanding constitutionalism (Tully 2001a, 123–47). However, the situation within the EU is much more radical. Usually, multinationalism and to a lesser extent multiculturalism challenge 'polity' legitimacy indirectly and incrementally through ever more extensive changes to the 'regime'. By contrast, the EU's 'polity' legitimacy is both fragile and fragmented and has to contend with the much more robust existing 'polity' structures of the member states. Moreover, it involves a number of cross-cutting 'regimes' operating between different aggregations of 'polities'. Thus, the legitimacy of any EU constitution requires constitutional dialogues at both the 'polity' and 'regime' levels, with the two to some extent cutting across each other (Shaw 1999, 2000b, 2000c). The tensions currently present within the EU largely stem from attempts to block and circumnavigate such dialogues.

These fault lines are perhaps best illustrated by the series of confrontations between the ECJ and the German Federal Constitutional Court (BverfG). The ECJ has wished to make itself the guarantor of the external 'polity' and 'regime' legitimacy of community law, taking for granted that it possesses internal legitimacy as a distinct *sphere* with a determinate *scope*: most particularly the securing of the free movement of goods, services, labour and capital between the member states. Moreover, it argues European law has not only 'direct effect' but also 'supremacy' over even national constitutional law in these areas. However, the BverfG has carefully circumscribed these claims within an internal constitutional point of view of its own. Thus, the EU possesses internal 'polity' legitimacy because the BverfG accepts that Article 24 of the German constitution allows the transfer of certain legislative powers to international bodies (*'Solange I'*). 'But', the Court went on (540), 'Art 24 ... limits this possibility in that it nullifies any amendment of the Treaty which would destroy the identity of the valid constitutional structure of the Federal Republic of Germany'. Importantly, it noted in particular the lack of a democratically elected and accountable EU legislature and the absence of constitutionally entrenched fundamental rights. 'So long as' a conflict between European law and the rights recognised by the German constitution was possible, the latter would prevail. Having obliged the ECJ to affirm its acknowledgment of human rights considerations as general principles of law, the BverfG has also accepted that it need not review secondary community legislation for compatibility with the basic law (*'Solange II'*). Yet it has not accepted that it is for the ECJ to decide what are community and what national matters, nor that it could not adjudicate on the constitutionality (within the German legal order) of either further extensions of the Community or even changes in the practices of the ECJ (*Solange II; Brunner*).

Though less fully expressed, most other national constitutional courts arguably hold a similar position (MacCormick 1995). The differences between the ECJ and the constitutional courts of the member states need not necessarily be a source of conflict if community law formed a 'discrete' order (eg Weiler 1999, ch 3). After all, unlike the US Supreme Court, the ECJ does not presume national law to be 'nested' within community law and so does not assess the bearing of rights in what it regards as non-Community areas, including those where a member state has obtained a derogation from Community obligations (eg *Cinéthèque v Fédèrations nationales des cinémas français*; *ERT v Dimotiki Etairia Piliroforissis*). However, difficulties still arise because, as we observed earlier, Community and national affairs remain almost impossible to disentangle from each other. Decisions in one *sphere* invariably have knock on effects for the other.

Thus, there are clashes not only over economic priorities but also between the predominately market-orientated community values and various of the non-market social and cultural values of the states (eg *Grogan*). It is on these occasions that dialogue becomes inescapable.

So far, the ECJ and national courts have neatly skirted around such problem areas through tacit mutual accommodations. However, courts are imperfect vehicles for expressing either a national or a European Community view that reveals how citizens identify with each other at either level.[10] The representative and accountable character of legislatures gives them an authority and legitimacy when seeking to accommodate different concerns and interests that courts do not possess (Waldron 1999). It is sometimes suggested that courts could acquire such qualities if their selection were more embedded in the political process. But that would be to subvert the separation of powers and the distinctive and valuable role courts play in upholding consistency, prospectivity and impartiality in the making and implementation of the law. It is these formal features of the rule of law that ensure that agreed policies are equitably and efficiently pursued. In this respect, EU law has provided the burgeoning body of European regulations with an all-important external legal-rational legitimacy (Majone 1996). However, as we noted earlier, to ensure that the law itself is 'for' the people in any substantive sense requires that it also possesses the internal legitimacy of having been made 'by' the people in ways that reflect the collective will. The relatively small number of judges cannot replicate the representative functions of a legislature and the diversity of opinions they normally contain. Moreover, their independence would be subverted if they were to be as accountable as we expect politicians to be. Yet in politics that accountability is crucial — for it is what obliges our representatives to take heed of the perspectives of ordinary citizens. None of this denies the vital role courts play in protecting the interests of individual citizens from the careless, inconsiderate and occasionally malicious actions of public and private agents and agencies. However, whilst litigation against an over-powerful state or corporation is an important feature of a democratic society, it is not a substitute for the democratic process. Courts properly focus on abuses of the law in individual cases. By contrast, democratic decision-making seeks to win the active assent of all citizens to a programme of collective policies. In circumstances where no consensus exists on what is the right or most just course of action, courts are in no position to take on this task. For it requires more than ensuring the law is equitably applied. It also involves

---

[10] In his study of the spread of constitutionally based judicial review in Europe, Stone Sweet (2000) notes how courts attempt to avoid legitimation problems by making pragmatic compromises that anticipate and so defer to what they presume will be the majority view. As we have noted elsewhere, and indicated above, this tactic is at best imperfect, see Bellamy (1999): ch 7; and (2001).

securing compromises amongst a whole range of concerns, balancing the knock on costs and benefits of pursuing policies in one area for those in others, and in consequence prioritising health and employment, say, over education and defence, and obtaining a willingness amongst citizens to pay for the requisite measures in one form or another.

It might be argued that the EU's unfolding constitutional order *is* the product of a political process — namely the intergovernmental conferences that decide changes to the treaties through political dialogue and compromise. The role of the courts, notably the ECJ, is then to simply interpret what 'we the people' have decided (Shaw 2000b, 24, 25–9). There are two difficulties with this view. First, it limits constitutional politics to specific transformative 'moments' rather than seeing it as on-going aspect of 'normal' politics. However, truly constitutional moments tend to occur in exceptional times, such as following a war, when there is a widespread desire for a new beginning and a sense of common purpose. The IGCs cannot be represented as genuine constitutional moments in this sense. Rather, they are continuations of the daily debates within Europe concerning the EU's purpose and membership as well as its form of governance. As we have noted, with the 'polity' issue still unsettled it is impossible to make settled decisions about its 'regime'. Moreover, this situation is exacerbated by virtue of there being different European peoples who view the 'polity' as well as the 'regime' questions very differently from each other. Secondly, IGCs are not especially open or democratic fora. Only occasional referenda force politicians to account, and these are usually quite crude and not universally held. Nevertheless, as those following Maastricht and most recently in Ireland after Nice have revealed, they often indicate a failure of politicians in even the most Europhile states to carry their populations with them. What is required is an improvement in the 'normal' European democratic process, not constitutional settlements that further reduce the daily involvement of European citizens in political debate about the shape and character of the EU.

The recent conventions to draft the European Charter of Fundamental Rights and a possible European Constitution have been greeted in some quarters as innovations that partly address these two difficulties. The conventions have been much more open and broadly based than the IGCs, with the government representatives outnumbered by national and European parliamentarians, along with representatives from the Commission. There has also been a relatively broad consultation of other EU bodies and groups from within civil society, with their deliberations and proposals being made widely available on dedicated web sites (De Búrca 2001, Shaw 2003). However, although they represent an improvement on the IGCs in these respects, they do not totally overcome their drawbacks and pose problems of their own. Though sometimes trumpeted as exercises in an exceptional and high-minded form of constitutional politics, in which the convention members deliberate to reach a consensus on truth and justice (Eriksen, Fossum and Menéndez, 2002), both conventions have in fact been characterised by the divisions and compromises typical of normal politics (Bellamy and Schönlau, forthcoming). Given our analysis, this comes as no surprise. Genuine ideological, pragmatic and principled differences remain over the various 'polity' and 'regime' dimensions of the EU. Naturally, these divisions were expressed within both conventions, so that it was to be expected that the resulting documents would seek to accommodate these differences rather than impose a unitary vision upon them. Indeed, fair compromises that reflect the range of views on an issue are, from a democratic point of view, no bad thing. However, there are dangers in constitutionalising such compromise agreements. For these bargains reflect what the current political power brokers within Europe find mutually acceptable. As ideals and interests change, we can expect the nature of what would be agreed to alter too — though in ways that cannot be anticipated, especially given Enlargement. From this point of view, there is a danger that entrenching a constitution (which looks set to incorporate the Charter too) would freeze and codify the status quo, rather than allowing rights policy and the governance structures to evolve along with the EU itself (Weiler 2000, Bellamy and Castiglione 2001). In this regard, it is an advantage rather than a drawback that the status and even the wording of the constitution is ultimately subject to agreement by the member states in an IGC, making it a treaty rather than a constitutional document in the strict sense, possessing a higher law status that regulates even the treaty-making process. Moreover, the most important parts of the constitution are not the lists detailing supposedly common European values and the respective competences of the Union and the member states that have thus far attracted most attention, but the design of the future political arrangements for implementing and policing them in the course of ordinary policy-making and, in extraordinary circumstances, amending them (Weiler 2002, 573–4). Here the opportunity exists for setting up continuous dialogues not only between member state constitutional courts but also between their legislatures — the latter facilitated by the empowerment of new transnational democratic fora.

Meanwhile, the enhancement of European democracy in such ways is subject to similar constraints to those we have highlighted with regard to a European constitution (Banchoff and Smith 1999). Within a relatively homogenous people, who accept the legitimacy of both 'polity' and 'regime', then government by simple majority rule is warranted, with minorities protected by the constitutional consensus. But when the contours of the 'polity' are in dispute, such hierarchical decision-making risks are coercive. Actors must achieve the higher threshold of a mutually acceptable compromise characteristic of systems of governance. By contrast to governmental arrangements, governance involves horizontal relations between actors who are sufficiently interdependent to desire a collective agreement, yet practically independent or normatively distinct enough to make imposed solutions impractical or unjustifiable (Hirst and Thompson 1996, 183–4; Schmitter 2001). Governance operates as a form of partnership in which each partner benefits from co-operation with the others and would be damaged by their non-involvement, even if not to the same degree. It involves regular interaction over a whole range of policies rather than being an *ad hoc* and sporadic arrangement, so that those involved share certain norms and have a commitment to the process itself, albeit not of the absolutely binding kind associated with obligations to a state.

The balance between Commission, Council and European Parliament and the various levels largely reflect such horizontal governance relationships. Their inadequacies result from the poor democratic control exerted by the relevant 'polity' constituency over each one of them. The democratic deficit tends to be analysed in terms of strengthening the European Parliament as the only directly elected institution. Once again, the difficulty with this solution lies in its introducing a hierarchical 'regime' without the requisite internal 'polity' legitimacy. As Weiler has pertinently remarked, in the absence of a unified European demos, asking the European peoples to accept legislation by majoritarian voting in the European Parliament would be like expecting the Danes to acknowledge the legitimate authority of a German Bundestag to which they had been granted voting rights (Weiler 1996, 111). Indeed, the legitimacy crisis posed by strengthening European parliamentary government is even more acute than Weiler's analogy suggests. For social differentiation has produced an ever more complex and diverse society and economy. It has become difficult for one body either to adequately represent the range of values and interests or to produce regulations that are sufficiently attuned to the peculiarities of particular case, let alone to implement and enforce them. As a result, there has been a dispersal of political authority amongst a whole range of private and semi-private actors, from privatised service providers, that increasingly run the once nationalised utilities within most of the member states, through specialised agencies and regulators, such as private standardisation bodies like CEN or CENELEC, to voluntary and special interest organisations (as employed in the fifth environmental programme). This shift from parliamentary democracy to a 'democracy of organisation' has gone further in the EU than in any state (Anderson and Burns 1996, 227–67). The promotion of social dialogue via Article 139EC has even produced an officially recognised partial privatisation of the legislative process (Bernard 2000, 279–80).

A situation of multiple European demoi operating across multiple polities requires a 'regime' that explicitly recognises and seeks to promote dialogue between them and the various ways in which they debate the changing dimensions of the proto-European 'polity'. As we have noted, the actual structure of the EU does in part reflect this concern. Thus, there are multiple channels of political representation for different sorts of political *subjects*: member states in the Intergovernmental Conferences and Council of Ministers, national political parties in the EP, selected functional interests in the Economic and Social Committee (ESC) and sub-national territorial units in the Committee of the Regions. The avenue for reform lies in strengthening the democratic accountability of each and facilitating a more equitable dialogue between them. Elsewhere (Bellamy 1999, ch 5; Bellamy and Castiglione 2000b; Bellamy 2001), we have argued that the most suitable norms for devising such a scheme derive from the neo-Roman republican tradition with its injunction that decision-making evades domination through 'hearing the other side'. The key to this approach lies in prioritising freedom rather than rights and justice. Given the latter are sources of disagreement, they cannot offer a framework for our political deliberations. By contrast, the emphasis on freedom stresses the importance of being able to continually re-negotiate and dispute any given settlement (Tully 2001b, 1–34). The focus is not on realising any particular end state so much as the capacity of the members of a political society to determine their way of life in a manner that reflects their diverse and evolving ideals, identities and interests. As a result, political arrangements have to be so structured to ensure each side engages with the concerns of others. The goal is to avoid domination by ensuring each affected group is a party to the decision and finds it mutually acceptable. The aim is not consensus but compromise through reciprocal accommodation.

Contestatory mechanisms are central to this scheme, providing the means for avoiding both false negatives and positives (Pettit 1999; Bellamy 2000b, 215–6). In parliamentary systems the ability to remove the government from office offers the best mechanism of this kind. In a system of governance, though, matters are not so straightforward because power is less centralised and the demos more fragmented (Anderson and Burns 1996). To some degree the dispersal of power is itself an aid. Multiple but interacting 'polities' and 'regimes' can offer checks and balances that can help secure mutual recognition. Such balancing largely justifies the weighted voting in the Council and distribution of seats within the EP, which biases representation against large states to ensure the smaller get a voice. However, EU institutions still leave grossly under-represented key concerns, from national legislatures and regions through to a whole series of non-business interests — from the unemployed, through ordinary consumers to public interest movements, including transnational coalitions of these groups. The more formal role granted national parliaments in the Protocol to the draft European Constitution at least gives some formal acknowledgement to one legislative level within the EU process (CONV 820/1/03 REV 1). Giving a legislative as opposed to purely consultative function to bodies such as the Committee of the Regions and the Economic and Social Committee, whilst employing electoral mechanisms to make them more accountable and representative, would further recognise the multiplicity of 'regimes' and 'polities' in the EU and strengthen the balance of powers within its decision-making. Though the Commission consults a large number of NGOs, both informally and within the context of the comitology process, the process of selection remains haphazard and obscure, whilst the representativeness and accountability of these organisations is deficient to say the least (Warleigh 2001, 619–39) In this respect, the White Paper on Governance promised (though it failed to deliver) a major step forward, not least in providing a catalogue of which organisations are consulted and in proposals for ensuring they are answerable to their members. Article 46 of the proposed constitution detailing the principle of participatory democracy is also a move in the right direction, particularly the citizens' initiative whereby a million citizens from a significant number of member states could invite the Commission to consider a legal act to implement an aspect of the Constitution overlooked by current policies (CONV 820/1/03 REV 1 46.4). The passing of an American-style Administrative Procedure Act, to ensure the participation of all interested parties in the framing of regulations, would further enhance the contestatory powers of citizens.[11] These suggestions are obviously indicative rather than exhaustive of what might be done. To the extent the EU continues to be characterised by several Europes rather than one, we claim merely that these sorts of mechanisms are vital to ensure the internal democratic legitimacy of the EU's ongoing constitutional process.

## 4.  CONCLUSION

Attention to the normative dimension of the EU has been stimulated by concern over its lack of legitimacy. We have argued that addressing this issue proves more complex than is sometimes supposed. Legitimacy operates across four dimensions, none of which are congruent within the EU or likely to become so. For different reasons, analysts of the EU have tended to ignore the interaction between 'polity' and 'regime', and to emphasise *external* at the expense of *internal* legitimacy. Putting all four dimensions together reveals the EU to be a polycentric 'polity' possessing a multi-level 'regime'. The result is that the EU conforms neither to the materialist realism of many theorists of intregration nor the high idealism of certain European federalists. Both descriptively and prescriptively it lies somewhere in between. As we have argued more fully elsewhere, this in between character of the EU is best captured by the 'republican' notion of a 'mixed constitution', within which sovereignty is horizontally dispersed between different parts of the body politic so as to force all parties to deliberate with

---

[11] These and other proposals are made in Curtin (1996); and Schmitter (2000). See also Craig (1997, 119–24) who draws out their republican potential.

each other.[12] In the terminology of the present chapter, this set up allows internal legitimacy to emerge via a series of dialogues amongst the multiple European constituencies, which serve to construct both the EU 'polity' and its 'regime'. From this perspective, the main avenues for reform should be to improve the ability of the EU's institutions to check and balance each other and to enhance the contestatory power of ordinary citizens: to the extent the new constitutional arrangements of the EU contain provisions moving in this direction they are to be welcomed.

## 5.   REFERENCES

### 5.1.   Cases

*Cinéthèque v Fédèrations nationales des cinémas français* Cases 60–1/84. 1985, ECR 2605.
*Cowan v Le Trésor public* Case 186/87. 1989, ECR 195.
*ERT v Dimotiki Etairia Piliroforissis* Case C–260/89. 1991, ECR I–2925.
*SPUC (Ireland) Ltd v Grogan* Case C–159/90. 1991, ECR I–4685.
*'Solange I'* Internationale Handelsgesellschaft. 1974, 2 CMLR 549.
*'Solange II'* Wunsche Handelsgesellschaft. 1987, 3 CMLR 225*Brunner*. 1994, 1 CMLR 57.
*UEAPME v Council* Case T–135/96. 1998, ECR II–2335.

### 5.2.   Bibliography

Anderson, S. and Burns, T. 1996, The European Union and the Erosion of Parliamentary Democracy: A Study of Post-parliamentary Governance. In S. Anderson and K. Eliassen (eds), *The European Union — How Democratic is It?* London: Sage, 227–67.
Austin, D. and O'Neill, M. 2000, *Democracy and Cultural Diversity*. Oxford: Oxford University Press.
Banchoff, T. and Smith, M. P. (eds) 1999, *Legitimacy and the European Union: The Contested Polity*. London: Routledge.
Bankowski, Z. and Scott, A. (eds) 2000, *The European Union and Its Order*. Oxford: Blackwell.

---

[12] See Bellamy and Castiglione (2000b) and Bellamy (2003, 180–88). Although Friese and Wagner (2002, 355) may be correct to describe our thesis as a 'weak' form of republicanism when compared to Habermas's 'strong' version, we trust it is evident from the above that they are mistaken to suggest that we 'take it for granted that there is agreement about the Europeanness of many questions'. Indeed, our scheme is motivated in large part by our disputing that such agreement exists, with us looking to deliberation within this multilayered setting to create it.

Barry, N. 1994, 'Sovereignty, the Rule of Recognition and Constitutional Stability in Britain', *Hume Papers on Public Policy*. 2: 1; 10–27.

Beetham, D. and Lord, C. 1998, *Legitimacy and the European Union*. Harlow: Longman.

Bellamy, R. (ed) 1996, *Constitutionalism, Democracy and Sovereignty: American and European Perspectives*. Aldershot: Avebury.

—— 1999, *Liberalism and Pluralism: Towards a Politics of Compromise*. London: Routledge.

—— 2000a, Citizenship Beyond the Nation State: The Case of Europe. In N. O'Sullivan (ed) *Political Theory in Transition*. London: Routledge. 91–112.

—— 2000b, 'Dealing with Difference: Four Models of Pluralist Politics', *Parliamentary Affairs: A Journal of Comparative Politics*. 53:1; 198–217.

—— 2001, 'The "Right to Have Rights": Citizenship Practice and the Political Constitution of the EU', Bellamy and Warleigh (2001), 41–70.

—— 2003, Sovereignty, Post-Sovereignty and Pre-Sovereignty: Reconceptualising the State, Rights and Democracy in the EU. In N. Walker (ed), *Sovereignty in Transition*, Oxford: Hart, 167–89.

Bellamy, R., Bufacchi V. and Castiglione, D. (eds) 1995, *Democracy and Constitutional Culture in the Union of Europe*, Lothian Foundation Press: London.

Bellamy, R. and Castiglione, D. (eds) 1996, *Constitutionalism in Transformation*, Oxford: Blackwell.

—— 1997a, The Normative Challenge of a European Polity: Cosmopolitan and Communitarian Models Compared, Criticised and Combined. In Føllesdal and Koslowski (1997), 254–84.

—— 1997b, 'Building the Union: The Nature of Sovereignty in the Political Architecture of Europe', *Law and Philosophy*, vol. 16, 421–45.

—— 2000a, 'The Normative Turn in European Studies: Legitimacy, Identity and Democracy'. SHIPSS, University of Exeter: RUSEL Working Paper 38/2000, http://www.ex.ac.uk/shipss/politics/research/rusel.htm.

—— 2000b, 'Democracy, Sovereignty and the Constitution of the European Union: The Republican Alternative to Liberalism'. In Bankowski and Scott (eds) (2000), 170–90.

—— 2001, 'Tra retorica e simbolismo: la Carta dei diritti fondamentali dell'Unione europea'. *La Carta dei diritti fondamentali. Verso una Costituzione europea?*, a cura di Barbara Henry e Anna Loretoni, *Quaderni Forum* XV, (2001), 2, 67–74.

—— 2003, 'Legitimizing the Euro-"Polity" and its "Regime": The Normative Turn in EU Studies', *European Journal of Political Theory*, 2: 7–34.

Bellamy, R. and Schönlau, J. forthcoming 'The Normality of Constitutional Politics: An Analysis of the Drafting of the EU Charter of Fundamental Rights', *Constellations*.

Bellamy, R. and Warleigh, A. 1998, 'From an Ethics of Integration to an Ethics of Participation: Citizenship and the Future of the European Union', *Millennium: Journal of International Studies*, 27; 447–70.

—— 2001, (eds) *Citizenship and Governance in the European Union*, London: Continuum.

Bernard, N. 2000, Legitimising EU Law: Is Social Dialogue the Way Forward? Some Reflections around the *UEAPME* Case. In J Shaw (ed) *Social Law and Policy in an Evolving European Union*. Hart: Oxford, 279–302.

Bork, R. H. 1990, *The Tempting of America*, New York: Free Press.

Checkel, J. 1999, 'Norms, Institutions, and National Identity in Contemporary Europe', *International Studies Quarterly*, 43: 83–114.

Checkel, J. 2001, Constructing European Institutions. In M. Aspinall, and G. Schneider, (eds) *The Rules of Integration: Institutionalist Approaches to the Study of Europe*, Manchester: Manchester University Press.

Christiansen, T., Jorgensen, K. and Wiener, A. 1999, 'The Social Construction of Europe', T. Christiansen, K. Jorgensen and A. Wiener (eds), *The Social Construction of Europe*, special issue of the *Journal of European Public Policy*, 6:4: 528–44.

Chryssochoou, D. 1998, *Democracy in the European Union*, London: I. B. Taurus.

——— 2000, 'Metatheory and the Study of the European Union: Capturing the Normative Turn', *European Integration* 22; 123–44.

——— 2001, *Theorizing European Integration*, London: Sage.

CONV 820/1/03 REV 1 Draft Treaty Establishing a Constitution for Europe, 27 June 2003.

Craig, P. 1997, 'Democracy and Rule-making Within the EC: An Empirical and Normative Assessment', *European Law Journal*. 3:2: 105–30.

Curtin, D. 1996, 'The European Union, Civil Society and Participatory Democracy', *Collected Courses of the Academy of European Law*, Florence: EUI.

——— 1997, *Postnational Democracy: The European Union in Search of a Political Philosophy*, The Hague: Kluwer Law International.

Dalton, R. J. 1999, Political Support in Advanced Industrial Democracies. In P. Norris, (ed) *Critical Citizens: Global Support for Democratic Governance*, Oxford: Oxford University Press, 75–6.

De Búrca, G. 1996, 'The Quest for Legitimacy in the European Union', *The Modern Law Review*. 59; 349–76.

——— 2001, 'The Drafting of the EU Charter of Fundamental Rights', *European Law Journal*. 26: 126–38.

De Witte, B. 1991, 'Droit communitarie et valeurs constitutionelles nationales', *Droits*. 14; 87–96.

Diez, T. 1999, 'Riding the AM-Track through Europe; or, The Pitfalls of a Rationalist Journey through European Integration'; *Millennium: Journal of International Studies*, 28:2: 355–69.

Duff, A. 1994, 'Building a Parliamentary Europe', *Government and Opposition*, 29: 147–65.

Dworkin, R. 1995, 'Constitutionalism and Democracy', *European Journal of Philosophy*, 3: 2–11.

Eriksen, Erik Oddvar and Fossum, John Erik, (eds) 2000, *Democracy in the European Union — Integration through Deliberation?* London: Routledge.

——— and Menéndez, Agustín José, 'The Chartering of a European Constitution', in Eriksen, Erik Oddvar, Fossum, John Erik and Menéndez, Agustín José (eds), *Constitution Making and Democratic Legitimacy*, Oslo: ARENA Report, No 5/2002, 1–11.

Elgström, O. and Jönsson, C. 2000, 'Negotiation in the European Union: Bargaining or Problem-Solving'? *Journal of European Public Policy*, 7:5: 684–704.

Føllesdal, A. and Koslowski, P. (eds) 1997, *Democracy and the European Union*, Berlin: Springer-Verlag.

Friese, H. and Wagner, P. 2002, 'Survey Article: The Nascent Political Philosophy of the European Polity', *The Journal of Political Philosophy*, 10:3: 342–64.

Greenwood, J. 1997, *Representing Interests in the European Union*, London: Macmillan.

Haas, E. 1975, *The Obsolescence of Regional Integration Theory*, Berkeley, CA: University of California Press.

Haas, E. 1958, *The Uniting of Europe: Political, Social and Economic Forces 1950–57*. Stanford: Stanford University Press.

Habermas, J. 1992, 'Citizenship and National Identity: Some Reflections on the Future of Europe'. *Praxis International*, 12:1: 1–19.

—— 1998, *The Inclusion of the Other: Studies in Political Theory*, Cambridge: Polity.

—— 1999, 'The European Nation-state and the Pressures of Globalisation', *New Left Review*, 235; 46–59.

—— 2001, 'Why Europe Needs a Constitution', *New Left Review*, 11: 5–26.

Held, D. McGrew, A. Goldblatt, D and Perraton, J. 1999, *Global Transformations: Politics, Economics and Culture*, Cambridge: Polity Press.

Hirst, P. and Thompson, G. 1996, *Globalisation in Question*, Cambridge: Polity.

Hollis, M. and Smith, S. 1990, *Explaining and Understanding International Relations*, Oxford: Clarendon Press.

Imig, D. and Tarrow. S. (eds) 2000, *Contentious Europeans: Protest and Politics in an Emerging Polity*, Boulder: Rowman and Littlefield.

James, A. 1999, 'The Practice of Sovereign Statehood in Contemporary International Society', *Political Studies*, 47:3; 457–73.

Jachtenfuchs, M., Diez, T. and Jung, S. 1998, 'Which Europe? Conflicting Models of a Legitimate European Political Order', *European Journal of International Relations*, 4:4; 409–45.

Jeffrey, C. 2000, 'Sub-National Mobilization and European Integration', *Journal of Common Market Studies*, 38:1; 1–25.

Klingemann, H-D. and Fuchs, D. (ed) 1995, *Citizens and the State: Beliefs in Government vol. 1*, Oxford: Oxford University Press.

Kymlicka, W. 1995, *Multicultural Citizenship: A Liberal Theory of Minority Rights*, Oxford: Oxford University Press.

Lehning, P. and Weale, A. (eds) 1997, *Citizenship, Democracy and Justice in the New Europe*, London: Routledge.

Lord, C. and Beetham, D. 2001, 'Legitimizing the EU: Is there a "Post-parliamentary Basis" for its Legitimation'? *Journal of Common Market Studies*, 39: 443–62.

MacCormick, N. 1995, 'The Maastricht-Urteil: Sovereignty Now', *European Law Journal*, 1; 255–62.

—— 1997, 'Democracy, Subsidiarity, and Citizenship in the "European Commonwealth"', *Law and Philosophy*, 16; 331–56.

Majone, G. 1996, 'Regulatory Legitimacy'. In G. Majone et al. *Regulating Europe*, London: Routledge, 284–301.

—— 1998, 'Europe's "Democratic Deficit": The Question of Standards', *European Law Journal*, 4: 5–28.

Marks, G., Hooghe L. and Blank, K. 1996, 'European Integration from the 1980s: State-Centric v Multi-level Governance', *Journal of Common Market Studies*, 34; 341–78.

Mazzini, G. 1907, *The Duties of Man and Other Essays*, London: J. M. Dent.

McAllister, I. 1999, The Economic Performance of Governments. In Norris, P. (1999).

Merlingen, M. 2001, 'Identity, Politics and Germany's Post-TEU Policy on EMU', *Journal of Common Market Studies*, 39: 463–83.

Mill, J. S. 1910, Considerations on Representative Government (1861). In J. S. Mill *Utilitarianism, Liberty, Representative Government*, London: J. M. Dent.

Milward, A. 1993, *The European Rescue of the Nation State*, London: Routledge.

Moravcsik, A. 1993, 'Preferences and Power in the European Community: A Liberal Intergovernmentalist Approach', *Journal of Common Market Studies*, 31:4; 473–524.

Moravcsik, A. 1999, *The Choice for Europe: Social Purpose and State Power From Messina to Maastricht*, London: UCL Press.

Nentwich, M. and Weale, A. 1998, *Political Theory and the European Union*, London: Routledge.

Parekh, B. 2000, *Rethinking Multiculturalism: Cultural Diversity and Political Theory*, Basingstoke: Macmillan.

Peterson, J. 1995, 'Decision-making in the European Union: Towards a Framework for Analysis', *Journal of European Public Policy*, 21:1; 69–93.

Pettit, P. 1999, Republican Liberty, Contestatory Democracy. In C. Hacker-Cordon and I. Shapiro (eds) *Democracy's Value*, Cambridge: Cambridge University Press.

Pierson, P. 1996, 'The Path to European Union: An Historical Institutionalist Account', *Comparative Political Studies*, 29: 123–64.

Pinder, J. 1994, Building the Union: Policy, Reform, Constitution. In A. Duff, J. Pinder and R. Pryce (eds). *Maastricht and Beyond: Building the European Union*, London: Routledge, 269–85.

Ruggie, J. G. 1993, 'Territoriality and Beyond: Problematizing Modernity in International Relations', *International Organisation*, 47:1; 139–74.

Scharpf, F. 1999, *Governing in Europe: Effective and Democratic?* Oxford: Oxford University Press.

Schmitter, P. C. 2000, *How to Democratize the European Union … And Why Bother?* Maryland: Rowman and Littlefield.

—— 2001, 'What is There to Legitimise in the European Union … And How Might This be Accomplished'? Florence: EUI mimeo.

Sharpf, F. W. 1988, 'The Joint Decision Trap', *Public Administration*, 66: 239–78.

Shaw, J. 1998, 'The Interpretation of European Union Citizenship', *The Modern Law Review*, 61:3; 293–317.

—— 1999, 'Constitutionalism in the European Union', *Journal of European Public Policy*, special issue 6: 4; 579–97.

—— 2000a, The "Governance" Research Agenda and the "Constitutional Question". In *Governance and Citizenship in Europe: Some Research Directions*, Brussels: European Commission, 22–5.

—— 2000b, 'Process and Constitutional Discourse in the European Union', *Journal of Law and Society*, 27:1; 4–37.

—— 2000c, Constitutionalism and Flexibility in the EU: Developing a Relational Approach. In G. De Búrca and J. Scott (eds) *Constitutional Change in the EU: From Uniformity to Flexibility*, Oxford: Hart. 337–58.

—— 2003, 'Process, Responsibility and Inclusion in EU Constitutionalism', *European Law Journal*, 9:1; 45–68.

Skinner, Q. 1974, 'Some Problems in the Analysis of Political thought and Action', *Political Theory*, 2; 277–303.

Smith, A. 1986, *The Ethnic Origins of Nations*, Oxford: Blackwell.

—— 1992, 'National Identity and the Idea of European Unity'. *International Affairs*, 68; 55–76.

Stone Sweet, A. and Sandholtz, W. 1997, 'European Integration and Supranational Governance'. *Journal of European Public Policy*, 4:3; 297–317.

Stone Sweet, A. 2000, *Governing with Judges: Constitutional Politics in Europe*, Oxford: Oxford University Press.

Sunstein, C. 1993, *The Partial Constitution*. Cambridge MA: Harvard University Press.

Tully, J. 1995, *Strange Multiplicity: Constitutionalism in an Age of Diversity*, Cambridge: Cambridge University Press.

—— 2001, 'La conception républicaine de la citoyenneté dans les sociétés multiculturelles et multinationales', *Politique et Sociétés*, 21:1, 123–47.

—— 2001b, Introduction. In Alain-G. Gagnon, C. Taylor, J. Tully (ed) *Multinational Democracy*, Cambridge: Cambridge University Press, 1–34.

—— 2002, 'The Unfreedom of the Moderns in Comparison to their Ideals of Constitutional Democracy', *Modern Law Review*, 65: 204–28.

Vink, M. P. 2001, 'The Limited Europeanisation of Domestic Citizenship Polity: Evidence from the Netherlands', *Journal of Common Market Studies*, 39: 875–96.

Waever, O. 1995, 'Identity, Integration and Security: Solving the Sovereignty Puzzle in EU Studies', *Journal of International Affairs*, 48:2; 389–431.

Waldron, J. 1999, *Law and Disagreement*, Oxford: Oxford University Press.

Walker, N. 1996, 'European Constitutionalism and European Integration', *Public Law*, 266–90.

Wallace, H. 1985, 'Negotiations and Coalition Formation in the European Community', *Government and Opposition*, 20: 453–72.

—— 1990, Making Multilateral Negotiations Work. In W. Wallace (ed), *The Dynamics of European Integration*, London: Pinter.

—— 1996, Politics and Policy in the EU: The Challenge of Governance. In H. Wallace and W. Wallace (eds). *Policy Making in the European Union*, 3rd ed Oxford: Oxford University Press.

Warleigh, A. 2000, 'The Hustle: Citizenship Practice, NGOs and "Policy Coalitions" in the European Union — The Cases of Auto Oil, Drinking Water and Unit Pricing', *Journal of European Public Policy*, 7:2; 229–43.

—— 2001, 'Europeanising' Civil Society: NGOs as Agents of Political Socialisation', *Journal of Common Market Studies*, 39: 619–39.

Weiler, J.H.H. 1996, European Neo-Constitutionalism: In Search of Foundations for the European Constitutional Order. In Bellamy and Castiglione (eds) 105–21.

—— 1999, *The Constitution of Europe: 'Do the New Clothes Have an Emperor?' and Other Essays on European Integration*, Cambridge: Cambridge University Press.

—— 2000, 'Does the EU Truly Need a Charter of Rights?', *European Law Journal*, 6:2; 95–7.

—— 2002, 'A Constitution for Europe? Some Hard Choices', *Journal of Common Market Studies*, 40:4; 563–80.

Wiener, A. 1998, *'European' Citizenship Practice: Building Institutions of a Non-State*. Oxford: Westview.

Wincott, D. 1995a, Political Theory, Law and European Union. In *New Legal Dynamics of European Union*, edited by J. Shaw and G. More, Oxford: Oxford University Press.

—— 1995b, 'Institutional Interaction and European Integration: Towards an Everyday Critique of Liberal Intergovernmentalism', *Journal of Common Market Studies*, 33; 597–609.

# 3

# The Juridification of Politics in the United States and Europe: Historical Roots, Contemporary Debates and Future Prospects

## LARS TRÄGÅRDH AND MICHAEL X. DELLI CARPINI

### 1. INTRODUCTION

IN AN ARTICLE prominently published a few years ago in *The New York Times*, Roger Cohen (2000) sounded a by now familiar theme: the nation-state is losing ground in Europe. But what was interesting about Cohen's article was not the general assertion, both commonplace and contested, that the European Union is characterised by the transgression of national sovereignties. Rather, its significance lay in his contention that a new European identity is in the process of being shaped that is based neither on the adoption of an elusive common 'culture', in the quasi ethnic sense of a common language, literature and history, nor on traditional nation-statist civic attributes such as mass political parties, the ritual of voting, the symbolism of flag, anthem, conscription, oath of allegiance, or passport. Rather, Cohen claimed, a new 'sense of European citizenship' is emerging, which is founded on the 'pre-eminence of European law over national legislation'.

And indeed, from its modest beginning in 1952 when the precursor to the European Court of Justice was created to settle rather technical disputes in the European Coal and Steal Community, the European Court has become a central and powerful institution within the emerging structure of the European Union, a Court whose jurisdiction has expanded to include not only narrowly defined economic issues, but also laws and rights that relate to areas like gender discrimination, human rights, working conditions, and the environment. As one official of the court notes, 'we used to be associated with abstruse things like fishing quotas, but increasingly European citizens see this as a place where they can uphold their rights', rights that are at times claimed against the national states on the basis of a developing EU charter of individual rights and anti-discrimination laws (in Cohen 2000). In other words, the European Court and the treaties on which the Court's rulings are based, has come to function in a manner similar to that of the American Supreme Court acting on the basis of the US Constitution and the Bill of Rights. This is an aspect of the EU that has been further strengthened through the work of the Laeken Convention, resulting in the proposed new Constitution for Europe that was presented in June 2003.

This leads us to a number of questions that we will seek to address in this chapter. To what extent is national parliamentary democracy in Europe in the process of being replaced or significantly complemented by a politico-legal culture where citizen action increasingly takes place through litigation within a transnational, European legal domain? Is the figure of the citizen, historically if not by definition bound up with the nation-state, about to be superceded by a new actor, a litigant acting within an emerging international 'community of law' (Wincott 2000) where both private and public conflicts will increasingly be fought out and resolved in international as well as national courts?

From the vantage point of normative political theory the question becomes one of assessing how one best conceives of and evaluates this newly empowered judicial realm: should this trend towards an increased juridification of politics be understood as an opening up of new opportunities for formerly disempowered individuals and groups to directly collect and exercise power, or should it, conversely, be critiqued as a debasement of deliberative and representative democracy, to put it provisionally in dichotomously charged polemical terms? We will return to these questions towards the end of the chapter.

However, let us first note that the juridification of politics to a considerable extent must be understood in empirical, rather than normative terms; that is, as one expression of the broad secular trend that is currently challenging the political order that we call 'national democracy'. From this point of view, the juridification of politics is a more or less unavoidable fact of modern political life, and the underlying assumption here is that Europeans could benefit from a deeper understanding of the American experience since there the close intertwining of law and politics has a much longer history and is far more firmly embedded in the constitutional framework and political culture.

What, then, are the secular trends that serve as the incubator for the juridification of politics? As discussed in more detail in the introduction to this book, at the broadest and most abstract level the context is that of 'globalization', first and foremost understood as the process whereby formerly sovereign or at least quasi-sovereign national economies have been overwhelmed by the emergence of a global economy. Since globalisation has occurred in the spirit of neo-liberal economic theory, this has in turn meant that the political sovereignty of the classical nation-state has been challenged as well, and that the space for national politics has shrunk.

In Europe the institutional context for this process, to which we will return, is the EU.[1]

A second crucial and related aspect of this secular trend is the rise of the modern individual, characterised by his and her reluctance to accept constraints imposed in the name of national community or state interest. Modern individualism is, like globalisation, best understood in terms of the victory of a market society that gives primacy to the individual in both political and economic terms. Thus, the globalised market society is challenging the nation-state both from above and from below.

The EU is in this context a particularly intriguing case to study since it can be understood simultaneously as an attempt to redress the lost balance between politics and the market and as an accommodation to the secular trends towards market society individualism. At one level, to be sure, it involves asserting the primacy of politics over the market. Especially with the Maastricht Treaty and the introduction of the so-called 'social dimension', ie an acknowledgement that the Union is not simply a common market but something more, a political society in which concerns about social justice must play a role along with the traditional emphasis on creating an open economy and a freer market, it has become clear that the ambitions of the EU include not only making the market safe from politics, but also its citizens secure from the uncertainties of the market. In this respect the EU is, not surprisingly, following in the footsteps of the nation-states that make up the Union. One might say that the German notion of the 'social market economy', with its dual agenda of promoting an efficient and productive economy as well as a substantial measure of social security, has been imported into the EU as a political objective.

However, the construction of the EU also entails the emergence of a political system that is profoundly different from the classical European nation-state with its affective base in a relatively homogenous national community and a corresponding politics of social solidarity. Instead, the EU is in fundamental ways more like the US, a political regime that seeks to balance the interests of the (federal) state with that of individuals, market actors, the institutions of civil society, and the governmental institutions at the (national) state and sub-national and local levels.

One key aspect of this 'Americanized' Europe is the emergence of a new juridified political culture. While neither the nation-state, nor majoritarian democracy is likely to disappear anytime soon, new avenues for collecting and exercising power are emerging that are far more complex and decentred as well as more amenable to the champions of individual and minority rights. An American style 'rights revolution' is unfolding in Europe, involving the use of the courts to claim rights and settle disputes, to seek protection

[1] For a more detailed discussion of the EU from this perspective, see ch 4 by Wincott in this volume.

from discrimination, to battle states and corporations as well as fellow citizens and citizens' organisations.

This shift signals not simply the empowering of individuals qua individuals, but also, and perhaps more importantly, the rise of identity politics. While no longer content to accept the universal and uniform identity of the imagined community of the nation, many of the modern individuals do not simply choose the path of atomised consumer individualism on a classical liberal model, but rather embrace identity politics and assert minority and group rights. Thus all manner of minority groups, defined ethnically, in terms of sexual proclivity, on the basis of (dis)abilities, age, gender, religion, and so on, have mobilised politically to further and protect group interests.

The proliferation of such groups has complicated the old political order based on a small number of class based parties and a politics that often sacrificed individual and minority rights at the altars of class solidarity, social rights, and national community. Given that a political system based on the idea of majoritarian, parliamentary democracy is not easily adaptable to the demands for protection of individual and minority rights, it is not surprising that many groups representing minority and individual rights increasingly turn to the courts, rather than to the parliaments, to claim their rights, be it the negative right to escape discrimination or the positive right to receive compensation for past acts of discrimination and oppression.

The social diversification of the body politic has been further deepened by a third crucial secular trend associated with both globalisation at large and European integration in particular, that is, increased migration within Europe and immigration from outside Europe. The central principle of the market society — the free movement of goods, people, and capital — intrinsically favours increased migration in the abstract. Concretely, the pull of European prosperity and the demand for cheap labour has translated there, as in the US, into real and large inflows of legal and illegal immigrants. These groups are even less likely to be easily integrated on the terms provided by a majoritarian social contract based on the ideal of an ethnically inflected national community.

The rationale for a comparative approach rests on the notion that the US and Europe represent two different traditions and two different historical legacies when it comes to political systems and the social contracts that inform their constitutional structures. Thus both the character of citizenship and the relation between law and politics differ. While issues of immigration are contentious on both sides of the Atlantic, the constructions of citizenship and national identity have generally been more open to immigrants and to ethnic and cultural diversity in the US than in Europe, where much 'thicker' theory and practice prevails.[2] Furthermore, the American constitutional

---

[2] This is not say that issues these issues have been unproblematic in the US, as we discuss in more detail later in this chapter.

structure has given a much greater place to individual rights and to the power of the judiciary. At the same time both the US and the EU are currently subject to the same secular trend, one that is putting the future of national citizenship in question while it globally tends to juridify politics.

In order to provide a meaningful comparative context for the discussion of the current situation, we will, in the next two sections, contrast what we call the 'anti-juridical' tradition characteristic of European political culture with the American political system that in stark contrast is characterised by a close intertwining of politics and law. We argue that this intertwining is rooted in the natural law-like status of the Constitution and the Bill of Rights as 'higher' law located beyond the purview of ordinary politics. In these sections we in turn consider the long-term historical legacies stretching back to the eighteenth and nineteenth centuries, the crucial developments that have taken place more recently during the twentieth century, and the current debates that are challenging notions of citizenship, the state and politics in both Europe and the United States.

In the concluding section we will consider, within this empirical context, the normative implications for the future. On the one hand one can imagine a decentralised power grid with new opportunity structures that may empower individuals and minorities. On the other, one might detect a hollowing out of democracy as a deliberative and consensus building process, leaving in its wake on the one hand single issue populism and on the other a legal proceduralism, both fatally disconnected from broader concerns with community welfare and social cohesion. We conclude by making a number of theoretical observations. The first set will focus on state/civil society relations, suggesting that law and courts constitute a connecting ground between the state and civil society, institutions and processes that allow for a market-like flow of information and power negotiation. The second set will focus on the relationship between democracy and law, and most particularly on the idea of thin versus thick conceptions of citizenship and citizenship practices.

## 2.  THE ANTI-JURIDICAL TRADITION IN EUROPE

As one begins to consider the varying views on the proper place of law in the political constitutional order, a startling but revealing difference between Americans and Europeans leaps out. Whereas in the US most of the voices expressing alarm when it comes to the power of lawyers and judges tend to come from the right, the opposite is true in Europe. Conversely, one looks largely in vain for the near equivalent of the American civil rights movement in the European context, at least until the very recent past. Of course, it might be tempting, not least for European

Social Democrats, to see this simply as yet another proof of the superiority of European-style democracy; had there been a properly functioning Social Democratic Party and a political system that was not rigged to give the rich and propertied undue influence; had American workers been less inclined to fall into states of false consciousness, incapable of seeing their proper class interest, lapsing into an optimistic middle class mentality; had there not been the tragic legacy of the enslavement of African-Americans and the genocidal war against the native American; then there would have been no need for a civil rights movement that had to rely on courts rather than parliaments, and on dubious metaphysical notions of 'self-evident' truths and rights rather than the force of objective historical movement. However, while there is indeed a great deal one can critically say about the American left's reliance on the courts,[3] the strong anti-juridical bent of the European left is fact rooted within the European tradition itself, and carries with it its own set of political limitations and social exclusions.[4]

## 2.1.   The Historical Legacy: Marx and the Law

To understand the long-standing and widespread suspicion of the idea of an independent judiciary that has prevailed in continental Europe, one must begin by noting that the dominant tradition has been legal positivism. That is, unlike the English and American common law tradition, with its emphasis on adversarial proceedings, the crucial role played by the jury, and the law-making powers of the judges, in Europe courts and judges have primarily served as officials of the state, applying positive, written, codified law. Law was not independent of state power, nor was there a higher law to appeal to, no independent source of authority, no basis for judicial review, whether a constitution or some species of natural law. Given this, it is not surprising that once opposition to authoritarian regimes began to emerge in earnest during the nineteenth century, critics often viewed the law simply as a matter of state power or anti-majoritarian class interest.

To make this point more fully, one might usefully begin by considering the towering figure of Karl Marx himself. As Donald Kelley (1978, 350) has pointed out, law was in fact 'the profession first chosen by Marx'. Marx had begun his legal studies in Bonn in 1835, and transferred in 1836 to Berlin where he studied with both the famous leader of the 'historical school', Friedrich Karl von Savigny and his critic, the Hegelian Eduard Gans.

---

[3] Unlike the right in the United States, which bases its attacks on juridical politics largely on the economic costs involved, critiques originating from the liberal or left-leaning side of the ideological spectrum tend to emphasise its non-democratic nature. See, for example, Beard 1957; Lowi 1979; Putnam 2000; Kagan 2001.

[4] On this theme, also see the contributions by Hilbink and Wincott in this volume.

However, after three hundred pages of what he in a famous confessional letter (10 November 1837) to his father referred to as 'unhappy work', Marx soon 'saw the falsity of the whole thing', and according to Kelley, 'broke off the project' (Kelley 1978, 354). The fundamental problem, according to Marx, was what he called the 'metaphysics of law', the divorce of law from its material base in 'reality'. Even as Savigny and other members of the historical school criticised natural law theories and attempts at creating rational, codified law along the lines of the Napoleonic code, they instead turned to history itself as a metaphysical source of law, as 'embodied natural law'. Analysing Savigny's elder colleague, Gustav Hugo, Marx argued that this

> is the frank, naïve reckless method of the historical school ... Hugo, therefore, profanes all that the just, moral political man regards as holy, but he smashes these things only to be able to honour them as historical relics; he desecrates them in the eyes of reason in order afterwards to make them honourable in the eyes of history and at the same time to make the eyes of the historical school honourable.
>
> (Kelley 1978, 360)

In particular, Marx fastened upon the problem of property and the manner in which Savigny had used the historicist line of argumentation to derive right from fact and thus lapse into what Marx deemed to be an immoral position, one that justified 'the right of arbitrary power' and 'legitimates the baseness of today by the baseness of yesterday' (Marx cited in Kelley 1978, 361).

Where this rejection of the study of law, as taught by Savigny, led was not to an embrace of some version of natural law however, but to a rejection of law altogether and a turn towards the study of 'the realities of possession and property', that is, to the studies of political economy that would serve as the basis for Marx' mature work. Nonetheless, as Kelley points out, Marx' youthful engagement with and rejection of law 'continued to possess at least a negative importance' as a target for his general attack on idealist social thought (Kelley 1978, 367). Just as religion was but the 'opium of the people', law was but a system for justifying and legitimising the power of the propertied classes, through which might was turned into right. And this denigration of law as lacking an autonomous source of legitimacy came to deeply inform the way in which the European left has historically viewed the law and the judiciary. Thus rights, in the classical Marxist analysis, were seen as 'merely the ideological reflex of capitalist property and exchange relations' (Cohen 1988, 43).

While Marx rejected ordinary politics as hopelessly naïve with respect to the fundamental nature of power, he retained — betraying here his debts to the 'utopian' socialism of the Saint-Simonians — a longing for a return to the non-alienated state that he associated with original communal property. Indeed, according to Marx 'civil law developed simultaneously with private property from the disintegration of the natural community' (cited in Kelley 1978, 365). Thus social revolution entailed the destruction not only of capitalism and private property, but also of the state and the right of might; the return of sorts to the happy state of affairs that pertained before the emergence of private property, the state, and law.

This 'realist' vision of law and rights is shared, if in different forms, by later, post-Marxist thinkers of the left, such as Michel Foucault. As Jean Cohen has pointed out, rights are in the Foucauldian scheme simply conceived as 'the product of the will of the sovereign state, articulated through the medium of positive law and facilitating the surveillance of all aspects of society' (Cohen 1988, 43). However, Foucault, influenced by Georges Bataille, made an additional move that would have been foreign to Marx. Bataille, the eminent philosopher of eroticism, had declared that the incest taboo — the orginary law that thrust man from a state of nature into a state of civilisation — simultaneously gave birth to the possibility of transgression, ie, the breaking of the taboo and breaching of the social contract (Bataille 1993). Along these lines, Foucault imagined the modern democratic welfare state not only as a regime that used power/knowledge to discipline and normalise, but also in terms of the endless possibilities for resistance and transgression that by necessity were produced at the same time. To break the law thus becomes an erotic act, a gesture in which *servile* man — who lived according to the social contract within the bounds of the law — for a moment could become *sovereign* man — the transgressor — to use Bataille's categories. However, for our purposes it is sufficient to emphasise that Foucault shared with Marx a view of law and rights that denied that rights originated, and thus derived their legitimacy from, outside the statist production of power/knowledge.

## 2.2.   The Place of Law in Twentieth Century European Political Systems

Of course, in the day to day world of European Social Democracy, neither an outright rejection of the state, nor politics as a form of eroticised rebellion, came to be the norm, even if a colourful minority within the left subscribed to varying versions of such attitudes, from the anarchists and syndicalists of the late nineteenth century, via the 68ers to contemporary queer theory activists, for whom protest, rebellion, resistance, revolution, romance, and eroticism were intimately linked. Rather, the enduring suspicion of the law and the judiciary found expression in the rather more humdrum conviction that the political objective of a serious socialist party must be to conquer the state rather than to rely on the laws created by a state controlled by the enemies of the working class. Indeed, 'rights' came to be associated with 'bourgeois' privileges, thinly veiled forms of protection of the property rights of the ruling class.

Once the formerly revolutionary movements had been transformed into stolid reformist and parliamentary parties, this attitude remained even if the language was toned down. Constitutional restrictions on the power of the parliament, formulated in terms of separation of powers and individual rights, were perceived as anti-democratic. The case of Sweden is in this respect emblematic. Since, as one observer has somewhat facetiously noted with respect to the Swedish Social Democrats, they imagined themselves as the builders of a 'good society', the so-called 'people's home' (*folkhemmet*), their view was that

> all constitutionally embedded rights make it more difficult for the government to at will and at any given moment do the right thing for society at large. Furthermore, such protections are unnecessary for ordinary citizens since the Social Democrats would never do them any harm.[5]

The hostility towards the judiciary was also based on the sociologically plausible assumption that lawyers and judges belonged to the bourgeois class, and that they thus were likely to more or less consciously act on behalf of their class brethren. In this context the idea of judicial review, for example, was viewed with deep suspicion and the notion that judges should be able to overturn decisions made by a democratically elected parliament was held to be too undemocratic to be given much weight. Finally, it must be added that the lack of an independent judiciary in Sweden, even the lack of a serious discussion of this absence among lawyers, judges, and jurists themselves, is a consequence of the dominance of the Uppsala school of legal philosophy associated with Axel Hägerström. In this tradition, the law and the judiciary was subject to the power of politics, there were no rights, or right to rights, beyond what was given by the parliament. That is, in Sweden as elsewhere in Europe, suspicion of the law among left-wing democrats must be understood in the context of the dominance of legal positivism.

Since the Second World War, the anti-juridical bent typical of the European tradition in general, and of those on the left in particular, has been modified. To be sure, in countries with untarnished confidence in their own democratic traditions — the Scandinavian countries, for example — a skeptical attitude towards the power of the courts in general and judicial review in particular remains. A recent major study of the role of the courts and of judicial review in England, France and Germany by the

---

[5] The quote is by the influential Swedish jurist, Gustaf Petrén, quoted in Zaremba 1992, 75.

Swedish political scientist Barry Holmström is a good example. Holmström recognises that the weightiest argument in favour of strong and independent courts concerns not so much the deepening of democracy but rather the protection of civil and human rights. Nonetheless he arrives at the conclusion that

> Politically active courts, and the judicialization of politics in democratic states, should rather be regretted than commended. It is part of a more general phenomenon, the professionalization of democratic rule, which steadily removes modern democracies from the core meaning of democracy, relieves elected representatives of their responsibilities towards the citizens, and places political power in unaccountable bodies.
>
> (Holmström 1998)

It is symptomatic that Holmström sees the juridification of politics in terms of professionalisation and increased distance between citizens and the democratic process. As we shall see soon, this is a point of view that stands at some distance from the US experience when it comes to, for example, the civil rights movement. Indeed, Holmström here is speaking from the perspective of the European experience, and it is indeed true that European judges have by tradition been civil servants of the State, applying positive law, rather than autonomous interpreters of the law who are open to legal arguments made by lawyers representing political actors whose base is in organisations independent of the State, that is, whose location is in civil society.

However, the faith in parliamentary democracy that underlies this kind of critique of a strong and autonomous judiciary, was severely challenged in mid-twentieth century Europe. In Germany in particular, a crucial legacy of the Nazi era was a new found distrust of majoritarian democracy. After all, Hitler himself had gained power not through a violent coup but by making skillful use of the democratic apparatus set up through the Weimar constitution, one of the most democratic ever written. With the experience of the Weimar Republic in fresh memory, Germans were determined not to go too far in the direction of unadulterated democracy. Under the influence of the United States, the Germans thus have their Basic Law and Constitutional Court, there to safeguard fundamental liberal values, from (majoritarian) democracy itself if necessary.

Furthermore, the behaviour of German judges, doctors, lawyers, and other servants of the state during the Nazi period in general and the Holocaust in particular, fatally undermined confidence in the positive law tradition, and conversely opened up a constitutional door for hitherto foreign notions like judicial review and individual and human rights charters. And this experience was not limited to Germany or even to the other states that fell under fascist or authoritarian regimes. In democratic and unoccupied Sweden, eugenics laws were passed that allowed for the forced sterilisation of thousands of Swedish women on the grounds of genetic and social unfitness. In a situation in which the courts were subservient to the parliament, and the clergy and the medical professionals were all servants of the state, there existed de facto no contending legal, political or even moral authority that effectively could have questioned the laws passed by the majority of the members of parliament, under the leadership of the Social Democrats (Zaremba 1992). This shows that in a system in which all power ultimately issues from the parliamentary majority, vulnerable individuals and members of minorities may well stand to suffer. Remarkably, the laws remained in effect as late as the 1970s, long after the defeat of Nazi Germany.

Thus the current emergence of a juridified political system has its roots not only in the victory of the global market society, but also in a distrust of state power, positive law, and unfettered democracy that goes back to the trauma of European fascism, if not to the excesses of ostensibly benign social engineering. Indeed, the construction of the EU must be understood partly as a reaction to the experience of the Holocaust and the horrors of the Second World War. It is a project not merely devoted to establish a European-wide free market, but also driven by the twin desires to ensure peace in Europe, on the one hand, and to prevent the abuse of human and minority rights, on the other.

Either way, the history of the EU has to a great extent been the history of the European Court and the legal system at large (Weiler 1999; Wincott 2000). And with the emergence of the European Court of Justice as a key motor in the process of European integration, the questions of judicial review, rights, and the use of litigation in the pursuit of political ends have come to occupy a more central place in Europe, if not yet to the same extent as in the US. The courts have gained a new status and a far more powerful role. Thanks to the power of the European Court to stand in judgment of national laws and serve as a vehicle for citizens of the EU to pursue grievances and claim rights — not only in conflicts with other individuals, organisations, and corporations but also in disputes with the institutions of the national member states of the EU — the political playing field in Europe has truly changed. The courts are thus offering new possibilities for European individuals and minority groups to assert power in a political and legal zone that escapes traditional European politics where the voters vote and the (elected) rulers rule.[6] Even in Sweden, so long resistant to judicial power, it is today possible to hear voices in support of increased power for the courts, both from those who belong to minorities such as the disabled, and from those who more generally are in favour of the separation

---

[6] On the role of the European Court of Justice in the protection of individual rights against the state, see Burley and Mattli (1993); Leleux (1982).

of powers and judicial review.[7] Not surprisingly, it has been only during this last decade that the laws allowing for the forced sterilisation of women deemed to be less worthy for genetic, social, or moral reasons have become the focus of intense scrutiny in the mass media and the academy.

We will return to these matters, but let us first consider the American experience and a juridico-political system that now appears as not simply very different from the European, but also as a possible source of lessons, both of warning and inspiration.

### 3.   THE ROLE OF THE LAW, THE COURTS AND LAWYERS IN THE UNITED STATES

While in Europe the law has ideally been kept at arm's length from politics, law and litigation are in the US so politicised that the judiciary arguably competes with the legislature and the executive for prominence in the political arena. This intersection of law and politics is evident in a number of ways. For example, in the United States, in addition to the national (ie, federal) court system, each state has its own set of trial and appellate courts for enforcing state laws. Thirty-nine of the 50 US states select a substantial portion of the judges for these courts in much the same way that candidates for office are selected — that is, through public campaigns and elections — making them directly accountable to the voting public. In addition, according to one recent study, between 60 and 73 per cent of federal judges from the 1930s through to the 1980s were prominently active in partisan politics prior to their court appointments (Goldman 1997). The intersection of law and politics also can be seen in the legislative branch. For example, lawyers are the most common profession of elected officials in the United States — currently 37 per cent of members of the US House of Representatives and 59 per cent of US Senators hold law degrees (*Politics in America* 2003). Indeed, the crucial role played by lawyers, judges, and the law in the US has been noted ever since European observers first made the trek to America to compare, criticise, and learn. Thus Alexis de Tocqueville, for one, noted with wonder that it was the judicial branch, not the legislature, which held the key to understanding democracy in America. Lawyers, currently the object of so much disdain in many quarters, were seen by Tocqueville as crucial to the health of American democracy because they linked the

---

[7] On the latter, see for example the recently completed parliamentary commission on democracy, among whose many published reports several dealt with this matter, including Nergelius, Peczenik, Wiklund (1999:58). Nergelius champions more power for the courts and has also featured in a face-off against Holmström in an issue of the official organ of the Swedish parliament, R&D, which focused on the question of how much judicial power would be good for democracy (Nergelius and Holmström, 2000).

popular and aristocratic classes and infused the republic with what Tocqueville called the 'legal spirit' (Tocqueville 1969/1848, 263–70).

## 3.1. The Historical Legacy: The American Constitutional Regime

The key reason for this startling difference is that while in Europe majority rule is taken for granted, there is at the heart of the American political system the belief that no one institution or process can or should represent the 'public will'. To the contrary, the system was from the outset designed to explicitly distribute power among individual citizens, various organised interests, the 50 states, and the different branches of national government. This design was meant to check the abuses of any one individual, group or institution, while at the same time forcing these various sites of power to interact with each other in order to create and execute public policy. According to James Madison, one of the principal architects of the US Constitution, through this complex system of checks and balances 'it may well be that the public voice ... will be more consonant to the public good than if pronounced by the people themselves, convened for that purpose' (Hamilton, Madison and Jay 1961/1787–88, 82).

Nowhere is this American experiment in preserving democracy by limiting its excesses more evident than in the principle of judicial review — the power of appellate courts to strike down laws they deem unconstitutional. As noted by Tocqueville, this power is a crucial protection against the 'tyranny of the majority' (Tocqueville 1969/1848, 262–76). Such a system is very different from what is customary in Europe, where legislatures monopolise the law-making power and where courts function as mere administrative agencies, applying and enforcing rules and regulations to the letter of the law. In contrast, American judges are bestowed with law-making capacities as they engage in constitutional adjudication, even if these capacities differ from those of the ordinary legislative powers of Congress. The basis for this power at the national level is the US Constitution — the 'supreme' law of the land — a document perceived as a source of law independent of and able to trump the will of the legislature. Thus, through the power of judicial review the Supreme Court can overturn decisions of presidents, national legislatures, and the 50 state governments. They can also force the national and state governments — the elected representatives of the people — to act in ways they would prefer not to.

This aspect of the US political system is often criticised as thwarting the will of the people, expressed through the 'normal' democratic process of elections and legislative action. But this argument both overestimates the power of the courts to dictate, and conflates majority rule with the public will. In fact, the courts neither function as purely administrative agencies, nor do they operate independently of normal politics. The law-making power of the judicial branch is ultimately determined not by its ability to enforce decisions (which is controlled by the executive branch), but by its relationship to other sites of political discourse and struggle. Lacking the power of the sword or the purse, the Court is heavily dependant on both the willingness of the other branches and levels of government to support their decisions and, ultimately, on citizens' willingness to accept and comply with its rulings even if they disagree. This normative authority of the so-called 'least dangerous branch'[8] of the government depends on its capacity to walk the fine line between avoiding capture by short-term victors in ordinary politics while also not moving too far afield from the larger public sentiment.

Thus the 'higher law' of the Constitution and the Bill of Rights is not a species of natural law in the strict sense since it both changes over time and is obviously subject to shifting political pressures from the outside and openly political struggles within the courts themselves. Indeed, we are here far removed from any notion that the law and judges somehow stand above politics.[9] Although there are those in the US who envy the European model in which, as Kathleen Sullivan has put it in a review article, 'opinions of the high court are issued without concurrences or dissents', symbolising the objective, 'positive' nature of the law, 'a distinctive feature of the modern US Supreme Court is its proud tradition of vigorous and open disagreement' (Sullivan 1998, 18). Indeed, the dissenting opinion in one court decision often becomes the basis for future majority opinions, as constitutional interpretation reacts to changing social and political views, as well as to changing membership on the courts. While European observers often are struck by the spectacle of 'liberal' and 'conservative' judges facing off, the public authority of the Court remains surprisingly undiminished in this openly political process.[10]

This is the case, we would argue, because the Constitution and Bill of Rights nonetheless constitute the functional equivalent of such a higher, natural law that legitimately can trump ordinary laws passed by the legislature according to the democratic will of the people (or, rather, their

---

[8] *The Least Dangerous Branch* is the title of Bickel's (1962) influential book about the US Supreme Court. Bickel in turn borrowed the formulation from Alexander Hamilton's essay, 'The Judges as Guardians of the Constitution', in the 78th Federalist Paper.

[9] For one example of a discussion of the question of the court's relation to politics by a leading legal scholar, see Sunstein (1992).

[10] One recent example of this is the way in which the highly controversial decision by the Supreme Court that ended the attempts by the Gore campaign staff to contest the disputed Bush victory in Florida in November 2000 Presidential elections, while bitterly contested, was quickly accepted (by all but the most ardent partisans) across party lines, not only among the general public but also among political elites, including Gore himself. Similar examples include the Supreme Court's 1974 decision that the Nixon administration had to release the audio tapes implicating the President in the Watergate cover up.

representatives). If you will, this higher law passes the 'duck' test: since it quacks and walks like a duck, it probably should be best thought of as a duck, even though it strictly speaking fails the formal test to qualify as natural law. The often rather arcane attempts to interpret the original intent of the authors of the constitution in the modern context strike outside observers as quite odd until it is grasped that such quasi-theological exercises must be viewed in terms of paying heed to the American civil religion in general and to its fundamental and effectively 'sacred' texts in particular. As James Bryce, writing in the early part of the twentieth century, noted, the American people 'are profoundly attached to the form which their national life has taken. The Federal Constitution has been, to their eyes, an almost sacred thing, an Ark of the Covenant, whereon no man may lay rash hands' (Bryce 1920, 642). Such religious references have not abated, with a more recent book describing the Constitution and Bill of Rights as 'our two sacred national documents' (Black 1988, 15). The power of the courts thus rests on a paradox: on the one hand the law is viewed as stable and sacred, as above ordinary 'dirty' politics, while on the other it is nonetheless constantly subject to and changing in reaction to precisely such political struggles.

A second feature of the American politico-juridical system that sets it apart from European practices is the notion of 'trial by a jury of peers', which Tocqueville regarded as the 'most eminently republican element of government' (Tocqueville 1969/1848, 272). That is, this is an aspect of the American system that serves to politicise the legal domain in a rather different way than is the case with judicial review. Rather than pitting one elite group (members of Congress) against another elite group (members of the Supreme Court), this provision hands over considerable power from legal experts to lay-people. Not surprisingly, this is also a controversial aspect of the American politico-juridical regime. While few Americans advocate abolishing the jury system, there are many who question the ability of lay people to make informed decisions when it comes to, for example, the proper size of punitive damages in tort cases, a matter to which we shall return. Others, conversely, celebrate *pace* Tocqueville the jury as a much-needed democratic counterweight to the rule by experts, elites, and big corporations. As with much of the theory and practice of the courts in United States these debates over the strengths and weaknesses of the jury system are at heart ideological, serving as one of several arenas in which the process and substance of politics is played out.

A third characteristic aspect of the American legal and political system is the Bill of Rights and the primacy and protection of individual and minority rights. Not only are specific rights enumerated in the Bill of Rights, but also enshrined is the general principle that individual rights and freedoms are protected unless explicitly excluded from protection in the constitution. For example, the 9th amendment to the constitution states that the 'enumeration in the Constitution, of certain rights, shall not be construed to deny or disparage others retained by the people', and the 10th amendment states that the 'powers not delegated to the United States by the Constitution, nor prohibited by it to the states, are reserved to the states respectively, *or to the people*' (emphasis added). Again, we are dealing with a fundamental difference between the European and American traditions. The Americans' insistence on such protections against state power is derived from the experience of the many colonists who left Europe to escape religious and political persecution. In comparison, Europeans appear to have a more optimistic view of the ability of the State to do good for its citizens, expressing the general will in Rousseauian language or universal interest in Hegelian ones. Americans, in sharp contrast, subscribe to the notion that the government that governs the least governs the best, that power corrupts, and that liberty must be safeguarded through elaborate constitutional measures in the form of separation of powers. At heart, Americans are more populist in their democratic political instincts, while European are more trusting in the state and the elite dominated political institutions and processes.

The institutional locus for the exercise of this constitutionally embedded individual rights tradition is the courts, even though the Bill of Rights and the ethos that is associated with it in fact lay dormant for a long time and only became truly significant in the twentieth century when societal changes, a shift in the balance of power in favour of the federal government relative to the states, and a more activist Supreme Court led to a more aggressive application of these amendments (known as 'incorporation') to state politics, policy and law through the belated use of the 14th amendment, added to the constitution in 1868. As Michael Kent Curtis notes:

> From 1833 to 1868 the Supreme Court held that none of the rights in the *Bill of Rights* limited the states. From 1868 to 1925 it found very few of these liberties protected from state action. Those the states were free to flout (so far as federal limitations were concerned) seemed to include free speech, press, religion, the right to jury trial, freedom from self-incrimination, from infliction of cruel and unusual punishments, and more. State constitutions, with their own bills of rights, were available to protect the individual, but too often they proved to be paper barriers. ... [The notion that the 14th Amendment was intended to apply the Bill of Rights to the states] has never, for instance, been accepted by the United States Supreme Court, although the Court has haltingly reached much the same result by gradual incorporation of most of the rights in the *Bill of Rights* as limits on the states under the due process clause, a development that reached fruition in the 1960s.
>
> (Curtis 1986, 1–2)

The same is true for a fourth crucial dimension of the American politico-legal system, related to the centrality of individual rights, namely tort law, the ability of citizens (as individuals or groups) to bring civil suits against other individuals as well as against economic and political institutions to seek compensatory and punitive damages for injuries and losses. While tort law has deep roots within the common law tradition, it has also evolved and changed in significant ways in more recent times. To appreciate the political role of tort law and the Bill of Rights, we now turn to a closer analysis of twentieth century developments.

## 3.2. The Rights Revolution and the Litigation Explosion: Law and Politics in Twentieth Century US

As Charles Epp (1998) has shown, the rights revolution, while it certainly does have roots in the American constitutional regime, in fact developed over time in a manner that was rather more complex and historically contingent than is often understood. Crucial to the successes of the civil rights movements of the post-WWII era was the prior building of what he calls 'support structures', without which the potential of the laws and the courts could not have been fully realised. Indeed, as late as the 1920s and 1930s the Supreme Court and the legal profession at large tended to serve the interests of not only the white majority as in the era of reconstruction, but also of Big Business in its struggle against unions and the budding working class movement, a far cry from the latter day associations of the courts with the civil rights movement (see, for example, Irons 2003, ch 21–24). A dramatic example of the Supreme Court's ability to thwart the will of a democratically-elected government came in the mid-1930s, when it overturned a series of laws passed as part of the Roosevelt administration's efforts to pull the US out of a deep and lingering economic depression. Telling of the ultimately political nature of the legal process in the US, Roosevelt responded to these decisions by proposing to add six new (and presumably more liberal) members to the Supreme Court. While this 'court packing' plan was severely criticised as being too blatantly political, it had its intended impact — the Supreme Court reversed its earlier decisions, allowing Roosevelt's New Deal legislation to be implemented.

One reason for the courts' largely conservative bent was the make up of the legal profession itself. However, beginning in the 1920s organisations like the ACLU, the NAACP, the American Jewish Congress, International Labor Defense, the American Fund for Public Service, and the Legal Defense and Educational Fund developed a strategy that combined fundraising for the purpose of supporting sustained efforts to push test cases through the court system with encouraging minority individuals to pursue law degrees. The result was something of a revolution when it comes to the sociological make-up of the legal profession as first Jews and Blacks and later women flocked to the law schools, and by the 1950s these efforts were to bear fruit as the civil rights movement began to win a series of victories in the courts as well as through Congress (Epp 1998, ch four).

The ability of Americans to bring lawsuits is, however, not limited to the anti-discrimination cases that were central to the civil rights movement. Over the last 50 years tort litigation has come to be increasingly used by individuals and groups committed to a variety of political issues, such as product liability, work place safety, the environment, and medical malpractice. This power to use the courts and tort law to advance political agendas and pursue collective goods is based on a number of rules and practices that have developed and changed over time; the establishment of the notion of the 'private Attorney General', the liberal rules governing class action lawsuits, and the contingency fee system.

With respect to the first — the right of private citizens to bring action — it has in theory a long history, but in practice a rather much shorter one. As Shep Melnick has pointed out, it was not until 1964 when the Supreme Court changed directions, from an earlier approach that required a specific authorisation in a statutory law to allowed private right of action, to one that first 'encouraged courts to find private rights of action implicit in federal statutes', and then claimed to have discovered a general right to private action in an all but forgotten law passed as part of the Civil Rights Act of 1870 (see Melnik 1989, 205). The effect of these decisions was to open up the legal arena to individuals and groups, in the spirit of 'participatory democracy', at a time when judicial activism and the rights revolution had already radically reshaped the place of the courts and litigation in the broader field of politics.

Similarly, class action litigation — the possibility to file a suit on behalf of a large number of individuals who do not actually know each other or participate actively in the suit — has a history that is simultaneously long and short. On the one hand, this practice, unknown in continental Europe, is 'as old as the medieval English roots of the United States civil legal system', to cite the authors of a report issued by the Rand Institute for Civil Justice (Hensler et al. 1999, 1). On the other, the current controversy over class action litigation can be traced back to 1966 when the so-called Rule 23, which provides for federal class actions, was revised in a crucial respect. Previously the rule had mandated that all individuals seeking damages in this manner must sign on (or "opt in"), but after the rule-change every member of the class were to be considered part of the suit unless they explicitly declined ("opted out"). The revised Rule 23 thus made it possible to launch much larger suits with much greater ease (Hensler et al 1999, 1).

Finally, it must be noted that the great frequency of litigation, whether of the individual or class action variety, also depends on the for Europeans odd practice of not paying lawyers outright for their work, but for the lawyers to accept work on the contingency fee principle. If the lawyers win the suit, they routinely collect some 30 per cent of the damages, if they lose they do not receive any pay. This is a system that allows the poor to use the legal system; it is also a system that potentially rewards the lawyers with windfall awards if they win cases and the plaintiff is rewarded large damage amounts. Again, while most Americans today take contingency fee financing for granted, this was in fact not always the case, but the emergence of current practices has to be understood in historical terms.

As Peter Karsten notes in his history of the contingency fee, such contracts were in fact prohibited since the Middle Ages in England, according to the common law doctrine of champerty (Karsten 1998, 231). It is only during the nineteenth century that the English rule with respect to both champerty and the requirement that the losing party pay the attorney fees of the winning party were overturned in the Unites States. According to Karsten the use of the contingency fee can be traced back to at least the first few decades of the century, if not before, but it is only by the end of the century and the beginning of the twentieth century that the contingency fee can be said to have become truly acceptable in most of the country.

While taking into account other factors, such as the principle that lawyers should be free to contract, the main explanation for this momentous shift Karsten traces to the political and religious history of the US. Beginning with the Age of Jackson, a new spirit of democracy, distrust of corporations, a partly religiously informed concern for equality and the rights of the little man, and the method of electing jurists and judges translated into what Karsten calls the 'Jurisprudence of the Heart'. The right of the poor man to pursue his just claims were, it was argued, more important than the risk that such fee arrangements could encourage an increase in frivolous lawsuits. Judges who had to stand for election, Karsten argues, were far more sensitive to this type of argument than appointed judges at a further remove from the will of popular assemblies and more beholden to elite political actors.[11]

The contingency fee remained highly controversial, however, and symptomatically the concept of 'ambulance chasing' goes all the way back to the end of the nineteenth century and the breakthrough of the contingency fee principle on a larger scale. However, the increased rate of civil litigation in recent decades and the relatively improved position of the plaintiff's bar in relation to the defendant's bar is the consequence of a number of other changes as well, including the abolishment of immunities for charities and the rise of the principle of comparative fault in place of the doctrine of contributory negligence (see Yeazell 2001; White 1985). Equally important has been the spread of consumer credit, which in turn has led to a steep increase in mandatory homeowners' and automobile owners' liability insurance.

---

[11] By 1860, Karsten notes, 'jurists in just ten of thirty-four states were appointed' (Karsten 1998, 247).

As Stephen C Yeazell notes, 'the large expansion of consumer credit and insurance created a vast pool of solvent potential defendants' (Yeazell 2001, 184).

In combination, social, political and legal changes in the twentieth century such as those discussed above dramatically expanded what was already a fundamental acceptance of the central role of judges and lawyers in the political process. As one indicator of this, consider that the legal profession in the United States grew at three times the rate of other professions from 1970 to the present, and that the number of lawyers per capita doubled during this period (Putnam 2000, 145–46).

### 3.3.   The Current Debate: Pros and Cons of Adversarial Legalism

Advances in the position of plaintiffs and their lawyers notwithstanding, it is not the case that the plaintiff's bar today is in the position occupied by the defense bar 75 years ago, when the latter truly dominated. Rather, as Yeazell puts it, plaintiffs' and defendants' lawyers are simply 'more evenly matched than they were in the first quarter of the century' (Yaezell 2001, 183). In fact, most cases never go to trial, and the defendants win most of those that do. What is more typical is that both sides engage in risk management and settle out-of-court based on available information according to economic rationality. However, what is visible in the media are the exceptional cases involving verdicts with large punitive damages awarded to plaintiffs.

Nonetheless litigation, or the threat thereof, is very much part of American political culture, and this litigatory approach to politics is the subject of intense feeling and debate. Critics and legal scholars, as well as civic minded citizens, have written many passionate accounts in which the central actors are not the high-minded private Attorney Generals, but rather the trial lawyers, described as 'bounty hunters', behaving like 'vultures' extorting money from corporations in the name of faceless victims who end up with little money from the settlement while ultimately having to pay it back, as consumers, as the companies raise their prices to compensate for the high costs of settlements and liability insurance (see, for example, Khavari 1990; Wills 1990; O'Connell 1979).

However, if what critics like Walter Olson (1991) decry as the 'litigation explosion' is one side of the coin, the other side is the 'rights revolution' that we have discussed above. From this perspective individual or class action litigation is viewed as a powerful strategy available to relatively powerless people, not least minorities, when they want to assert their individual or group rights, and in doing so produce changes in the behaviour of powerful institutions that also have collective benefits. By either challenging specific interpretations of the law, or using the law as already interpreted to demand in fact what is due in theory, individuals and groups have become empowered to claim rights, push emerging new issues on to the political agenda, and influence the behaviour of powerful élites. It is through this channel that civil rights activists have claimed many victories, and it is impossible to understand the advances made in areas like consumer rights, patients' rights, environmental protection, and gender equality, without first understanding the power of the court as a political institution. For this reason it is no accident that the most fervent opponents of 'rights' in the United States often come from the right side of the political spectrum. It is, for example, the powerful health-care industry that currently opposes moves to strengthen patients' rights to pursue their complaints through litigation, and a similar situation pertains when it comes to environmental issues, the rights of the disabled, or the attempts to address the harm created by the tobacco and gun industries.

But the question of how well litigation can serve the political agenda of those seeking to promote social reform and to protect the position of the weak is a contested one, even among those who argue from a left perspective. For each sympathetic account, for example the classic account by Donald Horowitz (1977) or, more recently, the book by Charles Epp referred to above, there can be found far more pessimistic ones, like Gerald Rosenberg's book *The Hollow Hope* (1991). One of the most prominent contemporary leftist critics of the litigatory approach is Robert A Kagan, who has coined the term 'adversarial legalism' to characterise what he also terms 'the American way of law' in a recent book (Kagan 2001) that brings together years of his work in this field.[12]

Kagan sees in the increased use of the courts and litigation a symptom of a political culture in which 'the people' have lost faith in the government and the ordinary political process. The cost of this turn towards courts and litigation is, according to Kagan, very high. Comparing the American adversarial and lawyer dominated system with Europe, where experts, impartial judges, and compromise prone parliamentary parties play the key role, he concludes that the American model is both inefficient and costly in economic terms, and unfair and unequal in its exercise of justice.

He notes that it is popular to blame lawyers for this seemingly irrational state of affairs, but he firmly rejects the thesis that lawyers cause adversarial legalism. The 'blame' ought to be shared rather more widely, Kagan suggests:

> Lawyers are not the only or even the primary source of American adversarial
> legalism. Far more important are the preferences of their clients and of the

---

[12] Also see Kagan, (1991), especially on the question of the costs associated with adversarial legalism.

political interest groups and leaders who seek to shape public policy. Adversarial legalism is the product of a populist political culture, inclined to trust courts rather than "big business" and "big government" and reluctant to finance European-style social insurance programs that could displace much civil litigation. Adversarial legalism is also stimulated by a constitutional tradition that has limited central bureaucratic government and encouraged litigation as a mode of checking governmental arbitrariness.

(Kagan 1994, 60)[13]

Thus Kagan traces adversarial legalism to the same constitutional structure and political culture that we have discussed above, with its radical separation of powers and divided government, on the one hand, and penchant for activist, populist, and anti-statist politics, on the other. To these features he largely ascribes negative values. Clearly, Kagan prefers the European-style Social Democratic or Social Liberal system, with its emphasis on social insurance paid or mandated by the state. When one turns to his recipes for reform, one also finds, not surprisingly, that he favours a broad shift from market-based provisions of social services, private contract, and tort litigation, towards universal health-care, no-fault insurance schemes, and social insurance as an alternative to litigation. As one avenue for discouraging litigation he furthermore proposes the return to the English Rule, ie requiring the loser to pay the court and litigation costs of the winner. He also calls for a diminished role of the jury in civil law trials, claiming that the jury is a 'source of inconsistency and unpredictability', here displaying his preference for judge and expert dominated resolutions of conflicts.

While Kagan's critique at times echoes the arguments often rehearsed by the right-wing, he differs sharply with them in that his objective is not to diminish legal restrictions on business, in particular, or decrease the power of the state, in general, but quite the opposite. He in fact seeks to promote and strengthen the role and power of government, refashioning public law and administration so as to shift power from courts to bureaucrats by drafting statues in such a way as to narrow the possibilities for judicial interpretation and review. The need for democratic oversight would instead be satisfied through greater participation by interest groups and citizen's organisations in the process of policy formulation, and the general quality of the administrative bureaucracy would be improved by investing more money in job-training, education, and staffing.

One of Kagan's students, Thomas Burke, has recently offered an analysis that builds on but also departs from Kagan's. In his book *Lawyers, Lawsuits, and Legal Rights*, Burke seeks to show that the prominence of lawyers and litigation in the US is not the result of some peculiarly American lust for litigation and lawsuits, rooted in distrust, alienation, and

---

[13] Also see Kagan 1991.

the collapse of communitarian values, but rather a function of what he calls litigious policies, that is, 'laws that promote the use of litigation in resolving disputes and implementing public policies' (Burke 2002, 4).

Elaborating what he calls the 'Constitutional Theory' of litigious policy-making, Burke largely restates the essence of Kagan's thinking, emphasising the structural factors — federalism, separation of powers, and judicial independence — along with 'the significance of the distrust of centralized governmental power' that underlies 'American activists support of court-based schemes' (Burke 2002, 14). In particular, he focuses on three incentives that he sees as central for this activist support of litigious policies. First, what he calls the insulation incentive, how implementation of public policy can be insulated from political enemies by taking it out of the hands of vulnerable federal bureaucracies and granting implementation power to the courts. Secondly, the control incentive, that is the use of federal court orders to force the hand of local and state government that otherwise are relatively free from federal control through the national government. And finally, the cost-shifting incentive that allows activists and policy-makers to create rights than are not directly funded through taxation, but rather are enforced through litigation which ends up shifting cost to others, often to private actors. ADA is one example of this strategy, and the current proposal to strengthen patients' rights in relation to HMOs is another one. As Burke notes, the deep choice here is one between creating a fully funded health-care system to replace the HMOs or to 'create a "patients' bill of rights" to allow individuals to sue HMOs for their sins'. One solution would involve tax money, the other would not. One would strengthen top-down government, the other relies on activists and from-below litigation, or differently put, one would rely on a classical indirect and deliberative democratic process, the other on a more direct, even populist approach. The tension and dynamic between these two modes is, however, complex. Certainly the lack of efficacy of traditional social policy and bureaucratic agencies helps create the environment in which litigation becomes attractive. But the story is not simply about the weakness of governance or the lack of trust in government; it is also, to put it in more positive terms, about grassroots activism and individual empowerment.

While Burke, as the above discussion of the health care and patients' rights dilemma indicates, is sensitive to the paradoxes and weaknesses of American style litigious policies and at times shows a great deal of sympathy for Kagan's proposals to move towards a more European-style approach to social policy, his is nonetheless more even handed in his account. He departs, complements, and extends Kagan's analysis in two key respects. To begin with he reasons that even if one deems what he refers to as 'replacements reforms' — first and foremost involving a move towards European-style regulation or socialisation — necessary, the odds against such reform to succeed in the US are very long indeed. This, Burke argues, follows from the constitutional theory that he promotes, one which places emphasis on what Burke calls 'the deep roots of litigious policy' in the American constitutional regime and its attendant political culture. But aside from this pragmatic argument, he also raises a second, more normative point, namely that even as many Americans bemoan what they see as a sue-prone society in which litigation is out of control, it may well be that 'the extension of litigation to more and more realms is a sign not of weakness, but rather a conjunction of traits many consider strengths' (Burke 2002, 203). Among these, Burke counts on the one hand the drive to extend justice, fairness and the power to redress to more and often formerly disadvantaged people, on the other the American constitutional tradition, which few Americans would appear to be willing to undermine or replace. 'Litigation', Burke concludes, may well be 'the price that Americans pay for aspects of their nation that many hold dear' (Burke 2002, 204).

In his review of Kagan, Frank Cross similarly takes Kagan to task for not sufficiently recognising the virtues of adversarial legalism while overstating the supposed evils of this system. While acknowledging the validity of many of Kagan's specific points of criticism, and embracing some of the proposed reforms, Cross argues that adversarial legalism 'as a more general matter has served America well, and should be celebrated more often than condemned' (Cross 2003, 191). In particular, Cross questions Kagan's thesis that the American system is particularly inefficient and costly from a comparative perspective, and he also seeks to defend the jury as well as other procedural values that Kagan tends to disparage.

On the first point, Cross posits that 'for Professor Kagan, economic efficiency seems to be paramount', and then goes on to argue on the basis of his (Cross') own statistical evidence that while 'American legalism may seem more time consuming, costly, and inefficient, […] this perception is misleading' (Cross 2003, 200). In fact, although there are indeed many more lawyers per capita in the US, the evidence also suggest that the system works well, with fewer delays than in European countries, and with a perception among business people of policy stability. Indeed, Cross more generally tries to make the case that at the aggregate level the economic consequences of the decentralised American common-law legal system, with its numerous points of entry and access, through tort law, private right of action and litigation, seem to be positive, not negative. He marshals evidence that on the average economies with common-law, and pluralistic political systems do better than the European style, civil-law, corporatist system celebrated by Kagan. He also alludes to a link between the common-law and the market, a point to which we will return below.

Like Burke, Cross does not dispute the argument that the US has an adversarial legal system. On the contrary he states in no uncertain terms that 'in the United States, litigation is a form of politics, and the courts are involved in governance, not in a ministerial bureaucracy. In this country, at least, litigation is a "political exercise"' (Cross 2003, 203). But this is, he argues not necessarily a bad thing. He notes that even Kagan acknowledges that in comparison 'American judiciaries are particularly flexible and creative', and that 'American lawyers, litigation, and courts serve as powerful checks against official corruption and arbitrariness'. Further on he also cites Kagan's comment that 'the litigiousness of Americans has made for antidiscrimination laws far more potent than comparable laws in nations that do not foster the private enforcement of public law' (Kagan 2002, 170, as cited in Cross 2003, 201).

Kagan discounts these positives while Cross takes them as a point of departure for his defense of American legalism. Thus he argues that even if it was the case that the American system was inefficient, which, as we have just seen, he doubts, there are other values than simple economic efficiency or even redistribution. He rejects what he sees as Kagan's utilitarianism, a vision of human welfare he deems 'a bit cramped', and raises the question of whether 'adversarial legalism might actually have some intrinsic value to Americans, independent of its economic consequences' (Cross 2003, 206). Cross suggests that the answer is yes, that procedure is of crucial, intrinsic worth. Americans value their 'day in court', as the saying goes, and 'they sue not just to recover an award, but also to vindicate their own behavior, to punish those they consider wrongdoers, to effect justice, and to obtain a dispassionate ruling in disputes' (Cross 2003 207).

It is in this context that Cross comes out in defense of the jury, which Kagan appears to want to diminish in stature in favour of expert and judge opinion. Cross suggests, recalling Tocqueville, that 'the right to trial by jury is a matter of fundamental liberty', that 'the jury is a key democratic institution', and that 'jurors may directly benefit from participation as jurors' (Cross 2003, 207). He goes on to cite studies that indicate that individuals see this experience as important, and that in fact even judges when asked to choose would prefer to be judged by a jury (59.3%) than by a fellow judge (20.7%). In conclusion, Cross admits that this system is messy, that it tends towards populism and perhaps excessive distrust of the state, that it may indeed stand in need of some reform, but also that on balance it has done more good than bad for America so far.

Some of the themes that Cross took up in his review of Kagan have also been forcefully argued by Carl T Bogus in his recent book, *Why Lawsuits are Good for America* (Bogus 2001). According to Bogus, the common-law tradition, with a powerful jury and broad right to litigate, is central to what he calls 'disciplined democracy'. In a world dominated by rich and powerful corporations, lawsuits remain as one of the few powerful means at the disposal to the relatively powerless. Bogus concedes that this system is far from perfect, but he maintains that it is a crucial complement to the right-to-vote and the power to make choices in the market place.

It is no accident, Bogus argues, that Big Business in co-operation with allies in the political world fabricate what he calls 'tales' about the fantastic abuse of the legal system. Thus he seeks to show that most of the stories about enormous 'frivolous lawsuits', such as the infamous case in which a woman reportedly received close to $ 3 millions in a jury verdict after having spilled hot coffee on herself, in fact are false or at best incomplete, failing to take into account later corrective action by higher courts or by judges. The real purpose behind these tales is in fact itself deeply political and partisan, designed to create public opinion in favour of limiting American citizens' rights to sue companies for producing bad products or offering dangerous services (Bogus 2001). Thus, beyond the formal calculations that inform economic cost-benefit analyses and concerns of transaction costs, lay deeper political questions about who gets to have access to power in the form of legal and politico-legal action. If one turns to the debate about the rule-of-law in the United States, it is from this perspective noteworthy that, as Bill Scheurman has pointed out, adversarial legalism has two enemies. From the right there are the conservatives who want to 'cut the rule-of-law down to a guarantee of economic liberty for the economically privileged', and from the left there are those liberals who, like Kagan, conversely appear willing to trade-in some aspects of American style of rule-of-law 'for a (vaguely conceived) promise of greater social and economic equality' (Scheuerman 1997, 740), an attitude towards law reminiscent of the one taken by European Social Democrats, rooted in the anti-juridical tradition of the European left.

## 4.   CONCLUSIONS

Should Europeans care about adversarial legalism? If, as Burke argues, chances are slim that Americans will adopt a European-style system to replace their litigious policies because of the deep constitutional and cultural roots of the American system, does not the same argument hold for the Europeans? Why would, from a European point of view, our analysis of the American way of laws and politics be more than a more or less interesting tale of a sue-crazy America with too many lawyers in search of at times preposterous lawsuits? Indeed, until recently comparisons between Europe and the United States have largely constituted an exercise in comparing several varieties of apples with an orange, often amounting to little more than attempts at showing that one system is better than the other. Europeans and europhiles have been able to boast of higher voter turnouts, stronger unions, and a more complete welfare state. Champions of the American model have, on the other hand, been in a position to emphasise a strong tradition of protecting civil liberties, religious freedom, and individual and property rights, a tradition ultimately based on the constitutionally embedded separation of powers and the strength of the judiciary.

However, it now appears that this fundamental difference between Europe and the US, while still very real, is gradually giving ways to signs of convergence. The secular trend in Europe today points to what may be termed the Americanisation of the European Union, as the ethos and values, as well as the institutions and rules, of the market society spread, and individuals and minorities search for new ways to collect and assert power. As we have noted, the emergence of the EU has gone hand in hand with a new and far more independent role of the courts of the New Europe, as well as with a more general challenge to the corporatist social contract that has underpinned the national democracies and their attendant welfare states. There are indications that Europeans vote less, that they have less trust in the governments and the elites, and even that they are turning more and more towards the language or rights and the politics of litigation.

For example, one of the strongest pieces of evidence often used to distinguish the health of European democracy from that of the United States has been voter turnout in elections. While it remains true that turnout in national elections in Western Europe remains high (averaging approximately 80 per cent over the past 20 years) as compared to the US (where turnout in presidential elections has hovered at around 50 per cent), in *both* Europe and the US turnout has declined an average of some 5 to 6 per cent over this period as compared to the years from 1945 to 1979 (Franklin, Lyons and Marsh 2001). And according to a recent survey, less than half of citizens in European Union countries report having 'some' or 'a lot' of trust in their respective nation's government (49 per cent) or their national parliaments (46 per cent), and only a third (33 per cent) report believing that their country is governed by 'the will of the people'. Tellingly, these percentages were as or lower than those found in the United States for the same questions (Voice of the People 2002). At the same time there is evidence that civil suits are becoming more common in Europe. For example, civil suits in France increased by 50 per cent between 1985 and 2000. Commenting on this trend, Noëlle Lenoir, a judge on the Conseil Constitutionnel (France's constitutional watchdog) noted that 'Cultural changes are allowing people to take a more active role in seeking justice and, in some cases, to profit financially from rulings. It's in part a result of the general Americanisation of French society, a social and legal change that is not over yet'.[14]

How then may we attempt to evaluate this trend from a normative perspective? Many Europeans are struck by what is often seen as the arbitrary powers of American judges and courts. And indeed the virtues of the

---

[14] As quoted in *Time Europe*, 2000.

traditional European approach are considerable, as we have already seen Kagan and others argue. Litigation is messy, and it at least appears to be a far more ineffectual approach than European-style no-fault insurance schemes. For one, if we consider the case of health-care or disability services, it is clear that doling out social rights within the logic of majoritarian democracy allows for a rational and orderly system of prioritising in an era of rising health-care costs. Furthermore, the considerable transaction costs associated with individual rights that are grounded in civil contract law — litigation, malpractice insurance, defensive medicine, etc — can largely be avoided.

However, the question remains whether such a system is able to deal with the complex and competing demands that characterise a modern society, with its socially diverse body politic, with its ethos of individual and minority rights. A comparative analysis of disability politics and policy in Sweden and the US is in this respect quite illuminating when it comes to the relative merits and limitations of the American and European models. Surprisingly to those who associate Sweden with generous social programmes and policies, the Swedish disability rights movement has looked to the Americans with Disabilities Act (ADA) for inspiration. Thus Adolph Ratzka, the leading figure within the Swedish Independent Living Movement has for years been calling for ADA-like legislation in Sweden to replace what he sees as discriminatory and paternalistic policies (Ratzka 1998). But even the more mainstream organisations representing the interests of the disabled have over time come to take a similar view. Perhaps symptomatic in this respect are comments made by Lars Lindberg, a leading force within the Swedish movement for the rights of the disabled. While himself a Social Democrat and no knee-jerk enthusiast of the litigatory approach, he nonetheless notes what he refers to as the greater vitality of the American movement that succeeded in pushing through the ADA legislation, emphasising the empowerment of the disabled themselves as opposed to the more passive approach typical in Sweden, which relied on benevolent bureaucracies rather than the actions of the disabled themselves. Not that Lindberg would like give up the Swedish approach entirely: what he would like to see is a combination of 'negative' American-style anti-discrimination rights pursuable in courts *and* Swedish-style 'positive' social rights that involves transfer payments (Lindberg 1996, 54).

The relative disempowerment of the Swedish individual in relation to the state and the social services provided by the government has come in to focus in recent years. Swedish citizens may have rights to a variety of social services but their power when it comes to seeking redress in case of conflict or if something goes wrong is far more limited. This is true when it comes to health-care, for example. Thus, while Swedish patients have extensive access to national health-care, they have relatively few rights within the system as such (Trägårdh 1999). Similarly, victims of traffic accidents often find themselves unable to pursue their grievances since the cost of lawyers are too high, the legal assistance provided by the state is too meagre, and the contingency fee system does not exist. Indeed, in a recent article in the leading Swedish daily newspaper *Dagens Nyheter*, a physician working with a group that seeks to advance the rights of accident victims went as far as to claim that Sweden is de facto denying these persons their fundamental human rights (Wong 2003).[15]

None of this is to say that the American system is ideal, or that it always succeeds in finding the proper balance between the competing interests that exist in American society. Throughout US history the political nature of the legal system has worked to privileged individuals or minority interests over the majority in ways that seem contrary to democracy. The judicial system has also worked at times to privilege the majority over the interests of minorities or individuals in ways that show the oppressive power of the state. Nowhere is this darker side of US jurisprudence more evident than in the aftermath of the September 11 terrorist attacks and the subsequent passage of the so-called 'Patriot Act', which significantly increases the surveillance power of the federal government on its citizens. But it is a system that at other points has been used by individuals and groups to gain access to public discourse about fundamental issues of fairness, justice, and equality, to protect the rights of these individuals and groups from tyrannical majorities or coercive state power, and to ultimately reshape the direction of public policy in ways that, as Madison suggested, are 'more consonant to the public good' (Hamilton, Madison and Jay, 1961/1787–88: 82). This system is messy and chaotic to be sure, but the politics of modern pluralist democracy is inherently messy and chaotic.

As we have seen in the discussion of the ADA legislation, it is only by looking at specific empirical cases that we can determine whether litigation is better or worse from a normative perspective. To be sure litigation can in some cases justly be interpreted as a desperate measure signaling a populist frustration with politics, a lack of confidence and trust in the state and the government. In other cases, such as the disastrous and largely counter-productive history of lawsuits related to asbestos, the litigatory approach has been dysfunctional. But at other times it can also be seen as a legitimate avenue for empowerment in the context of a political process that also includes deliberative democracy and a broader, long-term political vision. It is, we would argue, not possible to either glorify or demonise the juridifiation of politics *in toto*. It is, however, possible to claim that the secular trends that we have identified as linked to the juridification of politics are so strong that whether we like it or not from a normative perspective, we must recognise the need to not simply condemn but to choose a more constructive approach, one that seeks to identity the conditions under which the litigatory approach is more likely be productive than dysfunctional.

---

[15] Bengt H. Johansson, quoted in (Wong 2003).

What critics of the American system often miss is that the US judiciary is not simply a loose legal canon beyond the reach of democratic votes and sentiments. It is also very much part of the democratic political process. In this light, we would like to provisionally make three arguments. First, we would like to suggest that the legal system operates in a manner that is similar to the market, an open power grid accessible to a large number of actors seeking to settle disputes and come to agreements, and a system that is both flexible and self-correcting. Secondly, we would like to advance the notion that the courts can be viewed as a mediating, connecting institution, an arm of the state that is, de facto, located within or at least closely linked to civil society, extending the political realm into the daily life of citizen, simultaneously debasing and legitimising law as popular and accessible to ordinary people, even in litigation against the state itself. Thirdly, we will argue that in an empirical context where European style national democracy is under duress, litigation can be viewed as a citizenship practice. It is different from voting, but consistent with the logic of the market society in which politics and power negotiations occur in a more decentralised fashion among many actors within a pluralistic and individualistic civil society.

## 4.1.   Courts and Markets

Central to Adam Smith's analysis of the market economy is the seeming paradox that a large number of individuals bent on the pursuit of narrow self-interest in the aggregate also tended to produce a greater common good, or as Adam Smith put it, to increase the 'wealth of the nation'. It is our contention that the American politico-legal system at heart works according to an analogous logic. Thus, as Tocqueville noted, in a political system like the American one, it is the case that even though the individuals who partake in the dirty business of power and politics often are selfish, even contemptible, the final result from the point of view of society is mostly good. He detected a 'secret tendency' — the equivalent of Adam Smith's 'silent hand' in the economic domain — in the American political system that made the exertions of the citizens subservient to the prosperity of the community, in spite of their vices and mistakes.[16] This he contrasted with societies ruled by virtuous men, with pretensions of expressing the

---

[16] Frank Cross makes a similar point in his review of Kagan's book, making the following comment: 'Adam Smith famously observed how individual self-interested decisions could, via the invisible hand of competition, promote the general welfare. Likewise, the competitive legal environment of adversarial legalism might have indirect positive effects in improving the law and governance' (Cross 2003, 214).

general will or the voice of the people. There, he argued, public men might frequently do harm without intending it, notwithstanding their talents and virtues, whereas in a democratic state like the US, 'they bring about good results which they never thought of'. In Europe the era of the authoritarian state, with its fixed legal codes serving as the ultimate tool of state power, may be over. But the longing for a single source of highly formalised, 'non political' law survived into the democratic age. Only now the monopoly of law-making shifted from the King to the Parliament, representing the sovereignty of the people in the form of the majoritarian will expressed through the sovereign legislature.

Thus there exists, we would argue, an elective affinity between the liberal market society, on the one hand, and private contract, courts, and litigation, on the other. Both are built on the individual as the central unit, both are decentralised systems for passing information and trafficking in power, while the alternative — social rights administered by the state — is more akin to the command economy model. This is a point that we believe deserves further attention, but the literature already contains sprinkled references to this line of analysis.

For example, Cross notes in passing in his critique of Kagan that 'adversarial legalism is a populist libertarian approach to the law, while the European nations take more of a professional, statist, and elitist approach' (Cross 2003, 236). And while messy and seemingly chaotic this market-like dynamic may well have its advantages, Cross argues: 'Strife and uncertainty may produce progress and even greater efficiency. The common law system may be efficient due in part to its very instability, which enable inefficient or obsolete legal rules to be vacated or reversed due to the market incentives of the litigants' (Cross 2003, 217). Conversely, he notes elsewhere, 'the hermetically sealed doctrinal analysis' characteristic of European legal scholarship 'may be resistant to law and economics' (Cross 2003, 228). Crucial to this dynamic flexibility of the common law is the jury, which Cross, quoting Michael Saks, sees as an institution that 'allows the law to track changes in society with an efficiency that cannot be achieved by asking legislatures to rewrite laws every few months, or even by judges, who are inclined to give more deference to the legislatures than perhaps they always should' (Cross 2003, 231).[17] Thus the jury, the most democratic component of the legal system, provides a fluidity and flexibility that is lacking in the corporatist political systems in Europe, where, Cross suggests, policy is made 'by interlocking business associations together with governmental bureaucracies', which 'may be less likely to yield efficient and democratically flavored policies' (Cross 2003, 232).

---

[17] Original quote is from Michael J. Saks (1986).

John Hasnas (1996) has discussed tort reform in the US from a similar perspective. Hasnas celebrates what he, *pace* Hayek, calls 'the spontaneous order', which he sees as the hallmark of the market-like common law system. According to him, tort law is at heart a method for resolving conflict peacefully, it is a system that is 'consumer driven', *ad hoc*, ever changing, and not guided by some definite, final, and abstract idea of social justice. He bemoans attempts at tort reform that are driven by what he (again borrowing from Hayek) calls the 'reformer's conceit', the notion that jurists, judges, law professors and other intellectuals could conceive of a perfect law according to a rational plan. Such attempts at 'centrally planned legal reforms' are doomed to fail just as are centrally planned economies. Instead he calls for a return to 'true common law', a system 'that is never correct, but always self-correcting', that is constantly evolving 'through a process of trial and error' as opposed to centrally planned legal reforms that 'are inherently static in nature' (Hasnas 1996, 571–73). Like Cross, he sees the jury as the crucial institution, and the one reform that he does call for is 'the liberation of the jury', that is, no longer restricting the jury to finding the facts and assessing damages, but instead allowing them to 'fully decide cases according to the conscience of the members' (Hasnas 1996, 574).

## 4.2.　Courts as Links between State and Civil Society

If, then, we view the American politico-legal system as a market-like order, the courts (at least those handling civil law cases) themselves no longer simply appear as instruments of state power. Although they formally are part of the state apparatus, the availability and the daily use of the courts suggest that they also, in fact, function as institutions that seamlessly blend with civil society. While it is true that citizens can vote for members of Congress, the President, and other elected officials, this is only possible on rare and carefully specified occasions. And while members of Congress can also be lobbied, citizens have no legal right to have their particular cases heard and addressed. The courts, on the other hand, have an obligation to hear cases brought before them, and cases can furthermore be brought at any time, not just every two or four or six years. The courts thus function as arenas in which civil society actors routinely seek redress, settle disputes, and claim rights in an orderly and civil fashion. Because the courts provide a space of adversarial legalism, with each party represented by its own set of lawyers, the state (in the form of judge and jury) can appear as neutral and democratic, rather than heavy handed. Furthermore, since judgements can be appealed the process is also viewed as open-ended.

Thus, while European critics often point to the fact that Europeans vote more often in elections than do Americans, voting is not the only relevant measure of political activity. Indeed, if citizenship were to be reduced to a matter of (sometimes) voting for a party or a candidate for office, this would miss much of what constitutes citizenship in the eyes of many, certainly those who champion participatory democracy. Social and political capital is a function not only of individuals going to a polling booth, but also of their day-to-day involvement in politics and power negotiations. In this context it may be that Europeans need perhaps to focus not only on the supposed ills of American litigational culture, but also ponder the paradoxical fact that as of 1973 'there were more lawyers in New York City than in all of Germany, but more judges in Germany than in the entire United States' (Haskell 1997, 49).[18] The question is what this means in terms of the exercise of power from the point of view of the individual citizen, and one possibility is that there exists a larger number of entry points to the political power grid, seen from the point of view of citizens as *activists in civil society*, not only as *voters in political society*.

### 4.3.   From National Citizenship to Post-National Legal Personhood?

If the courts and the litigatory system thus are linked to the secular trends that are associated with the primacy of the market society and a vibrant and pluralistic civil society, the question is what becomes of the citizen, a figure that is historically if not by definition tightly linked to the emergence of national democracy.

As political theorists such as Jean Cohen (1996; 1999) or legal scholars like Linda Bosniak (2000) have pointed out, the modern idea of citizenship contains several, partly conflicting components. Thus both Bosniak and Cohen, in discussing the possibility of 'global', 'transnational', or 'postnational' citizenship, distinguish between three related but analytically separate aspects of citizenship. First, there is the idea of citizenship as denoting the formal legal, civil, political and social rights an individual has in relationship to a state. The first two dimensions — civil and political rights — inform what often is referred to as the liberal idea of citizenship, the third one — social rights — we associate with European-style social democracy. Secondly, there is the notion of a certain personality type, ie, the active, virtuous citizen, deeply engaged in community life under the sign of civic-minded duty. This is the idea of citizenship that is most commonly associated with the civic republican tradition, with Aristotle, Machiavelli,

---

[18] Haskel's source was Dietrich Rueschemeyer, *Lawyers and Their Society: A Comparative Study of the Legal Profession in Germany and United States,* Harvard University Press, 1973.

Rousseau, and the civic communitarians of today. Finally, there is the idea of citizenship as identity and the affective basis for a politics of solidarity in both the warfare and the welfare state. This is the point at which the idea of citizenship bleeds into the notion of nationhood, and where the history of citizenship merges with the history of nationalism.

Looking at citizenship from the point of view of the current challenge to the nation-state as the hegemonic political form, it is clear that these three aspects of citizenship stand in tense relations to one another. In particular, one can identify what we may call 'thinner' and 'thicker' variants of citizenship. Thus, the figure of the citizen as a legal person tends towards the inclusive and universal, that is, a very open but also very thin conception of citizenship. On the other hand, the idea of the citizen as a member of a national community or the citizen as a virtuous, active, and civic-minded member of a polis, both suggest a much thicker and exclusionary notion of citizenship.

Looking at these distinctions from a comparative US/European perspective, it becomes clear that in the 'old' Europe of national democracies, the thicker notion of citizenship has been tightly linked to identity, social solidarity and nationhood, whereas in the US the tension between thick and thin ideals of citizenship can be seen more in the debates between liberals and communitarians, with the latter celebrating the virtues of community and thick citizenship and the former preferring a more open and thus thinner variant. The bottom line is, however, that in Europe the thicker variant associated with nationhood and national democracy has come to dominate. Associated with this emphasis on national community has been the emergence of the welfare state. The politics of national solidarity has thus translated into what Marshall called social citizenship, ie a number of substantial social benefits and rights.

In the US, on the other hand, the thinner conception of citizenship has prevailed, centred on the liberal ideas about individual rights, even though the communitarian ethos still resonates in the political discourse. In sharp contrast to the Europe of the nation-states, not only has state and church been separated, but also state and nation(alities). Thus, while communal identities have been shaped on the basis of religion and ethnic/national identity, such communities have been and remain institutionally located in civil society and kept carefully separated from the state itself. And the provision of social welfare has been carried out to a much greater extent through such civil society institutions.

This has meant that it has been easier for immigrants to find a place within the far more diverse and individualistic American society, even if this point must not be overdrawn.[19] Indeed, the US — at least until the

---

[19] Thus there are plenty of examples in the US of how a more identity based conception of citizenship has dominated, for example the discrimination against non-English immigrants, at first Irish and German, later Eastern European, and during the 1920s Asian ones.

September 11 attack pushed citizenship to the fore again — has been a country in which many people could live at least reasonably well without the benefit of citizenship, where the law in fact applied to every denizen, and where the material benefits of citizenship were sparse. In fact, as Bosniak has noted, 'the tension between personhood and citizenship as the basis for rights is, in fact, a chronic national preoccupation' (Bosniak 2000, 461).[20]

From this perspective it would appear that we in the EU are witnessing a move towards a much thinner version of citizenship, away from the thicker conception of classical European national citizenship that is becoming less and less able to fully account for the individualism and pluralism of post-modern market societies. Indeed, we may be witnessing the emergence of a notion of post-national legal personhood that quite possibly will be thinner even than the one associated with the US, and what the American juridified political order holds out for the framers of a new European constitution is in this context, and for better or worse, an alternative to the classical European model, a far more decentralised and messy system for negotiating conflict in civil society. Having said this, the question remains whether the EU can attain minimum coherence as a polity, something at least close to a recognisable demos and quasi-national community, so as to be able to enjoy legitimacy as a governance regime.[21] Again, the American example is instructive. For all its 'thinness' when it comes to citizenship practices, the legitimacy of the United States' government and its fundamental institutions is beyond question. In fact, the US is currently, in the wake of the 9/11 attacks, becoming more and not less committed to the primacy of national sovereignty, expressed in foreign policy unilateralism and the refusal to submit to international treaties and institutions, such as the newly constituted international court, out of a primary concern with internal and external national security. This suggests then thin concepts of citizenship may well be an aspect of a strong national identity, leaving the Europeans with a double challenge: how to simultaneously strengthen, even create, a sense of European polity identity *and* to open its citizenship requirements to welcome and include the immigrants and other minorities it sorely needs to survive and prosper, politically, demographically, and economically, in the twenty-first century.

---

Or conversely, there is the outburst of a politics of national solidarity, most often associated with war-related patriotism, such as the programmes launched by Franklin D. Roosevelt.

[20] At the same time this commitment to offering legal standing and protection to aliens, and even illegal aliens, is grounded not in arguments referring to global, human rights doctrines, but rather by invoking the United States Constitution. This also means that the legal position of aliens is vulnerable to the changing political moods in the US, as Japanese-Americans experienced during World War II, and illegal and residents that are Moslems or of Arab descent have experienced post 9/11.

[21] For a discussion of this problematic, see the chapter of Bellamy and Castiglione in this volume, as well as the chapter by Breckman.

## 5.   REFERENCES

Bataille, Georges. 1993, *The Accursed Share*, vol II & III, New York: Zone.

Beard, Charles. 1957, *The Economic Basis of Politics and Related Writings by Charles A. Beard*, New York: Vintage Books.

Bickel, Alexander. 1962, *The Least Dangerous Branch*, New York: Bobbs-Merrill.

Black, Eric. 1988, *The Myth that Binds Us* Boulder, CO: Westview Press.

Bogus, Carl T. 2001, *Why Lawsuits are Good for America: Disciplined Democracy, Big Business, and Common Law*, New York: New York University Press.

Bork, Robert H. 1990, *The Tempting of America: The Political Seduction of the Law*, New York: The Free Press.

Bosniak, Linda. 2000, 'Citizenship Denationalized', *Indiana Journal of Global legal Studies*, 7.

Burke, Thomas. 2002, *Lawyers, Lawsuits, and Legal Rights*, Berkeley, CA: University of California Press.

Bryce, James. 1920, *The American Commonwealth* (vol II). New York: MacMillan.

Burley, Anne-Marie and Walter Mattli. 1993, 'Europe Before the Court: A Political Theory of Legal Integration', *International Organization*, (47, no 1): Winter.

Castells, Manuel. 1997, *The Power of Identity. The Information Age: Economy, Society and Culture, Volume Two*, Oxford: Blackwell Publishers.

Cohen, Jean. 1988, 'Civil Society and Social Theory', *Thesis Eleven*, no 21.

—— 1996, 'Rights, Citizenship, and the Modern Form of the Social: Dilemmas of Arendtian Republicanism', *Constellations*, 3 (no, 2).

—— 1999, 'Changing Paradigms of Citizenship and the Exclusiveness of the Demos', *International Sociology*, 14 (no 3).

Cohen, Roger. 2000, 'A European Identity: Nation-State Losing Ground', *New York Times*, 14 January.

Cross, Frank B. 2003, 'America the Adversarial', *Virginia Law Review*, 89.

Curtis, Michael Kent. 1986, *No State Shall Abridge: The 14th Amendment and the Bill of Rights*, Durham, NC: Duke University Press.

Epp, Charles R. 1998, *The Rights Revolution: Lawyers, Activists, and Supreme Courts in Comparative Perspective*, Chicago: The University of Chicago Press.

Franklin, Mark, Patrick Lyons and Michael Marsh. 2001, 'The Tally of Turnout: How the Changing Character of Elections Drives Voter Turnout Variations in Established Democracies', revised version of paper presented at The Harvard University Center for European Studies. (November).

Goldman, Sheldon. 1997, *Picking Federal Judges*, New Haven: Yale University Press.

Haskell, Thomas. 1997, 'The New Aristocracy', *New York Review of Books*, (4 December).

Hasnas, John. 1996, 'What's Wrong with a Little Tort Reform?' *Idaho Law Review*.

Hensler, Deborah H. et al. 1999, *Class Action Dilemmas: Pursuing Public Goals for Private Gain*, Executive summary. Rand Institute for Civil Justice.

Holmström, Barry. 1998, *Domstolar och demokrati*, Uppsala: Acta Universitatis Upsaliensis.

Horowitz, Donald L. 1977, *The Courts and Social Policy*, Washington, DC: The Brookings Institution.

Irons, Peter. 2003, *A People's History of the Supreme Court*, New York: Penguin Books.

Kagan, Robert A. 1991, 'Adversarial Legalism and American Government', *Journal of Policy Analysis and Management*, 10 (no 3).

—— 1994, 'Do Lawyers Cause Adversarial Legalism? A Preliminary Inquiry', *Law and Social Inquiry.*

Kagan, Robert A. 2001, *Adversarial Legalism*, Cambridge, MA: Harvard University Press.

Karsten, Peter. 1998, 'Enabling the Poor to Have Their Day in Court: The Sanctioning of Contingency Fee Contracts, a History to 1940', *DePaul Law Review*, 47 (Winter).

Kelley, Donald. 1978, 'The Metaphysics of Law: An Essay on the Very Young Marx', *American Historical Review*, 83 (April).

Khavari, Farid A. 1990, *Vultures: Doctors, Lawyers, Hospitals and Insurance Companies*, Malibu, CA: Roundtable Publishing.

Leleux, Paul. 1982, The Role of the European Court of Justice in Protecting Individual Rights in the Context of Free Movement of Persons and Service. In Eric Stein and Terence Sandalow (eds), *Courts and Free Markets*, vol 2, Oxford: Clarendon Press.

Lindberg, Lars. 1996, *Den amerikanska lösningen*, Stockholm: HSO.

Lowi, Ted. 1979, *The End of Liberalism*, New York: W. W. Norton.

Madison, James. Federalist Paper #10. In Hamilton, Alexander, James Madison and John Jay. (1961/1787–88), *The Federalist Papers*, New York: Penguin Press.

Melnik, R. Shep. 1989, The Courts, Congress, and Programmatic Rights. In R. Harris and S. Milkis, (eds), *Remaking American Politics*. Londo : Westview Press.

Nergelius, Joakim, Alexander Peczenik, and Ola Wiklund. 1998, *Löser juridiken demokratins problem?* Demokratiutredningens skrift nr 23, Stockholm: SOU.

Nergelius, Joakim and Barry Holstrom. 2000, 'Mer makt krävs till domstolarna', *R&D*, no 2, 28 January.

O'Connell, Jeffrey. 1979, *The Lawsuit Lottery*, New York: The Free Press.

Olson, Walter K. 1991, *The Litigation Explosion: What Happened when America Unleashed the Lawsuit*, New York: Truman Talley Books.

*Politics in America: 2004, The 108th Congress*, Washington DC: Congressional Quarterly Press, 2003.

Putnam, Robert. 2000, *Bowling Alone*, New York: Simon and Schuster.

Ratzka, Adolf. 1998, 'I kläm mellan laissez faire och den sociala ingenjörskonsten', *Socialpolitik*, no 2.

Rosenberg, Gerald N. 1991, *The Hollow Hope: Can Courts Bring About Social Change*, Chicago: The University of Chicago Press.

Rueschemeyer, Dietrich. 1973, *Lawyers and Their Society: A Comparative Study of the Legal Profession in Germany and United States*, Cambridge, MA: Harvard University Press.

Saks, Michael J. 1986, 'Blaming the Jury', *Georgetown Law Journal* 75, 693–704.

Scheuerman, William. 1997, 'The Rule of Law at Century's End', *Political Theory*, 25 (no 5, October): 740.

Soysal, Yasemin. 1994, *Limits of Citizenship: Migrants and Postnational Membership in Europe*, Chicago: The University of Chicago Press, 1994.

Sullivan, Kathleen. 1998, 'Behind the Crimson Curtain', *New York Review of Books*, (8 October).

Sunstein, Cass. 1992, 'How Independent is the Court', *New York Review of Books*, (22 October).

*Time Europe*. 2000, 'See Vous in Court: France is the Latest Nation to Join the Litigation Game', (vol 157): 15 January.

Tocqueville, Alexis de. (1969/1848), *Democracy in America*, edited by J.P. Mayer, New York: Doubleday and Company.

Trägårdh, Lars. 1999. *Patientmakt i Sverige, USA och Holland: Individuella kontra sociala rättigheter*, Stockholm: Spri.

'Voice of the People' survey. 2002, conducted by Gallup International for the World Economic Forum. Released 7 November 2002. (www.WEForum.org).

Weiler, J.H.H. 1999, *The Constitution of Europe. 'Do the New Clothes Have an Emperor?' and Other Essays on European Integration*, Cambridge: Cambridge University Press.

White, G. Edward. 1985, *Tort Law in America: An Intellectual History*, New York: Oxford University Press.

Wills, Robert V. 1990, *Lawyers are Killing America*, Santa Barbara: Capra Press.

Wincott, Daniel. 2000, 'A Community of Law? "European" Law and Judicial Politics: The Court of Justice and Beyond', *Government and Opposition*, 35; 3–26

Yeazell, Stephen C. 2001, 'Re-Financing Civil litigation', *DePaul Law Review*, 51.

Wong, Ola. 2003, 'Trafikskadade måste få stärkt rättskydd' in *Dagens Nyheter*, August 5.

Zaremba, Maciej. 1992, *Minken i folkhemmet*, Stockholm: Timbro.

# 4

## *Rights and Regulation in (the) Europe(an Union): After National Democracy?*

### DANIEL WINCOTT

### 1.   INTRODUCTION

RADITIONALLY THE EUROPEAN left has harboured considerable scepticism about both Judges and European Integration. The widespread assumption that the working class would eventually become a self-conscious majority (and hence choose to vote for social democracy) meant that the left often favoured systems in which the power of elected assemblies was relatively untrammelled. Unelected, judges were seen as a brake on the legitimate power of democratic assemblies, who characteristically privileged individual rights, especially property rights above collective action and interests. Yet judges have become increasingly influential in Europe, both at national and supranational levels. It is difficult effectively to separate out these two levels in theory or practice: national and supranational levels of law are fundamentally entangled with one another. Indeed, the operation of the supranational level is only possible through national systems.

Although judges themselves have been key players in these processes of 'judicialisation' (on which processes see Stone Sweet 2000), the processes have also been provided considerable support by politicians, support which may increase considerably in the near future. If completed, two political processes currently under way in Europe would tend to increase the political influence of its Courts. First, although the Charter of Fundamental Rights is not (yet) strictly justiciable, it may none the less become partially and informally incorporated into European Law through decisions of the European Court of Justice (ECJ). Discussions in the Convention on the Future of Europe and elsewhere point towards the formal incorporation of the Charter into European Law, a move which would obviously enhance the influence on judges within Europe. Secondly, there are currently considerable pressures partially to formalise a range of governance 'modes' within the EU, including the Open Method of Co-ordination (OMC), new forms of regulatory agency, partnership agreements of various sorts and so on.

At the same time it is proposed that EU's traditional 'Community method' (which produces its 'binding' legislation) should be reformed, in the direction of less detailed 'framework legislation' of a more general scope. The Commission would then be delegated powers to 'fill in the details' as appropriate. These tendencies are visible in the Commission's White Paper on Governance published in 2001 and the Convention's proposals (as at March 2003 — see Wincott 2003a for a discussion). Perhaps less obviously than in the case of a justiciable Charter of Rights, nonetheless the role of the Court would probably grow if these proposals are implemented. The Court is likely to be drawn into judging the boundaries between modes of governance and the overall balance between them.

I approach this chapter from the supranational level 'downwards', as it were. After this introduction I will go on to sketch an image of the EU's political system. I will then turn to more detailed analysis, first providing an account of the contingent process of the development of its judicial architecture, before considering the conceptualisation of the EU as an emergent 'regulatory polity'. Finally, I will consider how the left might respond to the EU.

Some analysts might see tendencies towards the judicialisation of supranational politics in Europe as a victory *for* and *won by* political forces of the right. After all, historically, it is the right that has sought to depoliticise key aspects of economic and social regulation, removing them from the more directly democratic domains of political life and placing them instead in specialised and expert contexts, explicitly insulated from majoritarian pressures. While I would endorse the first of these claims, it is much more difficult to find evidence for the second one. Political forces of the right have not been dominant in the construction of the European Union. At key moments in the construction of the Union, the political balance between left and right has been fairly even (between say Schmidt and Gisgard d'Estang or Mitterrand and Kohl). Ironically, key figures on the European right (de Gaulle and Thatcher being exemplary) have often been deeply sceptical about the European project, sometimes influencing it more by default than by explicit plan.

The creation of the Single Market is the period in the construction of the EC/EU that has received most attention in this context. As well as being analysed as an episode in the on-going battle between national control and supranational influence, in the 1980s politics and policy of the EC had an important 'left-right' dimension. This aspect has been most influentially analysed as a clash between 'projects' for regulated capitalism and neoliberalism (Marks and Hooghe 1999). Broadly the argument is that the 1980s represented a clear, perhaps even decisive, victory for neoliberalism over regulated capitalism. While not necessarily dissenting from the conclusion that the political economy of Europe moved sharply in a market-oriented direction during this period, the argument needs to be made more precisely.

The identification of political economy 'projects' suggests that key (coalitions of) actors can be attached to each project. Yet during the 1980s the Commission was led by Jacques Delors, whose background was centre-left, France was led from the left, as was Spain, and even Kohl's Christian Democracy was hardly a pioneer of neoliberalism.

In fact, the major European figures of the 1980s who might be regarded as neoliberal were mainly British. Yet Mrs Thatcher hardly regards the trajectory of European integration from the mid-1980s onwards as desirable. Indeed her attitude towards Europe appears to have been informed more by a visceral nationalism than a rational liberalism. Arguably *the* most significant neoliberal figure in the construction of 'Europe' was Leon Brittan, the Conservative Minster who became a European Commissioner after sacrificing his national career to save Mrs Thatcher. But it would stretch even the most generous account of Sir Leon's abilities to make him the key actor in a neoliberal victory in Europe. Perhaps we should not assume that the outcome of political integration must have resulted from the conscious, even strategic, vision of key actors guiding them to decisive victories over opponents. It may be more helpful to view integration as the complex and often contradictory precipitate of the clash of a variety of actors striving to achieve their objectives, none of which is fully achieved.

Moreover, part of the difficulty here may arise from misconceptions embedded in the terms of the debate. It is, of course, often helpful to describe some regimes as much more 'market'-oriented than others. It is also perfectly possible to describe a minimally regulated political economy regime. Nonetheless, in practice no regime dispenses with regulation to the point of approximating to the minimal model, never mind to an idealised 'free market'. Thus for example, in the US, a system disparaged in France as a species of Anglo-Saxon ultra-liberalism there is nonetheless considerable space for economic liberal critique of the 'heavy hand' of the state. In practical terms, it is probably more accurate to identify neoliberalism as a political project, rather than an 'actually existing' political economy regime. In any given context, a neoliberal project would seek to increase the scope of the market as a form of social organisation.

The other 'side' of the contrast also produces some conceptual confusion. Ironically, it is the dominance of the neoliberal trope that allows all alternatives to it to be homogenised into one form, variously labelled as social democratic, corporatist or 'regulated'. Only if we believe that a fairly pure market form is possible as a general mode of social organisation do the various political and social forms of political economy regime all appear similar. Thus the significant differences between the natalist traditions of France, the German Model and the Swedish Social Service State only appear similar when contrasted to an idealised image of market society.

While it may make sense to regard the European Union as moving in a more market-oriented direction during the 1980s, perhaps even at the expense of traditions of Socialism, Social Democracy and Christian Democracy, this movement hardly dispensed with the regulation of capitalism. Rather, complicated and often only half understood arguments about the precise character of the regulation of capitalism were the means by which the scope for the market was extended. Moreover, the significance of each particular piece of regulation is only revealed in the context of the overall emergent regulatory structure. Europe's evolving political economy regime was, then, hardly the consequence of the success of a self-conscious project. Instead, crucial aspects of the architecture of (the) Europe(an Union) seem to have depended on the contingent articulation of disparate elements, accidents of historical sequencing and a generalised and routine respect for the rule of law, rather than being explicitly endorsed in a coherent and clearly articulated right wing (re)construction of the EU as a means of de-politicising Europe. This seems to be the case both in respect of the history of key episodes in European integration and in the longer-term construction of aspects of the European architecture, such as its judicial system.

## 2.   THE POLITICAL SYSTEM OF EUROPE

The Political System of the European Union has a number of key features. First, it is a system within which Law and Courts bulk large. It is well known that since the early 1960s the European Court of Justice has sought to constitutionalise the legal framework of the European Union. If not a *rechtsstaat*, the EC has become a 'Community of Law'. Some of the steps on this journey have been large, but in general the development has been gradual but consistent.

Secondly, it has a relatively small budget, at least compared to most states, largely because the member states have been reluctant to allocate larger amounts of money to the European level. This means that most EU policies are regulatory rather than (re)distributive. The few areas in which significant funds are dispersed by the EU — such as agriculture and cohesion (regional) policy — are tightly defined by the states. If the Commission and Parliament made a concerted attempt to extend tax and spend style policies, their likelihood of success would be small.

Thirdly, it remains a system within which collective identities other than those of nations and states are only weakly articulated. In other words, nothing like the process of political identity formation characteristic of processes of nation and state building within its constituent states has yet occurred within the EU. For example, although political parties are organised along ideological lines within the European Parliament, each Euro-party remains a confederation of national party groupings and it is these national groupings that organise elections within in various states. In turn these elections typically revolve around national issues and debates, rather than taking up European themes that cut across national boundaries.

Together these features have resulted in a Union that is much more like the US than it is characteristic of the political forms of the European states as they developed between 1945 and 1980. Interest groups rather than political parties are the characteristic mode of collective action and legal processes play a comparatively large role in relation to political ones. Of course, there is a considerable and well-known body of scholarship that makes many of these points. Giandomenico Majone's analysis of the emergence of a Regulatory State in Europe is especially noteworthy here (1996). But even those more associated with the left recognise these points (at least implicitly) when they recommend strategies to 'make the most of European law' (Harlow 1992, see also the discussion in Mabbett 2000).

However, the existing discussion is too narrow. All too often the emergence of regulatory policies as the characteristic mode of European Governance is discussed as a technical matter — with at least two unfortunate consequences. First, the manner in which structural features of the Euro-Polity have privileged certain forms of policy is downplayed. This is the case both in the sense that other alternatives have been difficult to consider or pursue successfully and also that the existence of some structural pre-requisites of regulatory policies have been taken for granted. Secondly, it is sometimes assumed that regulatory policies are the upshot of some prior normative agreement. Indeed, sometimes the simple existence of such policies appears to be held to imply that they are normatively justified. According to this view only normatively acceptable regulations can come into existence and all desirable regulations will in fact emerge. Bizarrely this is a view that seems to embrace the critic's straw doll version of 1960s US pluralism.

How and why have regulatory policies and a certain sort of rights-oriented polity emerged in the EU? What are the institutional prerequisites and features of these developments? Current theories, I argue, pay insufficient attention to the importance of the judicial structure for the emergence of European regulatory policies. Succinctly put, the argument is 'no European law, no regulatory polity'. Having inserted the Law into its proper place in these developments, however, the waters begin to muddy. At first blush it might seem that emphasising the role of the Courts and the Law in these developments further solidifies the regulatory character of EU politics. If the EU is marked out as a distinctive political system by any of its individual features, it is surely the Law.

However, on closer investigation, the process of judicial construction appears to have been much more difficult and less 'complete' than is widely recognised. Now, to those familiar with analyses of the contingency of rights in the US context may find all this rather unsurprising. Of course, rights construction was much bloodier, messier and more political than the conventional sanitised, judge-centred version would have us believe, they might say (see, for example, Epp 1998). (Although the political character of the process of rights construction is much more detached from popular struggles in the EC than elsewhere.) However, in the European context, these observations may throw up the basic questions about the character and even the viability of the integration project in general. The challenge with which the EU is now faced as it is set to become continental in scope is much more fundamental than is commonly acknowledged. In general, rather than regulatory politics appearing as the inevitable, widely accepted and rational trajectory of European political development, my approach raises radical questions about this political form. Whether there are viable alternatives for the left is another matter.

## 3.  THE CONTINGENT DEVELOPMENT OF EUROPEAN COMMUNITY LAW[1]

The story of the emergence of the European Community legal system is well known, but can be interpreted in a number of different ways. In its bare bones, the story concerns the construction of a 'new legal order' — and a *constitutional* legal order at that — out of a body of international law. Crucial features of the new legal order included its potential direct effect as such on individuals within the territory of the Community and its supremacy over contradictory provisions of national law. The ideas of direct effect and supremacy are conventionally treated (and taught to law students) as the two foundational principles of Community law.

Examining a process of *construction* we should always look for the *constructors*. Neither direct effect nor supremacy was created by the states that signed the Treaties on which the Community was founded. Both 'principles' came into existence through judicial decisions. A more detailed historical examination of the cases on which these principles were developed seems to show that the Legal Service of the Commission played a central role — it suggested that the Community law might be both directly effective and supreme over relevant provisions of national law. The Court proceeded more cautiously. First, in preparing the case, its Advocate-General argued that EC law was not supreme over national law, therefore it could not be directly effective for individuals. Instead, in general European rules had to be transposed into national rules on which individuals could

---

[1] In the subsequent sections I will refer to 'Community' law rather than 'Union' law. This is not because I take a particular position in the extensive debates on the relationship between the Union and the Community. Instead, because many of the author's I cite refer to 'Community law' in the interests of stylistic consistency I will also use it.

then rely. Secondly, while both the Commission's legal service and the Advocate-General recognised that direct effectiveness and supremacy were two faces of the same coin, when the Court itself came to decide on this issue, it split them. In the *Van Gend* case, the Court decided that some of the provisions of the Treaties could have a direct effect for individuals within the Community. It was silent on the issue of supremacy. The following year, in *Costa*, it addressed the issue of supremacy. Despite no mention of supremacy in the Treaty of Rome, the ECJ found Community rules overrode contradictory provisions of national law. It is worth remembering that a number of member states specifically objected to the ideas of direct effect in the *Van Gend* and to supremacy in the *Costa* proceedings. That having been said, once the Court had come to its decision, no state sought to revisit these issues (see Stein 1981 and Wincott 1995).

In standard textbook accounts, the *Van Gend* and *Costa* cases are sometimes treated as if they established two fundamental principles of Community law and after the principles were established, only the details needed to be worked out. Yet the initial decision on direct effect only applied to Treaty provisions. Typically it applied to aspects of the Treaty that set out a matter of substantive policy to which all member states had — by definition — signed up. The initial decision on supremacy begged major questions about the scope of Community law (in its relation to national rules). More generally, a close look at the supremacy issue shows a more gradual process. One commentator has written of the cautious advance of the Court of Justice, moving 'through successive small steps'

> ... Initially it acknowledged the novelty, but stressed that it did not represent a new type of federalism. ... Instead of immediately proclaiming the supremacy of Community law over national law, the Court spoke more delicately of a subsequent, unilateral national provision's inability to prevail over a pre-existing Community law provision. Over time this prudence has been completely abandoned.
>
> (Mengozzi 1992; 61)

Perhaps more important, the shape of the doctrine of supremacy as a practical doctrine was necessarily defined relationally — particularly in interaction with various national courts. Moreover, many national legal systems refused to accept this principle for long periods of time. It was not accepted in France until 1989. While largely accepted in the German system by 1986, the issue was re-opened after the Maastricht Treaty.

Two sets of developments during the late 1960s and 1970s help to bring the development of the Community legal system into focus. First, in relation to direct effect, the Court sought to extend this notion to an important category of secondary legislation, the directive. Secondly, the issue of supremacy triggered a debate about the protection of fundamental rights within the Community. First, then, directives were designed to be a form of

European rule that would have a particular result across the territory of the Community, while leaving a large measure of discretion about the means by which national implementing legislation would achieve this objective. In practice, directives had proven to be a very widely used form of legislation. If directives were directly effective, then the general structure of Community secondary legislation would change and its significance increase dramatically. The Court first asserted that directives were directly effective in the *Van Duyn* case. The Court provided only weak arguments in support of this assertion. First, it suggested that because directives were 'binding' their potential direct effect should not be excluded. Secondly, it stated that directives would be more useful if they were directly effective — true, but hardly a justification for a change of principle. Finally, it argued that the role of national courts in the application of Community law suggested that directives might have direct effect. On the other hand the preliminary reference procedure, which gives national courts the opportunity to draw on the expertise of the ECJ in deciding cases raising issues of Community law could also be used for provisions of European law which have no binding effect (Wincott 1995).

It was fully five years later that the Court developed a more convincing argument that directives should be directly effective, at least in some ways. In the *Ratti* case, the Court argued that member states should not profit from their own failures to implement Community secondary legislation. In other words, in cases against individuals, states should not be able to rely on their own failure to have implemented a directive. However, this rationale only allows directives to be directly effective on relationships between an individual and the state, not on those between individuals or within Civil Society. Indeed, the subsequent development of direct effect of directives, focused tightly on this issue of making states liable for their failure to implement them within national law. It is also worth noting that the extension of direct effect to directives was received with much less ease than was direct effect of Treaty provisions within various national legal systems (especially those of Italy, France and Germany). Generally, however, these issues have now been resolved and the ECJ's approach prevails (Wincott 1995, 2000).

The supremacy of Community law over national laws is quite another matter. From the earliest days several national Courts strongly resisted the idea that Community law was supreme over national law. Moreover, in contrast to the conventional image of the ECJ as a far-sighted and heroic actor (see, for example, Burley and Mattli 1993: Dauses 1985, Weiler 1986 also discusses the courage of the Court — for an evaluation of this discourse see Wincott 2000), the European Court itself seems to have been initially reluctant to extend its role in key areas. Almost as soon as the ECJ announced its position on supremacy, several national constitutional courts perceived a potential threat to the protection of human rights afforded by their own national constitutions. If European laws are supreme over conflicting provisions of national law, how far up the hierarchy of national rules does this supremacy reach? As soon as the issues of national *constitutional* protection of *fundamental* or *human rights* are raised, very sensitive matters of identity, national independence and sovereignty are raised.

Building on the previous experience of the Court under the Coal and Steel Community, even after its initial decision on supremacy, the ECJ drew away from developing an independent jurisprudential position protecting fundamental rights. Instead, initially the Court seemed concerned to protect the *autonomy* of the Community legal order, rather than its *integrity, unity* or *uniformity*. It was only after national courts reacted to this position by placing clear and explicit limits on the Community legal order that the ECJ began to reconsider its position. The German Constitutional Court was the first to move here. On 18 October 1967 it issued an order stating that due to the absence of 1) a democratic basis and 2) protection of human rights in Community law, European rules could not be allowed to undermine the constitutional rights of Germans. As a consequence all Community rules would have to be reviewed at the national level to ensure that they were compatible with the national constitutional protection of human rights. Even faced with this challenge — and other national constitutional courts adopting similar stances — the ECJ did not immediately move to assert its own rights protection. Instead, various national courts persisted in asking human rights related questions of the ECJ (Wincott 1994).

When the ECJ did eventually move to acknowledge that it had a role in the protection of fundamental rights, it did so *sotto voce* stating that there was no barrier in the provision at issue to prejudice 'the fundamental human rights enshrined in the general principles of Community law'. One political analyst of Community law has argued that this statement was 'virtually wrenched' from the ECJ by a preliminary reference from a German administrative court 'which couched the question for interpretation in "or else" terms' (Volcansek 1992, 115–6). From these unpromising beginnings, the ECJ moved to develop its own positive conception fundamental rights protection through its case-law. So, rather than fundamental rights being an essential and permanent feature of the EC normative order, enthusiastically developed by the ECJ, the European Court resisted for some time, before moving reluctantly to develop a fundamental rights jurisprudence.

When it did begin to develop fundamental rights protection, the ECJ faced various national interlocutors who did not simply remain unpersuaded of the Court moving in the direction they had suggested — instead they actually hardened their line. In 1974 the *Bundesverfassungsgericht* argued that

> As long as the integration process has not progressed so far that Community law also receives a catalogue of fundamental rights decided on by a parliament and of settled validity, which is adequate in comparison with the catalogue of fundamental rights contained in the Constitution, a reference by a court in the Federal Republic of Germany to the Bundesverfassungsgericht

in the judicial review proceedings, *following* the obtaining of a ruling of the European court under Article 177 of the Treaty is admissible and necessary if the German court regards the rule of the Community law which is relevant to its decision as inapplicable in the interpretation given by the European Court, because and insofar as it conflicts with one of the fundamental rights in the Constitution.

('*Solange*' 29 May 1974 [1974] 2 CMLR 551)

Note that the German Constitutional Court was setting up at least two distinct hurdles its acceptance of the principle of the supremacy of Community law here. The first concerned a credible catalogue of rights, comparable to that in the Basic Law. The second is the insistence that this catalogue of rights could not be a judicial invention, instead it had to be decided upon by a parliament. Remember that, formally speaking, at this stage the EC had an Assembly which was made up of delegates from national parliaments, rather than a directly elected Parliament (although the Assembly had taken to calling itself a Parliament).

In reaction to this challenge to its interpretation of its prerogatives, the ECJ redoubled its efforts to find a 'fundamental rights' dimension to the cases that came before it. But it was only in 1979 in the *Hauer* that the Court engaged in a detailed analysis of the sources of and limits to its fundamental rights jusrisprudence. Prior to this case, the basis for its fundamental rights decisions sometimes appeared delphic. In the words of a distinguished commentator on European law, it was as if the Court wanted to 'give and object lesson in human rights analysis'. (Weiler 1986, 1132)

Yet there was little the Court could do to satisfy the German court (as well as some other national constitutional courts) on the other dimensions of its challenge. The move towards direct elections for the European Parliament, begun in the mid-1970s, and first put into practice in the new election of 1979, was the product of a quite independent dynamic. It certainly helped the case of the ECJ *vis-a-vis* the *Bundesverfassungsgericht*, to be sure, but it was hardly introduced to do so. In other areas, however, political moves were undertaken to bolster the ECJ's position. A number of means of formalising political support for the ECJ were considered. The option of the Community itself joining the European Convention on Human Rights was canvassed, but the debate thrown up by this suggestion was inconclusive. Both Community institutions and member states were ambivalent about it. Instead a Joint Declaration (of the EC Institutions) on Fundamental Rights was negotiated which lent some political support from the Council of Ministers, Parliament and Commission to developing rights jurisprudence of the ECJ. The Court seems to have taken this document as an important political support for its position, referring to it explicitly in its *Hauer* judgment. On closer investigation, however, the weakness and limits of the declaration might seem more significant than its existence.

First, it had no official status — it could not be relied upon by the Court in any formal sense. Secondly, although no more than a third of a page long, the declaration took a good year to negotiate. Several states were not enthusiastic about it (Wincott 1994).

Nonetheless, on the basis of these changes — the introduction of an (admittedly weak) directly democratic element in the structure of the Community, a general political declaration of support for the position developed by the Court, and, partially as a consequence, an emboldened jurisprudence on fundamental rights — as well as the general evolution of the Community system during the early and mid-1980s the German Constitutional Court eventually relented and seemed to acknowledge the supremacy of Community law. The German Court was particularly impressed with the case-law of the ECJ. It noted

(a) the court of justice's positions that (i) protection of fundamental rights is mandatory; (ii) such protection is based on Community law; and (iii) it is linked to the content of the Member States' constitutions and of the European convention for the Protection of Human Rights and Fundamental Freedoms;

and

(b) the *de facto* importance which protection of fundamental rights has acquired in the Court of Justice's activity.
                    (*Solange II* 22 Oct. 1986 [1987] 3 CMLR 262)

In a sense the German Court had lowered the barriers it had placed in the way of accepting the supremacy of Community law and the legitimacy of its fundamental rights jurisprudence, rather than, the ECJ having met the challenge in full as set out in the first *Solange* ruling. The relationship between the ECJ and other national constitutional courts followed broadly the same pattern. By the end of the 1980s, then, it might have appeared that the supremacy and fundamental rights protection saga was settled. After an initial reluctance, the ECJ had succeeded in persuading various national courts to accept its (new) position, that it could invent and adequately protect a catalogue of fundamental rights largely through its own activism (albeit with important, if weak and equivocal political support). But the idea that the saga was settled could hardly be further from the truth.

Notwithstanding its initial hesitance, once the ECJ's view on fundamental rights had been accepted by its key interlocutors, it began to open out the scope of its rules. Initially having been forced to develop a notion of fundamental rights protection in order to defend its own conception of the supremacy of Community law, it then began to use these rights as an element of the supremacy of the Community legal order. In the early cases, the ECJ examined the compatibility of Community rules with fundamental rights; later, the Court began to examine national laws that might interfere with Community principles against its own fundamental rights standards. In effect, the ECJ began to treat the foundational principles of Community law (particularly the four freedoms of movement — goods, labour, services and capital) as fundamental rights. This resulted in the emergence of a much wider range of potential conflicts between Community law and national rules than might once have been expected.

For example, although in 1986 a distinguished commentator on Community law had asserted that the issue of abortion 'did not touch on the EEC or its Court' (Weiler 1986, 1127) by the beginning of the 1990s, the ECJ had become embroiled in the *Grogan* case which was centrally concerned with this issue. The Irish Constitution affords human rights protection to the unborn *foetus*. Activists unhappy with the restrictions on abortion that this protection ensures sought to distribute information about clinics in England. When prosecuted, these activists sought to rely on their rights under Community law — on the grounds that abortion is a service, to which Europeans should have free access across state boundaries. Faced with this difficult issue, which was politically sensitive both because of its inherent qualities, but also as a matter of the relationship between the Community and the member states, the Court seemed to shrink away from the issue. Rather than engaging with the issues the Court made its decision turn on the fact that the activists in question were not employees of the relevant English clinics. The suggestion seems to be that had the economic relationship been clearer, then it would have trumped the normative position entrenched in the Irish constitution. Whatever view is taken of the substantive normative issues at stake here, the implication that they turn on whether or not activists involved were employed by overseas clinics hardly matches up to them (for a discussion see Wincott 1994).

In the late 1980s and early 1990s, after the second *Solange* judgment, the ECJ appeared relatively confident about its own position atop the normative and practical hierarchy of (the) Europe(an Community). Cases such as *Grogan* (and perhaps also the extended saga of the regulation of Sunday trading in England and Wales) drew the ECJ into difficult terrain. They underscored the difficulties of asserting what seemed to have been its view of the hierarchy of laws in Europe due variously to the sensitivity and absurdity of the material with which it found itself dealing. Both the general political reaction to the Maastricht Treaty as well as the specific circumstances of the challenge to the validity of the Treaty in the German courts pushed things further in this direction. The Court found itself in a general political context of a widespread — although by no means universal — suspicion about the legitimacy of the existing structure of the Union, never mind its possible future development. Moreover, creative jurisprudence with the purpose of further developing European level rights protection was as likely to deepen this suspicion as to allay it (Wincott 1994).

The *Brunner* case, in which a German national challenged the validity of the Maastricht Treaty requires more detailed attention. Although the upshot of this case was to allow the German government to ratify the Treaty, the German Constitutional Court sought to set clear normative limits to the future evolution of the Union in its judgment. In a sense, then, the German Court revisited its earlier concerns about the supremacy of Community law over national law in this case. At heart, the *Bundesverfassungsgericht* saw the Union as a union of states, with basic authority resting with the peoples of Europe, as a single European people did not (yet?) exist. In a ringing, if sexist, phrase the German Court depicted the states, rather than the union, as the 'Masters of the Treaty'. Absent a basic reworking of the social fabric of Europe, the German court seemed to place states and their peoples above Union/Community institutions (including the ECJ) in a legitimate normative hierarchy. As such, it seemed to set a limit of some sort to the possible future development of the Union. Of course, for almost all practical purposes, the operation of Community law and its relationship to national courts remained unaltered. There are, of course, a variety of interpretations of the normative significance of the *Brunner* case. Those wedded to strongly hierarchical conceptions of sovereignty understand it as a flat reassertion of the normative supremacy of national over Community laws (Herdengen 1994). Others perceive an essentially ethnic (and perhaps particularly German) conception of citizenship underpinning the judgment (Weiler 1995). Those developing more pluralistic conceptions of law detect a move away from hierarchy, towards a notion of national and Community law as co-evolving bodies of law in a complex competitive/co-operative relationship (MacCormick 1995).

In this re-reading of the role of the ECJ and the historical development of the Community legal system I have sought to move away from conventional, perhaps 'first generation', conceptions. Standard accounts of the emergence of this structure or these rights focus largely on the role of the Court and its teleological method of interpreting the Treaties (present in almost all 'first generation' or 'standard texts' on Community law for discussions see Kilpatrick 1998 and Wincott 2000, for a counterpoint to the 'first genera-tion' see the essays collected in Shaw and More 1995). These ideas are/were often rooted in background assumptions about the nature of the law, rather than explicitly theorised. Their influence has been none the weaker for that. Instead of viewing the ECJ as a court committed to defending an essential and unchanging body of rights and concept of law, the ECJ's vision of its own role and the character of Community law have altered. Changes to the scope and character of the policy programme and legal order over which it had jurisdiction changed (the growth of the scope and range of Community competences), national court challenges to the ECJ's evolving view of its own role and of Community law, and alterations to the social and economic *zeitgeist* have all been important influences.

We should not be surprised that either the general development of the Community's legal structure or the specific emergence of a jurisprudence of fundamental rights have been a complex, difficult and circuitous processes culminating in no definitive final form. But the alternative account of EC law at which I have hinted here begs questions beyond the domain of law narrowly defined. Partly this is a matter of analogy. In common with the received view of EC law, standard accounts of the EU as a regulatory polity tend to depict its emergence as a gradual but inexorable and rational process. More than that, however, they fail to attend to the core role of law within regulatory policies and polities. By taking the law for granted, they, too assume that its creation was unproblematic, or even that it had always been in existence. Once this assumption is problematised, new questions are begged about the processes by which the EU 'regulatory polity' emerged.

## 4.   THE REGULATORY POLITY

The idea is well entrenched that the European Union — or more precisely those parts of it that make up the European Community — is particularly successful in the development of regulatory policies. This is a double claim: that the EC is more successful at developing regulatory than other sorts of policies and that it is more successful at developing these sorts of policies than the European states have been. The EC is displacing states but also leading them towards an increasingly 'regulatory' role. For some, these developments mean that it is 'not misleading, but actually heuristically useful to think of the EC/EU as a "regulatory state"' (Majone 1996, 55). It is, of course, unusually bold to claim that the EC/EU is a state of any sort.

The claim is that the EU/EC is a *regulatory* state does not necessarily mean that it has all of the classic qualities of statehood. We would not necessarily expect a regulatory state to have an external military capacity. A key question about the EU/EC's regulatory statehood turns on one's view of the relationship between a state's internal coercive capacity, the functioning of its legal system and the reliance of regulation on the law. As it developed historically and for the moment, the EC's legal system has not relied upon an autonomous European coercive capacity. Those of an optimistic turn of mind might therefore see the EC legal system as at the cutting edge of a new kind of law. Others of more pessimistic disposition would suggest that the EC's legal order is not autonomous. If there are no European prisons or police officers, the EC's order relies upon its interpenetration of EC and national legal systems and the coercive resources of which they dispose. Because I do not want to be drawn on this issue now, I prefer to describe the EC as a regulatory polity here, rather than as a regulatory state.

What are regulatory policies? In the EU context most attention is focused on the contrast between rule based regulatory policies and distributive and redistributive policies that require direct expenditure. A further category of 'stablization policies', focused on the maintenance of satisfactory levels of economic growth and employment as well as price stability, is also sometimes identified (Majone 1996, 54–5). The core argument is that the EC has been more concerned with regulatory policies than those that require direct expenditure. However, this argument is sometimes augmented by a claim that it is not simply policies that are based on direct expenditure that are being superseded, so too are stabilisation policies. Here we begin to see the analytical case being clouded by being tied into a particular normative agenda, without sufficiently direct acknowledgement. The logic of the argument here seems to be displaced in order to make a particular point with some rhetorical force. By tying together direct expenditure and stabilisation as the functions of the modern European state that were historically central, Majone is able to claim that the traditional European Keynesian welfare state (concerned with stabilisation and (re)distribution respectively) is being replaced by the emergent regulatory state, operating largely at the European level and identified particularly by analogy with the US. Yet in his eagerness to make this point, Majone seems to forget that the macro-economic stabilisation function has hardly been eliminated in Europe. It is not so much that the stabilisation function has been superseded, as that its *form* and *purpose* have changed. Macro-economic stabilisation has taken an increasing regulatory, rule-based, form, which increasingly operates at the European level. The independent European Central Bank is based on the model of the *Bundesbank*, but carries the formal logic of that model even further than it has been carried in the German case. The purpose of 'stabilization', at the EU level as elsewhere, has shifted from maintaining high levels of employment to achieving low inflation.

Be that as it may, the core claim of regulatory analysts remains that rule-based rather than direct expenditure policies dominate the EC. While there is a good deal to this argument, it is important not to overstate the case. Certain key policies in Europe do dispose of significant direct expenditure. Agricultural policies are a case in point here, as are 'cohesion' or regional development policies. However, high levels of spending on agricultural policies is a legacy of its early institutionalisation and 'cohesion' funds, which redistribute from rich to poor regions within Europe, emerge as 'side payments' to bind poorer states into liberalising agreements sought by their better off neighbours. While it does show that there is more to the EC than regulation, the (admittedly brief) discussion of these other policy areas serves more to draw attention to the remarkable dominance of regulatory policies than to undercut the regulatory analysis.

Why have regulatory policies developed? A variety of arguments have been canvassed here. They range from issues of practicality to a fundamental change in popular values across Europe. My own preference is to emphasise the practicalities. In other words, given the structure of the EC/EU, regulatory policies were the easiest to achieve. However, proponents of the EC as a Regulatory State characteristically see its development in very positive normative terms. Arguments based on practicalities typically emphasise the comparatively small size of the EC's budget together with limited discretion or flexibility over how it can be spent. These characteristics may have stymied efforts on the part of some in the Commission and the representatives of some states to develop full-blooded redistributive policies, particularly during earlier phases of the integration process. Moreover, given the emphasis on unanimity among the member states for the introduction of new policy competences, if only one state wishes to block the development of a more redistributive approach, it is very difficult to achieve. The role of British governments between 1979 and 1997 is instructive here, as the Thatcherites threw roadblocks in the way of a series of social initiatives associated with Jacques Delors and his colleagues in the French Socialist Party.

However, in addition to the negative reasons for the development of regulatory policies (ie other forms of policy are very difficult to achieve), my emphasis on the importance of the legal framework suggests another argument based on practicalities, which is more 'positive', at least in one sense of the term. If redistributive policies make high demands of the capacity to tax, regulatory policies require a highly efficient and reliable legal framework. There is no point in attempting to achieve integration through regulation if no one obeys the rules. In other words, the development of regulatory policies requires a series of positive politico-legal achievements, in the form of the creation of a framework of law. It is not just that the achievement of other forms of policy was problematic, the EC/EU *had the specific resources necessary to develop relatively effective regulatory policies.* If EC policy-makers didn't have access to large-scale financial resources, from the mid-1970s onwards, they did have an unusually effective legal structure on which to draw. The timing of the development at the EC level of large scale and innovative regulatory policies from the mid-1970s onwards also supports this view. The neglect of the law may have something to do with traces of functionalist arguments in the regulatory framework (an issue to which we will return in a moment). The law exists in order to make efficient contracting possible (in civil society and between government and society). However, as I have shown in some detail in the previous section, the emergence of the EC legal system was hardly inevitable, instead being a highly contingent matter, which could easily have been blocked, or developed in a different direction. Moreover, the future viability of it is not assured.

Other causes of the shift to regulatory policies are also considered. These move through various seemingly technical issues, related to the importance of expertise in various specific policy areas, to questions of time-(in)consistency and credible commitments in public policy. Particularly as we shift to the latter set of issues, however, the tone begins to change, from one of technicality, to a mixture of normative argument and claims about shifts in (popular) values across Europe. One of the difficulties that advocates of the regulatory state need to address is the question of timing. Why should regulatory policies have developed *when* they did? Why did policy-makers become concerned with issues of policy credibility during the 1980s and 90s, to the point that they were prepared to design structures that would constrain their own future choices? This problem shows some analogy with the difficulties US analysts faced in accounting for the alleged shift from regulation to deregulation in the 1980s. Essentially, the more deterministic the theory that predicts the growth of regulation (or of intervention on the European side of the Atlantic) the more difficult it becomes to account for deregulation. One element of the attempt to account for this shift has been borrowed directly from the Chicago School attempt to explain deregulation in the US. Drawing on Gary Backer's work, the claim is that normative theories of desirable regulation are the best positive guide to the emergence of new forms of (de)regulation. Although underpinned by an account of the minimisation of deadweight losses, this normative analysis as a positive theory of regulatory emergence (known as NPT) essentially presents a functionalist and Panglossian analysis of politics. By asserting that politics as well as economics are efficient, this approach effectively loses all its critical edge and, ironically, provides little or no guide to the timing of changes to a regulatory regime (for a discussion of the NPT in a European context see Majone 1996, 31–7). We are left with a rather unsatisfactory and circular argument that regulatory policies exist because they are efficient, and we know that they are efficient because they exist.

By way of an aside, Majone's adoption of an analytic position of this sort sits uncomfortably with other positions that he takes. Elsewhere he is well known for focusing on the importance of rhetoric, argument and persuasion in policy-making (1989), an approach that suggests an open vision of policy change. Moreover, while he associates the emergence of the EC regulatory state with a neo-liberal turn, nonetheless, he suggests that this position is compatible with the development of considerable social and environmental regulation (so long as it does not take a redistributive form). In other words, there seems to be some scope for a *politics* of rights, particularly in defence of diffuse interests which he claims are better protected at the EC/EU as a site of non-majoritarian politics than in the more majoritarian settings of national parliamentary democracy. Moreover, in the context of the protection of diffuse interests of this sort, the scope for political/policy entrepreneurship is, he claims much greater. In this context, it would perhaps be fair to argue that he deploys the NPT theory at a rather high level of abstraction, accounting for the broad features of a general shift. Within these broad parameters there might be considerable scope for a variety of policy trajectories and configurations to develop. Perhaps general issues of efficiency are understood as calling forth a political reaction *of some sort*, but the precise form of that reaction is much more contingent. Cast in terms of the specific matters at issue, Majone considers the neo-liberal turn as dictated by the general requirements of efficiency, while leaving the precise mixture and form of deregulation and re-regulation and of economic, social, consumer and environmental regulation as a matter of political contingencies and policy entrepreneurship.

As we have just seen, the emergence of the regulatory model in Europe is associated with a neo-liberal turn, which affects both the national and supranational levels (Jobert 1994). This shift is characteristically identified as a broad set of changes that can be summed up as an increasing (although compared to the US relatively late) acceptance of the basic legitimacy of the market. All in all there is evidence of the shift from the Keynesian welfare state (focused on stabilisation and redistribution) towards a regulatory state at the national level as well as the European one (Majone 1996, 54–55). Although it seems fair to acknowledge that some sort of a shift of this sort has occurred, the change is hardly complete or uncontested. Moreover, the precise relationship between changes at the EC and the national levels requires careful consideration for two related reasons. First, although popular values concerning economic and social policies have undoubtedly changed in Europe since 1980, in aggregate Europeans appear to remain strongly wedded to at least some form of their (national) welfare states. If, at least at this national level, the welfare state has some enduring appeal and legitimacy, then the neo-liberal turn is hardly complete, at least in terms of popular values. Secondly, advocates of the regulatory polity/state model tend to depict the EC as at the cutting edge of the development of regulatory policy in Europe (not least because a series of European level agencies exist that are broadly independent of partisan politics).

Advocates of the regulatory model seek to resolve the tensions thrown up by the differences perceived at the national and EC levels by distinguishing (re)distribution from efficiency, wealth claiming from wealth creating or politics from economics (Majone 1996, 294–5, 1998). Effectively the argument is that while a national politics of redistribution may be legitimate, such an approach could/should not be transposed to the European level, which instead is a domain governed by norms of economic efficiency. The affective ties of identity that are required to sustain and legitimise redistribution simply do not exist at the European level. Arguably the absence of such ties limits the legitimate possibilities for the introduction of European level parliamentary democracy. Equally, any attempt to introduce welfare state policies at the European level might provoke and aggravate social conflict, rather than ameliorate it (see Majone 1998). To the extent that policies can call forth politics, the creation of redistributive welfare policies at the European level might provoke seismic political conflict, rather than smoothing over problems of legitimacy at the Union level. This sort of argument has considerable neg ative force; that is, it points to political limits to redistributive politics at the European level. Advocates of a European welfare state would do well to remember the seismic events associated with the development of national welfare states across Europe. No such passionate movements appear to be springing up to create its equivalent for the EC/EU.

However, the negative claim that there is no mandate for a European level welfare state (and perhaps also for European level majoritarian parliamentary democracy) of itself hardly justifies the pattern of deep integration, limited to the economic. We have seen that the distinct rationale for regulatory/economic integration itself is somewhat circular. A further difficulty exists. The issue becomes more problematic, if EC regulation/liberalisation undercuts national social policy. And there is considerable evidence of a subversive liberalism in EC policy (indeed Majone himself points to a process of national deregulation followed by European re-regulation see *inter alia* 1994 for a discussion). We have already noted that notwithstanding some evidence of a tendential shift towards regulatory modes of governance at the national level in Europe, European publics appear to be powerfully attached to their national welfare states. To the extent that this attachment still exists then politics has hardly been successfully separated from economics. If, in other words, 'European' economics undercuts national politics, then the legitimacy of European regulation can no longer be grounded on the separation of economics and politics. Again, we are thrown back on a pragmatic and contingent historical account of the emergence of the European regulatory polity, throwing its legitimacy back into question.

Even at the EU level, emerging forms of policy again bear witness to the difficulty of separating politics from economics. Some advocates of monetary union argued that the 'economics' of monetary policy could be separated from the 'politics' of tax and (re)distribution. Yet, once in place, the monetary union has not been allowed to operate in isolation from fiscal policy — the relationship between (independent European) monetary policy and (nationally controlled) fiscal policies continues, to be debated. Although some have sought to deploy monetary policy as a means of creating pressure for a formal shift of (at least some aspects of) tax policy to the supranational level, the immediate reaction to monetary union has been to develop elaborate processes for fiscal policy co-ordination across Europe, which includes important disciplinary elements. When these are used (as they have been recently with respect to Ireland) they seem to be much resented. Similar policies have emerged in other policy areas on which monetary union has an impact, albeit an indirect one. For example, building on the Amsterdam Treaty (especially Arts 125–129), the Luxembourg 'Jobs Summit' of 1997 and various other initiatives have attempted to co-ordinate (and introduce cross national 'benchmarking') into a range of national social and labour market policies, including strategies to combat social exclusion, policies on child poverty and attempts to activate labour market policies.

At the Lisbon summit in 2000, several new projects for policy co-ordination of this sort, avoiding recourse to the full community method of policy-making, were proposed under the rubric of an 'Open Method of Coordination'. The precise meaning and scope of the OMC remains unclear. In particular, the role of Community institutions, especially the Commission, in such policies has yet to be hammered out. Moreover, there is some confusion about whether the OMC encompasses policies to co-ordinate fiscal/economic policies and the Luxembourg (labour market policy) Process. One question here concerns the role of the Commission. It has a substantial role to play in economic policy co-ordination and the Luxembourg Process (albeit much more limited a one than in the traditional 'Community' method). But if the OMC is a new form of co-ordination distinct from these processes, the member states may be seeking largely to exclude the Commission from it. The key point about all of these policies is that national governments are caught on the horns of a dilemma, having to react to pressure for further, more 'political', integration as a consequence of the economic integration they have already accepted. Recently, the reaction has been to devise forms of policy-making that make national governments more and more central to European policy-making processes.

## 5.   IN *LIEU* OF A CONCLUSION

The structural claims of the regulatory polity approach are generally well founded, although I believe that its normative claims concerning the legitimacy of the European Regulatory State are much less convincing. The general attempt to separate economics from politics, efficiency from (re)distribution or wealth creating from wealth claiming is problematic, in my view. In the particular European context, the attempt to identify the 'Community' parts of the EU as a sphere of economic efficiency, isolated from politics, is most powerfully challenged by the subversively liberal impact of European integration on national welfare states. Although there is little doubt that the market is increasingly legitimate across Europe,

Europeans have hardly renounced their welfarist traditions. But the prospects for a 'European' welfare state are poor. There is little evidence that promethean political forces are emerging at the European level that are broadly equivalent to those that called national systems of social protection into being. In other words, the strong tension between European level market/regulatory integration and the welfarist norms held to be legitimate in most European states, which are broadly institutionalised in various national systems of social protection. For those concerned to expand the scope of the market and constrain the political sphere, living through the problems thrown up by this tension might be accepted as a feature of a transitional period. But what should the left do?

The left will have to accept (and may be in the process of accepting) that several of its traditional objectives need to be abandoned or reconceived. Such acceptance notwithstanding, there is some evidence that other possible strategies are emerging. These fall into two or three broad categories. First, as regulatory theorists have emphasised, although the emergence of patterns of public policy increasingly dominated by regulation is part of a broad 'neoliberal turn', nonetheless, a variety of possible configurations of regulatory policy are possible. Indeed, regulation may be an effective means of pursuing some political objectives dear to the left. The left, in other words, could contest the form or character of European regulatory policies. One possible option would be to develop strategies to influence regulation — probably through lobbying and litigation — so as to maximise the scope for the protection or enhancement of, say, the environment or the interests of women. Such an approach could emulate similar moves made in the US. More precisely, the question here is whether and how existing tendencies of this sort should be enhanced, co-ordinated and perhaps politicised. Some ten years ago, Carole Harlow (1992) recommended a strategy of this sort, saying that 'we' should 'make the most of European law' rather than bemoaning the Union's democratic deficit. In this context it is important to emphasise the *political* element of rights construction — particularly the impact that politics can have on the scope of rights. Majone correctly stresses the necessity of regulation for market making and the maintenance of markets, but he also notes the scope for *social* regulations, which help to structure the interaction of individuals within market — and civic — fora. One dimension of a left — or left liberal — project in Europe might concentrate on, as Harlow suggested, is an expansion of the scope of social regulation. This strategy appears to 'go with the grain' of the current politics of the Union as manifest in the Convention.

However, if and as regulatory strategies of this sort are pursued, it remains important to recognise that they reflect and probably enhance a structural shift in European politics (of which there are signs at the national as well as supranational levels). Democracy and rights are not functional equivalents. To be sure both address the question of how power is assembled, accessed, exercised and negotiated, yet they do so in different ways and with distinct consequences. Strongly majoritarian 'democratic' welfare states may be based on, and reinforce, a collectivist political imaginary in which social rights squash individual and minority rights. Equally, however, a one-sided emphasis on regulation over redistribution can generate a politics of social victimisation. Pierre Rosenvallon (1995) argues that the US has become a society of generalised compensation in which the central figure of social interaction is the victim rather than the citizen. For Rosenvallon, US politics is marked by a failure to recognise social rights and an associated *radicalisation* of civil rights, an attempt to realise distributive justice using principles and practices of commutative justice.

A second strategy would be to challenge some of the key features of the way that the regulatory polity has been/is being institutionalised in Europe, in particular to change the balance between EU led regulatory elements and national systems of distributive justice (which are themselves subject to change of a variety of reasons). Perhaps the most important site of such institutionalisation both currently and over the past decade has been monetary union. The broad structure of the institutions governing the monetary union is regulatory in the sense that they seek to take monetary policy out of the sphere of control of elected politicians (whether at the Union or collaborative-national level). However, the manner in which countries were chosen to qualify for membership of the union was re-politicised (hardly any states met the formal criteria for monetary union, but a political decision about 'good progress' having been made allowed several states to join). The fall in value of the Euro may reflect this weakening of the 'anti-inflation' membership criteria. Periodically pressure is exerted to enhance the degree of political control over monetary policy in the Euro-Zone. Whatever the merits of such a move, I remain sceptical about its prospects for success.

Finally, the left might be able to use the developing forms of policy co-ordination as a means of developing a common 'social' and 'economic' project for Europe. It remains too early to identify the full character and impact of these forms of national policy co-ordination, although some commentators are rather optimistic (see, for example de Búrca and Zeitlin 2003 — an important contribution to the Convention on the OMC). The Luxembourg Process has certainly been used in some states as a means of motivating welfare reforms of one kind or another (see Wincott 2003b). (Politics here is saturated by 'business' language of benchmarking and learning from best practice.) Whether such reforms modernise or replace historic national 'social models' is an open question. It does, however, remain possible that these forms of co-ordination are being or could be used to defend some key aspects of national 'welfare states' from the subversive liberalism of the European Union—perhaps even extend them. This may be a possibility, but it is by no means a certainty. First, intergovernmental co-ordination approach does not directly address dynamic issues of democratic or popular accountability. Instead, arguably it increases the potential slack that national leaders can gain from their domestic electorates, thus further exacerbating these problems. Moreover, the success of policy co-ordination and benchmarking processes is almost wholly contingent on sustained and convergent political will. Although OMC type processes have had some time to institutionalise themselves, the current political climate may be less propitious than that of the years leading up to the Lisbon Summit. Many on the left were critical of the character and perceived purposes of the social democratic politicians holding government office during those years in most of Europe's capital cities. Yet Europe did show an unusual balance of political forces then. Rarely have politicians broadly associated with the left been in power in so many states, including the largest and most powerful ones. Yet even in this setting serious questions were asked about the commitment to a common and co-ordinated social project across Europe. Non-binding co-ordination may be the best available means of protecting and re-developing some aspects of the policy regimes left by a century of national democracy, but how far it can temper the shift to a Europe of rights and regulation remains to be seen.

## 6. REFERENCES

Burley, A.M. and Mattli W. 1993, 'Europe Before the Court: A Political Theory of Legal Integration', *International Organization,* 47.

De Búrca, G. and Zeitlin, J. 2003, 'Constitutionalising the Open Method of Coordination: A Note for the Convention', Mimeo.

Dauses, M. 1985, 'The Protection of Fundamental Rights in the Community Legal Order', *European Law Review,* 10.

Harlow, C. 1992, 'A Community of interests? Making the most of European Law', *Modern Law Review,* 55; 331–50.

Herdengen, M. 1994, 'Maastricht and the German Constitutional Court: Constitutional Restraints for an "Ever Closer Union"', *Common Market Law Review,* 31; 235–49.

Hooghe, L. and Marks G. 1998, The Making of a Polity: The Struggle over European Integration. In *Continuity and Change in Contemporary Capitalism,* edited by H. Kitschelt et al, Cambridge: Cambridge University Press.

Jobert, B. (ed) 1994, *Le Tournant Néo-Libéral en Europe: Idées et recettes dans les pratiques gouvernementales,* Paris: Éditions L'Harmattan.

Kilpatrick, C. 1998, 'Community or Communities of Courts in European Integration? Sex Equality Dialogues between the UK Courts and the ECJ', *European Law Journal,* 4; 122–5.

Mabbett, D. 2000, 'Social Regulation and the Social Dimension in Europe: The Example of Insurance', *European Journal of Social Security,* 2: 241–57.

MacCormick, N. 1995, 'The Maastricht-Urteil: Sovereignty Now', *European Law Journal,* 1; 255–61.

Majone, G. 1989, *Evidence, Argument and Persuasion in the Policy Process*, New Haven: Yale University Press.

—— 1994, Communauté Economique Européenne: Déréglementation ou re-réglementation? La conduite des politiques publiques depuis L'Acte Unique. In *Le Tournant Néo-Libéral en Europe: Idées et recettes dans les pratiques gouvernementales*, edited by B. Jobert, Paris: Éditions L'Harmattan.

—— 1996, *Regulating Europe,* London: Routledge.

—— 1998, 'Europe's "Democratic Deficit": The Question of Standards", *European Law Journal*, 4; 5–28.

Mengozzi, P. 1992, *European Community Law,* London: Graham & Trotman.

Rosenvallon, P, 1995 *La Nouvelle Question Sociale,* Paris Seuil.

Shaw, J. and More G. (eds) 1995, *New Legal Dynamics of European Union,* Oxford: Clarendon Press.

Stone-Sweet, A. 2000, *Governing with Judges*, Oxford: Oxford University Press.

Weiler, J.H.H. 1986, 'Eurocracy and Distrust: some questions concerning the role of the European Court of Justice in the Protection of Fundamental Human Rights within the Legal Order of the European Communities', *Washington Law Review*, 61; 11.

—— 1995, 'Demos, Telos, Ethos and the Maastricht Decision', *European Law Journal*, 1; 265.

Wincott, D. 1994, 'Human rights, Democracy and the Role of the Court of Justice in European Integration', *Democratization*, 1; 252–71.

—— 1995, 'The role of law or the rule of the Court of Justice? An "institutional" account of judicial politics in European Community', *Journal of European Public Policy*, 2; 583–602.

—— 2000, 'A Community of Law? "European" Law and Judicial Politics: The Court of Justice and Beyond', *Government and Opposition*, 35; 3–26.

—— 2001, The Court of Justice and the European Policy Process. In *European Union: Power and Policymaking*, 2nd edn edited by J.J. Richardson, London: Routledge.

—— 2003a, Backing into the Future? Informality and the proliferation of governance modes (and policy participants) in the EU, in T. Chistiansen and S. Piattoni (eds) *Informal Governance in the European Union*, Cheltenham: Edwar Elgar forthcoming.

—— 2003b, 'Beyond Social Regulation? Social Policy at Lisbon: New Instruments or a New Agenda?', *Public Administration*, 81/3 forthcoming.

## ECJ Cases

Case 26/62 *Van Gend en Loos* [1963] ECR 1

Case 6/64 *Costa v. ENEL* [1964] ECR 585

Case 41/74 *Van Duyn* [1974] ECR 1337

Case 148/78 *Ratti* [1979] ECR 1629

Case 44/79 *Hauer* [1979] ECR 3727

Case 159/90 *Grogan* [1991] 3 CMLR 893

# 5

## Constitutional Moments

### JULIET WILLIAMS

FOLLOWING TWO YEARS of deliberation by members of the Laeken Convention, in May 2003 the much-anticipated draft of a constitution for the European Union finally was unveiled. When the European Council first convened the Laeken convention, its members were responding to accusations that the European Union suffered from a so-called 'democratic deficit'. In recent years, the EU increasingly has been perceived as a bureaucratic behemoth controlled by elites, far removed from the will of the people it claims to represent. The popular mandate handed to members of Europe's constitutional convention was to clarify the scope and reach of the EU's power over individual states and citizens, and to provide a basis for 'a clear, open, effective, democratically controlled Community approach' to decision-making (Bogdanor 2003). Almost immediately, analogies were drawn between the EU's 'constitutional moment' and the US's 'Philadelphian Moment' some two hundred years earlier, playing on the strong association between the US Constitution and the principle of popular sovereignty. Just as is the case in Europe today, fears of a democratic deficit were widespread at the time of the US founding, as significant sectors of the public viewed the proposed constitution as a thinly-veiled plan for a centralised, bureaucratic state. Similarly as well, great hopes were pitched on the promise of constitutional guarantees of popular sovereignty and individual rights. While it is easy to draw parallels between the European and American constitutional moments, does the comparison point to anything more than superficial similarities — and if so, are there lessons for Europeans to learn from the US founding?

In this chapter, I return to the period of the US founding to more closely consider the relationship between ideas of constitutionalism and democracy prevalent at the time. Taking the ratification debate as a point of departure, I focus on the controversy surrounding demands for the addition of a bill of rights. I suggest that this struggle reflected a conflict between two competing visions of constitutionalism circulating at the time. On one side were those who advocated for what we might think of as a model of dynamic constitutionalism, in which rights emerge in the political process as various factions, as well as different branches of government, compete to create constitutional meaning. On the other side of the debate were advocates of the 'pre-settlement' account of constitutionalism — the view that a constitution creates fixed and settled guarantees, anchors of stability set against the shifting and uncertain tides of political will. The peculiarity of the American case, I suggest, is that while the document which was eventually ratified functions dynamically, the rhetoric of pre-settlement took hold as the dominant discourse of American constitutionalism. Ironically, however, the idea of constitutional pre-settlement may do more to disable than to protect democracy by creating the comforting illusion that democracy can be protected by constitutional guarantees. The story I tell in the following pages is offered, then, as a cautionary tale for Europeans seeking to salve a democratic deficit with a constitutional cure. In Europe today, as in the United States in 1787, it is not just a constitution that is being forged, but a narrative of constitutionalism as well. Careful consideration of US founding reveals the way that ideas about constitutionalism can preempt the kind of ongoing political engagement necessary to sustain democratic governance.

## 1.   REVOLUTIONARY BEGINNINGS

Since the very beginning, a concern with tyranny and a commitment to popular sovereignty have been prominent themes in US politics. In *The Declaration of Independence*, Thomas Jefferson memorably chronicled the excesses of British rule, enumerating for posterity the 'history of repeated injuries and usurpations' which sustained 'an absolute tyranny over the States'. Beyond the egregious outrage of taxation without representation, Jefferson catalogued a host of other indignities suffered by the colonists: compulsory quartering of 'swarms of Officers' sent by the King to 'harass our People, and eat out their Substance'; the dissolution of representative legislatures; interference with the establishment of independent courts; and the revocation of colonial charters. Denying British claims of sovereignty, Jefferson declared that legitimate authority can be derived only from 'the consent of the governed'.

The American Revolution was widely viewed as a victory for the principle of self-rule. In the glow of success, the revolutionaries-turned-Founders were supremely confident in the prospects for a regime rooted in the will of the people. Naively, they assumed that British-style tyranny was the only real threat worth worrying about. The nation's first constitution, *The Articles of Confederation*, reflected the single-mindedness of their concerns. The basic idea was to prevent the emergence of a king-like figure, and so under the *Articles*, no provision was made for an executive branch, let alone an executive officer. Nor was a central court established — there would be no robed despots in this new land. Instead, the *Articles* delegated all federal power to a unicameral Continental Congress, granting this body only modest and clearly circumscribed powers. While sharply limiting the reach of the new central government, however, the *Articles* created enormous latitude for the state legislatures. Isaac Kramnick describes the result as a prescription for nothing less than 'the absolute dominance of the legislature' within each of the states (Kramnick 1987, 21). Consistent with the optimistic mood of the day, the risk of legislative overreaching was deemed remote. Electoral accountability was virtually the only safeguard taken against legislative excess. No serious attempt was made to balance powers; state constitutions provided for virtually powerless governors to head the executive branch. Likewise, the judicial branch was made to depend on the legislature for decisions regarding appointments, terms of service, and salaries, and legislatures claimed for themselves discretion over traditionally judicial questions (Kramnick 1987, 22–23). Though the state constitutions included bills of rights imposing strict constraints on the executive power, it was widely understood that these rights were not meant to limit the power of the legislatures. As Jack Rakove explains, the purpose of these early bills of rights was merely 'to guide [the legislature] in exercising its discretionary authority rather than to restrain legislative power by creating an armory of judicially enforceable rights' (Rakove 1996, 307).

While deeply committed to legislative supremacy, many observers recognised a potential danger in over-compensating for the representational deficits of the British system. Precautions like frequent elections for representatives and rotation of office bespeak underlying concerns about concentrating power in the hands of any one individual for too long (Rakove 1996, 303). And as it happened, quite quickly the possibility of democratic pathology became a reality. The *Articles'* novel plan for a loose confederation of states proved itself a design for chaos. In the years following its adoption, isolated charges of legislative excess billowed into urgent demands for reform. The powerful state legislatures alienated constituents from all sides: the well-off grew incensed as more and more redistributive legislation was passed to allay the debts of the war, while the less privileged began to suspect that representative rule would never be more than a highly imperfect substitute for direct democracy. Once again, it was time for a change.

As disappointment with the *Articles* spread, state legislatures ceased to enjoy uncritical approval. But even as complaints about state governments multiplied, would-be reformers struggled to gather momentum for change. With memories of the indignities suffered under British rule still vivid and the revolutionary spirit still strong, any proposal to shift power away from the people was sure to encounter almost mechanical resistance, regardless of how disappointing the actual experience of self-governance had proven itself to be. Indeed, in confronting the failure of a regime based on the principle of legislative supremacy, the constitutional architects found themselves facing head-on a constitutive ambivalence at the very centre of the young republic's self-understanding. The ambivalence concerns popular sovereignty, which the revolutionaries regarded as both their greatest accomplishment and their most serious liability. For then as now, the ideal of rule by the people was exalted even as the reality of popular sovereignty was despised. In such a climate, the case for reform had to be broached with delicacy and discretion. In the end, the Framers would settle on a strategy which would demand an extraordinary feat of rhetorical finesse, a strategy which would tax the skills even of this consummately gifted cohort of politician-philosophers: they would have to convince the public that their campaign to limit 'the people's legislatures' was being waged in the name of popular sovereignty itself.

When the ratification debates began in earnest in the fall of 1787, advocates for the proposed constitution took their case to the public. Central in the effort was the publication of the *Federalist Papers*, a series of short essays appearing in New York newspapers under the pseudonym 'Publius', authored by Alexander Hamilton, John Jay, and James Madison. The task of defending the seemingly contradictory plan for a stronger yet more limited government fell largely to James Madison. While affirming the principle of popular sovereignty, Madison challenged the standing assumption of an equivalence between popular sovereignty and rule by popular legislatures. Based on recent experience, Madison proclaimed it to be undeniably the case that 'the instability, injustice, and confusion introduced into the public councils have, in truth, been the mortal diseases under which popular governments have everywhere perished' (Kramnick 1987, 122). While acknowledging that the people 'seem never for a moment to have turned their eyes from the danger, to liberty, from the overgrown and all-grasping prerogative of an hereditary magistrate, supported and fortified by an hereditary branch of the legislative authority', he noted with dismay that '[t]hey seem never to have recollected the danger from legislative usurpations, which, by assembling all power in the same hands, must lead to the same tyranny as is threatened by executive usurpations' (Kramnick 1987, 309). Regrettably, it had turned out that individual rights were as insecure in a regime ruled by popular legislatures as they had been under monarchical rule. The question now was how to bring the legislatures back into line. Towards an answer, Madison began with a study of the problem of private citizens organised into 'factions', understood as 'a number of citizens, whether amounting to a majority or minority of the whole, who are united and actuated by some common impulse of passion, or of interest, adverse to the rights of other citizens, or to the permanent and aggregate interests of the community' (Kramnick 1987, 123). In a regime resting on the will of the majority, minority factions are easy to control — provided that the majority of the citizens can be relied upon to fulfill their civic obligation to participate. As Madison explained in *Federalist 10*, 'if a faction consists of less than a majority, relief is supplied by the republican principle, which enables the majority to defeat its sinister views by regular vote' (Kramnick 1987, 125). But what about the problem of majority factions? Making a virtue of a potential vice, Madison argued that the more vigorous and engaged the citizenry is, the less chance there is that any one faction will come to dominate the others. Advocating for representative rule over direct democracy, Madison sought to insure that government would represent a population large and diverse enough to produce competing factions, for as the number of citizens increases, so does the number of factions, and hence the likelihood of mutual checks. Crucially, Madison's scheme depends on a variety of interests being represented in everyday legislative politics. In *Federalist 39*, he declared it '*essential*' (emphasis in the original) for a republican government to 'be derived from the great body of the society, not from an inconsiderable proportion or a favored class of it' (Kramnick 1987, 255). Though political participation is an essential feature of Madison's plan for limiting government, his theory does not rest on a romantic vision of republican citizenship. Participation is encouraged neither because it is supposed to be intrinsically edifying nor because citizens are considered likely to act out of civic commitment, but rather because the more energy the people direct towards politics, the lower the likelihood that any particular measure will get through the legislature. The aim of such a system is not to produce the best laws, but rather to prevent passage of bad laws, revealing that inefficiency was a price the Federalists were more than willing to pay for stability.

In considering matters further, Madison recognised that factionalism is an inevitable tendency not only among citizens, but within official circles as well. Extending the logic of *Federalist 10* to government itself, Madison defends a scheme of institutional checks and balances. As he explains in *Federalist 51*, the legislature can be contained only 'by so contriving the interior structure of the government as that its several constituent parts may, by their mutual relations, be the means of keeping each other in their proper places' (Kramnick 1987, 318–19). Rather than attempting to enumerate each branches' powers, Madison defended an elaborate institutional structure in which interests would be checked and balanced, within the citizenry and amongst the various branches of government.

It is essential to understand that Madison's constitutional plan rests on a dynamic theory of limited government. Under his scheme, limits on government are produced in the course of political contest, rather than prescribed at the outset. In seeking to explain Madison's preference for dynamic as opposed to pre-settled limits, it is commonplace to observe that Madison feared that a written constitution would erect nothing more than 'parchment barriers' against abuses of power. But his reasons for adopting a dynamic view of constitutionalism are decidedly more complex. To fully appreciate Madison's commitment, it is vital to understand the *strategic* appeal of this approach in the context of the political scene at the time.

For Madison and his Federalist brethren, a constitution based on dynamic limits accomplished three aims. First, dynamic limits held out the promise that legislative power could be constrained in a way that did not appear to challenge the primacy of the principle of popular sovereignty. In a regime based on dynamic limits, majoritarian politics and limited government are seen as mutually reinforcing, and vigorous citizen participation is encouraged rather than feared, for as Madison explains in *Federalist 51*, the best way to prevent tyranny of the majority is 'by comprehending in the society so many separate descriptions of citizens as will render an unjust combination of a majority of the whole very improbable, if not impracticable' (Kramnick 1987, 319). Rather than foregrounding his own grave mistrust of local legislative politics, then, provision for dynamic limits enabled Madison to portray himself as an advocate of the assertion of popular will at every level. Given the strong popular attachment to the right to self-rule at the time, this feature of dynamic limits should not be underestimated.

Secondly, dynamic limits provide the perfect justification for strengthening the federal government. By 1776, the notion of separated powers was firmly entrenched as a necessary structural precaution against tyranny. Having read their Montesquieu, many early Americans believed that separated powers could limit government by insuring that power would never be concentrated in one set of hands. They also knew that the separation between branches must not be total; otherwise, limits would be impossible to enforce. The question, then, was just how much mingling to allow. The experience under the *Articles* suggested that when the branches were divided but unequal the strongest would prevail and a system of separated powers would quickly give way to a monopoly of power. For this reason, the Federalists insisted that each branch must be strong enough to function as a meaningful check against the others (Kramnick 1987, 302–308). The political significance of this institutional insight is profound. Balanced powers provided the perfect justification (excuse?) for enhancing the power of the executive branch in particular in a nation of citizens skittish about centralisation. To advocate bluntly for a powerful executive would surely have triggered analogies with monarchy, but to argue for a strong executive in the name of limiting the legislature was a different matter all together.

Finally, dynamic limits facilitated compromise by leaving vital issues regarding the distribution of power between the states and the federal government unresolved, allowing the Federalists to indefinitely defer debate on just the kind of divisive questions that would likely derail the ratification campaign. In this way, equivocation, if not outright evasiveness, came to define the Federalists' strategy for ratification. Faced with controversial questions, they preferred to take their chances, leaving key matters unsettled so as to avoid the kind of confrontation which could result in a decisive defeat. Vesting their hope in dynamic limits, the Federalists wagered that as long as a rough balance of powers was maintained, they could achieve their desired objectives without showcasing their own profound doubts about the desirability of popular sovereignty.

## 2. A TALE OF TWO TRADITIONS

Though the original Constitution rested on a scheme for dynamic limits, the discourse of dynamic constitutionalism did not prevail; instead, constitutionalism is most often conceived in terms of pre-settlement. That is, constitutionalism in the US mode is understood to be a regime which rests on fixed and settled rights, legally entrenched in a written constitution. To understand how the rhetoric of pre-settlement came to dominate, one must turn to a consideration of the controversy surrounding the addition of a bill of rights.

When the proposed constitution entered the forum of public opinion in the fall of 1787, it was met by immediate and vigorous attacks. Led by the Anti-Federalists, opponents charged that the Federalist plan for dynamic limits was a thinly-veiled elitist ploy to divest the people of their rights. In an angry letter published in a New York newspaper on 1 November 1787, the pseudonymous 'Brutus' made an impassioned plea for the addition of a bill of rights. Reminding the Americans that even in Britain 'the magna charta and bill of rights have long been the boast, as well as the security of the nation', Brutus chastised the Federalists for their 'astonishing' oversight (Kammen 1986, 315). Brutus suggested that for the Federalists, the real appeal of dynamic limits lay in the promise of tilting power in favour of the national government, which he was convinced would lead to eventual evisceration of the autonomy of the state governments.

Although the Anti-Federalists tried to pitch the public debate as a choice between the uncertainty of dynamic limits versus the security of pre-settled ones, the differences dividing the two camps were not nearly so stark. Looking beyond the public rhetoric, it is clear that the Anti-Federalists were no more sanguine about the efficacy of pre-settlement than were their Federalist counterparts. Indeed, the Anti-Federalists were as committed to dynamic constitutionalism as were the Federalists. In this regard, consider Akhil Amar's contention that the underlying purpose of the Bill of Rights was not to fix and settle limits once and for all, but rather to ensure that the people would retain the power to participate in the political decisions central to their lives. He explains:

> The Bill of Rights protected the ability of local governments to monitor and deter federal abuse, ensured that ordinary citizens would participate in

the federal administration of justice through various jury provisions, and preserved the transcendent sovereign right of a majority of the people themselves to alter or abolish government and thereby pronounce the last word on constitutional questions. The essence of the Bill of Rights was more structural than not, and more majoritarian than counter.

(Amar 1998, xiii)

Amar goes on to stress the significance of the oft-neglected Ninth and Tenth Amendments, which speak volumes about the underlying Anti-Federalist agenda. Both of these amendments are intended to shift power back to the states in anticipation of just the kind of ongoing power struggles characteristic of a system built on a dynamic edifice. The purpose of the Bill of Rights is twofold, then: to enshrine certain specific rights, but more importantly, to shift power back to popular majorities so they can more effectively counter elite rule at the national level. While the Anti-Federalists favoured more explicit limits on the federal government than did the Federalists, they, too, realised that in the last instance, popular majorities, not pre-settled rights, are the best and only defense against the encroaching power of government.

As the ratification debates wore on, the Federalists found the relentless demands for a bill of rights impossible to ignore. In addressing their critics, however, the Federalists had to choose their arguments carefully, for the Anti-Federalists would be quick to exploit any opportunity to charge that the smooth rhetoric of the Federalists masked an elitist agenda (Wood 1969, 537). Stressing their unwavering commitment to rights, the Federalists explained that there is a significant distinction to be drawn between opposition to the proposed bill of rights and a disregard for rights altogether. The Federalists contended that the campaign for a national bill of rights rested on a fundamental misunderstanding of the proposed constitution, one drawn from a false analogy made between the more familiar state constitutions and the novel federal constitution. Since state governments adopted the principle of legislative supremacy, it was necessary to reserve specific rights for the people. This practice followed the pattern of earlier bills of rights like the Magna Charta which were understood as dispensations made to the people by an all-powerful ruler (Wood 1969, 537). But the proposed Constitution was a different kind of document altogether, the Federalists explained. In the case of the national government, the guiding assumption would be that all powers not specifically granted to the federal government were reserved to the people. In other words, it should go without saying (figuratively and literally) that the people retained all the rights the amendments sought to protect, and many more.

This argument did little to mollify the critics. Gordon Wood attributes the Anti-Federalist intransigence to a failure of the imagination: 'Unable to grasp the sweeping significance the Federalists were attributing to the sovereignty of the people, the Anti-Federalists stood amazed at the Federalists' effrontery' (Wood 1969, 540–41). Wood's implication is that the Anti-Federalists simply could not accept the admittedly audacious claim that popular sovereignty could function as the ultimate check on government. But perhaps the problem lay in the fact that the Anti-Federalists grasped all too well what the Federalists were doing. It is hardly surprising that the Federalists' claim that in a regime built on popular sovereignty reserved rights are redundant rang hollow in a nation borne of the experience of promises broken and authority abused. In the end, the Federalist position was defeated by the force of plain old common sense. As Jefferson would write in a letter to Madison in 1789 with reference to the question of whether to include a bill of rights: 'Half a loaf is better than no bread'.[1] While a bill of rights might in some cases fall short, surely its adoption would be worthwhile if it proved helpful, at least some of the time.

To meet this argument, the Federalists were forced to shift their message from the warning that a bill of rights would not be a cure-all to the claim that a bill of rights might actually do more harm than good. Sounding a note of alarm, Hamilton argued in *Federalist 78* that adding a bill of rights would be 'dangerous' if it were to create the presumption that unenumerated rights warrant less respect than those specifically articulated. With no small measure of drama, Hamilton beseeched, 'why declare that things shall not be done which there is no power to do'?[2]

While Hamilton's concerns are reasonable enough, his worries hardly explain the adamancy of his opposition to including a bill of rights. If his primary concern truly was the problem of the ambiguous status of rights, why would he not have pushed for the inclusion of a statement clarifying the matter, as the 9th Amendment was meant, in fact, to do? There has to be something more behind Hamilton's resistance, but what? Was it simply that he harboured a suspicion that the genuine purpose of the proposed amendments was to shift power back to the states? The puzzle has only deepened with time, since history has proven the Bill of Rights much more innocuous than the Federalists warned, eventually evolving into a powerful weapon in the battle to *contain* state power. Far from promoting state sovereignty as the Anti-Federalists had hoped, the Bill of Rights languished in the hands of the courts for the first 100 or so years of its career. Only after

---

[1] Jefferson to James Madison, 15 March 1789. Quote is from Rakove (1998, 166).
[2] In an interesting variant on the 'dangerousness' argument, Madison remarked in a letter to Jefferson in 1788 that he feared that in defining rights specifically, their scope would quite possibly be diminished. 'I am sure that the rights of Conscience in particular, if submitted to public definition would be narrowed much more than they are likely ever to be by an assumed power. One of the objections in New England was that the constitution by prohibiting religious tests opened a door for Jews Turks and infidels' (Rakove 1998, 161). Once again, we see the strategic resort to vagueness as a way to prevent a political loss in the present.

the 14th Amendment was passed, opening the door to applying the Bill of Rights to the states, did the courts begin to champion its cause aggressively, and then as a means of limiting state power. And yet, Hamilton surely did believe that a bill of rights would do more harm than good.

I would suggest that his trepidation reflects his (mis)understanding of the underlying logic of dynamic checks. Hamilton likely reasoned that a bill of rights would turn out to function more as a constraint on the judiciary than on the legislature. By leaving rights vague, the courts were being handed enormous discretion. Perversely, a bill of rights might limit the court's power by constraining its interpretive freedom — a fatal liability in the uncertain environment of a dynamic regime. From the standpoint of enhancing the power of the courts, it might have appeared unwise, then, to hamstring judges to a text which would inevitably prove inadequate as a literal source of limits on state power. This logic proved, of course, to be dead wrong, for Hamilton could not anticipate that the mere presence of written rules, would redound to the enormous benefit of the courts. In spite of its deficiencies as a descriptive theory, pre-settlement would prove itself invaluable as a rhetorical tool in the public campaign fought to win support for enhancing national power.

### 3.    ABOUT FACE

In the end, the Federalists backed down. In exchange for ratifying the Constitution, the Federalists promised that they would see to the passage of a bill of rights as the first order of business once the new Congress convened. Crucial to the Anti-Federalist victory was James Madison, once a staunch opponent but ultimately a 'reluctant champion' of the Bill of Rights (Mathews 1995, 30). Madison's change of heart rests not so much on a principled conversion as a pragmatic calculation. Once the drift of public opinion became clear, Madison would insist that 'my own opinion has always been in favor of a bill of rights'. But even as an advocate for the amendments, he would confess: 'I have never thought the omission a material defect, nor been anxious to supply it even by *subsequent* amendment, for any other reason than that it is anxiously desired by others'.[3] And anxious others were. So much so that Madison feared the matter would doom ratification, or almost as bad, force a second convention which would likely lead to an undoing of the fragile consensus he had laboured so tirelessly to build.

Once passage of the Bill of Rights seemed inevitable, the Federalists shifted their attention to damage control. The immediate goal was to

---

[3] Madison to Thomas Jefferson, 17 October 1788. Quote is from Rakove (1998, 161).

prevent the amendments from disrupting the equilibrium the original constitution established between the states and the federal government. Recall that the logic of dynamic limits dictates that power must be countered with power. Since the Bill of Rights was meant to shift power back to the states, the Federalists' imperative now was to bolster the strength of the federal government. It is in this context that the issue of role of the judiciary would move to the fore. As I have discussed, the proliferation of state bills of rights in the Revolutionary era challenged the prevailing doctrine of legislative supremacy, planting the seeds for a shift of authority to the courts as final interpreters of the law. But the question of what part the federal judiciary would play in checking state legislatures remained unresolved throughout the ratification debates. The judiciary loomed as a shadowy presence, the contours of its future role in the regime blurry. Robert McCloskey notes that 'enthusiasts for judicial review have never quite been able to explain why so formidable a power was granted by implication rather than by flat statement,' despite the 'ample evidence' attesting to the Framers' support for judicial review found in letters, notes, and other ancillary sources (McCloskey 1994, 24). If only the Framers had bothered to clearly articulate their position in the constitutional text, we might have been spared centuries of scholarly labour over the question of original intent on the matter of judicial power. But the omission hardly seems accidental. The Federalists had good reason to be cagey about their intentions if they hoped to forestall charges of judicial tyranny. Indeed, to deflect opposition the Federalists would go to great lengths to downplay the power of the judiciary. And so it is that in *Federalist 78* Hamilton stressed that 'the judiciary, from the nature of its function, will always be the least dangerous to the political rights of the Constitution; because it will be least in the capacity to annoy or injure them' (Kramnick 1987, 437). Knowing what we do of the Federalists' general disposition towards national power, this gloss must be understood at least in part as strategic. To present the courts as vigorous advocates for individual rights against the states would have been political suicide. Nonetheless, the Federalists clearly hoped that the 'least dangerous branch' would be powerful enough to function as a meaningful check against 'the impetuous vortex' of state legislative power.

As it turns out, the passage of the Bill of Rights was an unintended boon for Federalists seeking to enhance federal power over the states. Recall that during the ratification debates, the Federalists dismissed pre-settled rights as ineffectual and unnecessary. But in defending dynamic limits, the Federalists opened themselves up to the charge that they were tacitly sanctioning judicial tyranny. In the absence of clearly written constitutional limits, the courts' discretion seemed to be limited only by the notoriously fungible constraints of the common-law. In light of popular concerns about judicial discretion, the Federalists were wise to downplay the importance of the judiciary in a constitutional order, emphasising instead the crucial role played by the people in guiding the decisions of electorally accountable representatives.

The adoption of the Bill of Rights made it possible for the Federalists to defend a strong but limited legislature. Despite all they had done to discredit the idea of constitutional pre-settlement during the ratification debates, the Federalists now were in a position to benefit from the pervasive public faith — cultivated by their Anti-Federalist antagonists — in the promise of written guarantees. For with the addition of the Bill of Rights, the Federalists could argue for the augmentation of the power of the court as the defender of written guarantees, enhancing its power even if its ultimate ability to deliver on guaranteed rights remained limited.

There is perhaps no one who understood better the importance of the ideology of pre-settlement in legitimising the judiciary than the great Federalist Chief Justice John Marshall. In *Marbury v. Madison* (1803), Marshall proclaimed that 'the United States has been emphatically termed a government of laws, and not of men'. The Constitution sets limits on government 'and that those limits may not be mistaken, or forgotten, the constitution is written'. While in his opinion Marshall focuses on the question of *whether* the Constitution is 'the fundamental and paramount law of the nation,' the pressing issue in this case is *who* has final say over what the Constitution means — Congress or the Court? Marshall does not lose time declaring that 'it is emphatically the province and the duty of the judicial department to say what the law is'. But why? Marshall treats the implicit alternative — legislative supremacy — as too absurd to warrant serious engagement. In a few cursory paragraphs, he briskly rehearses the familiar case against legislative supremacy, contending that it would 'subvert the very foundation of all written constitutions' by granting 'to the legislature a practical and real omnipotence, with the same breath which professes to restrict their powers within narrow limits'. Marshall concludes that acceptance of a written constitution entails acceptance of judicial supremacy. But we know that at the time of ratification, his Federalist brethren did not see it this way at all. In fact, because the Framers doubted the likely efficacy of the courts, they argued that the best way to limit government was to create an institutional structure that would enforce limits against itself. But the Federalists also seemed to understand that the public willingness to abide by the authority of the courts might serve in practice as a kind of functional equivalent of the unattainable ideal of constitutional pre-settlement. For this reason, there was something to gain from proliferating the ideology of pre-settlement, however unfaithful such an act might be to the underlying reality.

Perhaps it is not surprising, then, that the Federalist embrace of the rhetoric of pre-settlement lasted only as long as it proved convenient. Just 15 years later, in the landmark case of *McCulloch v Maryland* (1819), their tune would once again change. In this case, the Supreme Court was asked to decide whether Congress had the right to establish a national bank under the broad powers granted by the 'necessary and proper' clause in Article I of the Constitution. On behalf of a unanimous Court, Marshall dismisses the claim that the absence of an explicit grant of power demonstrated an intent to deny that power. After all, he explains, 'it is a constitution we are expounding,' and by its very nature a constitution does not provide the level of detail one can expect from an ordinary statute (*McCulloch v Maryland*, 125). With this statement, Marshall reveals the fatal defect of his own reasoning in *Marbury*, in which he had argued that the true significance of the Constitution lies in the very fact that it is written. In cautioning against making too much of the distinction between written provisions of the Constitution and implied powers, Marshall discloses the fallacy of resting the authority of the courts in the fact of a written Constitution in the first place.

Ironically, then, in the end passage of the Bill of Rights helped the Federalist cause by buttressing the power of the federal judiciary. But however desirable the augmentation of judicial power may have been from the Federalist perspective, Madison knew it would be fatal to create the impression that his support for the amendments arose from a desire to bolster federal judicial power. After all, Madison's reason for championing a bill of rights in the first place was to prove his sympathy with the cause of *states'* rights. Rakove explains that in the debate over adding a bill of rights, Jefferson went out of his way to draw Madison's attention to a point he had seemingly neglected, 'that a bill of rights might strengthen the hands of the judiciary as an independent protector of rights'. Rakove reflects: 'To modern readers, it may seem surprising both that Madison overlooked this point and that Jefferson needed to call it to his attention' (Rakove 1998, 164). But knowing what we do of the political tensions of the time, it is not surprising at all, since no hearts were going to be won over championing the federal courts. As much as the state legislatures were distrusted, no one wanted to go on record advocating for a huge transfer of power to the federal judiciary. Legislative supremacy, having lost credibility, may have been for all intents and purposes a dead doctrine, but strong advocacy of judicial review would surely have appeared at the time to be the moral equivalent of dancing on the grave.

In the end, Madison invoked an altogether different and infinitely more politic explanation for his change of heart. As he explained in a letter to Jefferson written in 1788:

> What use then it may be asked can a bill of rights serve in popular Governments? I answer the two following which though less essential than in other Governments, sufficiently recommend the precaution. 1. The political truths declared in that solemn manner acquire by degrees the character of fundamental maxims of free Government, and as they become incorporated with the national sentiment, counteract the impulses of interest and passion.

2. Altho' it be generally true as above stated that the danger of oppression lies in the interested majorities of the people rather than in usurped acts of the Government, yet there may be occasions on which the evil may spring from the latter sources; and on such, a bill of rights will be a good ground for an appeal to the sense of community.[4]

Madison portrayed the Bill of Rights, then, not so much as a tool to guide the judiciary as an instrument of civic education. He hoped the amendments would foster a culture of respect for rights, which would in turn inspire citizens to sanction those officials who transgressed.

Why this emphasis on civic education? Madison's statement should not be read as an expression of a commitment to the principle of republicanism, for we know that in the end, Madison rested his hopes for limited government not on civic virtue, but rather on dynamic limits. Accepting this premise, the question becomes: what role does civic education play in a dynamic regime? The period of the Founding is generally remembered for the great faith the people placed in constitutional promises. It is easy to forget that the Framers were acutely aware of the inherent precariousness of constitutionalism. Indeed, recall that the ratification of the US Constitution itself was technically illegal, violating the procedures for amendment specified under the prevailing *Articles of Confederation*. This Founding breach served as a powerful reminder that the authority of a constitution would ultimately depend on the willingness of the people to recognise its authority. In this context, civic education served an especially important purpose in discouraging challenges to the constitutional order. Citizens would be encouraged to believe in the supremacy of constitutional principles, even though the very need to reinforce these values betrayed the fact that the Constitution really is not supreme in the first place. But in a dynamic regime, those vested in the *status quo* can only hope that the majority of the people do not realise how much power they are actually accorded in shaping the meaning of rights. If people understood that, could we ever feel secure in our freedom?

As an example of what Madison may have had in mind when he spoke of civic education, consider his reflections on the question of just how specific the provisions of the Bill of Rights should be. Madison explains in a letter to Jefferson, 'I am inclined to think that absolute restrictions in cases that are doubtful, or where emergencies may overrule them, ought to be avoided. The restrictions however strongly marked on paper will never be regarded when opposed to the decided sense of the public; and after repeated violations in extraordinary cases, they will lose even their ordinary efficacy'.[5] Based on his own understanding of the inherent fragility of constitutionalism, Madison thought it unwise to be too committal in the

---

[4] Madison to Thomas Jefferson, 17 October 1788. Quote is from Rakove (1998, 162).
[5] *Ibid*, 163.

Bill of Rights. If the lines were ambiguous in the first place, the public would have a hard time determining when they had been crossed. In other words, too much civic education might be as dangerous as too little, for a public too knowledgeable about the meaning of the Constitution would quickly realise just how fragile constitutional limits really are.

### 4. INTO THE FUTURE

Just a few years after ratification, following the passage of the Alien and Sedition Acts of 1798, Madison would become acutely aware of the political nature of the courts, and he did not hesitate to turn to the states to rally resistance to this offensive law. It was soon apparent that his faith in the national government as a tempering force on state government was rooted in a contingent assessment of the situation at the time, rather than a categorical trust in federal over state power, and so Madison's position would change as circumstances did. The Federalists supported a dynamic structure precisely because they recognised that power at any level could be abused. Because the Framers understood that judges ultimately are political actors, they did not mean to rest supreme power in them either. The Framers realised that any office of government can be abused and any branch of government can go astray. Rather than elevating one branch above all of the others, security was thought possible only in a system flexible enough to adapt to the unexpected. My point in noting that Madison sided with the states against the Alien and Sedition Acts is not to imply that he was fickle or inconsistent. In highlighting the Federalists' own oscillation on the question of which level of government poses the most serious threat to liberty (state vs. national) and where sovereignty ultimately lies (the judiciary vs. the people) I simply mean to suggest that in a system based on dynamic limits, one always must be suspicious of claims of pre-settlement, for such claims are often primarily strategic, meant to foreclose further debate.

Of course, with the passage of the 14th Amendment some 80 years after ratification of the Constitution, it became plausible to suggest that the Bill of Rights must now be extended to bind the states as it did the national government. In so doing, would not pre-settlement finally become a reality? Hardly. In 1868, we witness an almost perfect recapitulation of the debate over the Bill of Rights at the Founding. As before, the rhetorical stress is placed on protecting individual liberties and extending rights, and as before, the question of federalism lies at the core of the controversy. And once again, eventually the courts would be the big winners as power was reshuffled. Given the nature of a dynamic regime, it comes as no surprise that the federalism debate has continued to the present day. Passage of the 14th Amendment was, to be sure, a significant move in the game of negotiating the balance of power between the states and the national government, but it hardly put an end to the struggle.

Today, Madison's dire warnings about the futility of 'parchment barriers' have been all but forgotten. Preserved for posterity in a glass shrine, the constitutional parchment itself is considered nothing short of sacred. The Bill of Rights has emerged as the most cherished portion of the US Constitution, revered by the public precisely because it is widely believed to provide guarantees against governmental encroachments on individual rights.

## 5.   BEYOND AMERICAN CONSTITUTIONALISM?

Amongst scholars today, there is growing recognition that the pre-settlement account of constitutionalism is deeply flawed as a description of the constitutional experience in the United States. In recent years, there has been an outpouring of research by political scientists, historians, and legal scholars documenting the significant ways in which constitutional meaning — especially the meaning of rights — has changed over time.[6] This new scholarship offers a narrative of constitutional rights in the United States emphasising instability and innovation, not fixity and permanence. At first glance, the timing of this new wave of constitutional scholarship might seem puzzling, even paradoxical. While scholars proudly proclaim the ultimate dependence of the US political system on popular sovereignty, public confidence in democracy sinks to ever newer lows. Outside the idealised world of academic rumination, politics in the US is a dirty word. Congress, the branch closest to the people, is widely viewed as a bloated leviathan, bent on spending hard earned tax dollars to coddle special interests and promote pet projects. Elected officials are denounced as stewards of the rich, willing to work only for those with enough money to buy the privilege of representation. Under these circumstances, it is easy to see why the concept of constitutional pre-settlement remains so seductive today, why it continues to exert such a hold on the popular imagination. A dynamic constitution is one which rests responsibility for democracy in the hands of the people itself, rather than offering guarantees. Given the shaky footing of democracy in America today, Europeans should be wary of seeking an American-style cure for its own democratic deficit. Though the discourse of US constitutionalism offers the enticing promise of democratic guarantees,

---

[6] The origins of this movement are often traced back to Bruce Ackerman's *We the People* (Ackerman 1991). More recently, the notion of 'constitutional politics' has been given its most significant treatment by Stephen Griffin in *American Constitutionalism* (Griffin 1996). Other works that take a similar approach include Moore (1996), Tushnet (2000), and Whittington (2001).

the structure of the US Constitution places democracy on a significantly more precarious footing.

## 6. REFERENCES

Ackerman, Bruce. 1991, *We the People I: Foundations*, Cambridge, MA: Harvard University Press.

Amar, Akhil. 1998. *The Bill of Rights*, New Haven: Yale University Press.

Bellamy, Richard. 1996, 'The Political Form of the Constitution: The Separation of Powers, Rights, and Representative Democracy', *Political Studies*, XLIV: 437–57.

Bogdanor, Vernon. 28 May 2003, 'Comment & Analysis: Europe Needs a Rallying Cry: The Problem with the EU's Draft Constitution is Not That it is Too Radical, but Too Limited in its Vision', *The Guardian* (London).

Campos, Paul. 1998, *Jurismania: The Madness of American Law*, New York: Oxford University Press.

Gillman, Howard. 1998, 'From Fundamental Law to Constitutional Politics — and Back', *Law and Social Inquiry*, 185–202.

Griffin, Stephen. 1996, *American Constitutionalism: From Theory to Politics*, Princeton: Princeton University Press.

Holmes, Stephen. 1995, *Passions and Constraint*, Chicago: University of Chicago Press.

Horowitz, Martin. 1993, 'The Constitution of Change: Legal Fundamentality without Fundamentalism', *Harvard Law Review*, 107:30–117.

Kammen, Michael. 1986, *The Origins of the American Constitution: A Documentary History*, New York: Penguin USA.

Kramnick, Isaac (ed). 1987, *The Federalist Papers*, New York: Penguin Press.

—— 1987, Editor's Introduction, *The Federalist Papers*, New York: Penguin Press.

—— 1990, *Republicanism and Bourgeois Radicalism*, Ithaca: Cornell University Press.

Matthews, Richard K. 1995, *If Men Were Angels*, Lawrence: University of Kansas Press.

McCloskey, Robert C. 1994, *The American Supreme Court*, revised by Sanford Levinson, Chicago: University of Chicago Press.

*McCulloch v The State of Maryland et al.* 17 US 316. Lexis-Nexis.

Moore, Wayne. 1996, *Constitutional Rights and the Powers of the People*, Princeton: Princeton University Press.

Rakove, Jack. 1996, *Original Meanings: Politics and Ideas in the Making of the Constitution*, New York: Vintage Books.

—— 1998, *Declaring Rights: Brief History with Documents*, New York: Bedford Books.

Tarr, Alan. 1998, *Understanding State Constitutions*, Princeton: Princeton University Press.

Tushnet, Mark. 1999, *Taking the Constitution Away from the Courts*, Princeton: Princeton University Press.

Waldron, Jeremy. 1999, *Law and Disagreement*, New York: Oxford University Press.

—— 1999, *The Dignity of Legislation*, Cambridge, Cambridge University Press.

Whittington, Keith. 2000, 'In Defense of Legislatures'. *Political Theory*, 28: 690–702.

—— 2001, *Constitutional Construction: Divided Powers and Constitutional Meaning*, Cambridge, MA: Harvard University Press.

Wood, Gordon, 1969, *The Creation of the American Republic 1776–1787*, New York: Norton Press.

# 6

# *Law and Politics in a Madisonian Republic: Opportunities and Challenges for Judges and Citizens in the New Europe*[*]

## LISA HILBINK

> Law cannot endure as a world neutrally detached from the contests of political
> argument but must take its proper place as a facet of political society rather
> than as an autonomous and external force acting upon it. It is, and must be
> seen as, a necessary ingredient of the body of political ideas.
>
> (Harlow 2000, 366)

T HE FIRST DRAFT of the Constitution for Europe, presented with
much fanfare on 20 June 2003 in Thessaloniki, leaves many contested issues unresolved and many institutional powers ill-defined.
On at least one matter, however, it speaks quite clearly: the European Union
is and must remain a regime committed to the protection of fundamental
human rights. To that end, the draft Constitution directly authorises, for
the first time, the European Court of Justice (ECJ) to interpret and apply a
litany of codified rights. Although the text explicitly limits the jurisdiction
of the Court to Union-level law and institutions, implying that it cannot
issue decisions against alleged rights abuses by member state officials, it is
likely that in practice, 'it will extend access to those rights where it can'
(*The Economist*, 21 June 2003). Indeed, even without formal textual authorisation, the Court long ago entered the business of rights adjudication,
invoking rights standards from national and international sources to challenge the legitimacy of member state-level acts and policies (Kenney 1998;
Mancini 2000; Stone Sweet 2000; Conant 2002).

The Constitution's explicit empowerment of the ECJ reflects a relatively
new and growing enthusiasm for judicially-enforceable rights in Europe.

* For comments on earlier drafts of this chapter, I would like to thank Pablo De Grieff, Sally
Kenney, Diane Orentlicher, Keith Whittington, and the participants in the workshop 'After
National Democracy: Rights, Law, and Power in America and the New Europe', Oñati
International Institute for the Sociology of Law, Oñati, Spain, June 1–2, 2000. Special thanks
to Lars Trägårdh for his patience and support.

Whereas in the past, judicial review was viewed with suspicion, if not outright scorn, by many Europeans, who deemed it a betrayal of democratic principles, today the concept has gained broad acceptance across the continent (Favoreu 1990; Cappelletti 1989). In Western Europe, scholars now speak of a 'second democratic revolution', driven by a new consciousness on the part of citizens of their rights and a growing demand that governments enforce respect for these rights. This revolution 'from sovereignty to justiciability' entails a move away from a focus on political will and majority power toward an emphasis on law and the protection of minorities (Garapon 1999, 44; Toharia 2001, 29–30). In Eastern Europe, meanwhile, many citizens have understood democracy's promise to be that individual dignity would, at last, be respected and protected by the government. Kim Lane Scheppele (2001b, 32) notes that in Hungary in the 1990s, 'it was common ... for [citizens] to say that something was "undemocratic" when it violated basic rights'. Democracy 'was not associated with republicanism or elections' but rather 'with a substantive set of rights to be treated decently and with respect'. For these reasons, judges at many levels have been converted into central and powerful players in European political life (Garapon 1999, 43; Scheppele 2001, 2; Stone Sweet 2000, 130).

With this judicialisation of politics, Europe seems to be moving closer to the US model of democracy, in which courts have long played an important (albeit frequently controversial) role. It thus seems appropriate to consider the American judicial role in theory and practice, so as to highlight both its strengths and its limitations. This is what I propose to do, in very modest form, in this chapter. Through this discussion, I will argue that the lesson to take from the American experience is that while courts can offer an additional channel for individual citizens to stake claims and influence government, they should not be considered the ultimate or primary guarantors of individual rights. Although many theorists and average citizens conceive the American judiciary as a bulwark of liberal principle, standing outside and above the fray of ordinary politics to defend constitutional rights from democratic excess or abuse, in fact, American courts are, and were meant to be, very much *part of* the political process. Indeed, to the extent that the judicial defense of constitutional rights has been both legitimate and effective in the United States, it has been so precisely because of the political embeddedness of courts. Thus, European enthusiasts of judicially-enforceable rights should take care to ensure that the judges charged (directly or indirectly) with rights-based constitutional adjudication have the necessary 'democratic pedigree' (Eisgruber 2001) to fulfill successfully this new role, and, perhaps even more importantly, that citizens understand that the realisation of a regime of rights cannot be left to judges alone, but requires the sustained mobilisation of concerned actors in civil society. In short, they must accept that law is 'a facet of political society' (Harlow 2000, 366).

## 1. THE TRADITIONAL JUDICIAL ROLE AND THE LAW/POLITICS DISTINCTION IN (OLD) EUROPEAN DEMOCRACY

When speaking of a continent as large and diverse as Europe, it is difficult to generalise about 'its' political or legal traditions. Obviously, each member state of the European Union has its own particular blend of institutions and practices. Nonetheless, I think two things can safely be said about the continent as a whole: first, that 'democracy' has generally been understood in republican (rather than liberal) terms; and secondly, that legal positivism has been the dominant philosophy shaping the judicial sphere.

As Trägårdh and Delli Carpini note in their contribution to this volume, the democratic tradition in European countries has tended to be solidaristic in focus, privileging the 'general will' or the common good over minority rights and interests. While in some countries, institutional mechanisms have been developed to give voice and protection to ethnic and religious minorities (Lijphart 1977), the republican conviction that popular interests are best expressed through and protected by the legislature (ie, the elected representatives of the people) has, until recently, predominated (Favoreu 1990; Vick 2002). Concomitantly, the judicial function has traditionally been conceived in strictly positivist terms. Law — that is, the codes, statutes or decrees issued by elected representatives — has been understood as the expression of the sovereign people's will, and hence it has long been considered illegitimate for judges, as unelected, tenured actors, to exercise any discretionary or creative power in the application of the law. The proper role for the judge, on this view, is faithful agent of the legislature, or mere 'mouthpiece of the law'.[1] Adjudication is understood to be largely technical and passive, even bureaucratic (Merryman 1985; Damaska 1986).[2] In short, in this 'democratic positivist' model of adjudication (Dyzenhaus 1999), law (the judicial function) and politics (the legislative function) are constructed as completely distinct realms, with actors in the former subordinate to those in the latter.[3]

Since 1945, of course, a number of developments have challenged the understanding of both democracy and the judicial role in Europe. In the

---

[1] The term 'mouthpieces of the law' comes from Montesquieu (1989). However, it should be noted that Montesquieu advocated trial by jury, rather than by a bureaucratic caste of judges. In addition, Montesquieu's theory of the separation of powers served as the inspiration for the American system of 'checks and balances', to be discussed below.

[2] Indeed, in civil law countries (most of Euope), the judiciary is run like other branches of the civil service: judges enter the career through competitive examination, starting at the lowest rank, and then work their way up the institutional hierarchy on the basis of merit and seniority.

[3] This is not to say that judges are simply instruments of political actors in this model. In fact, judges are supposed to eschew all politics and be faithful only to 'the law'. However, when the democratic political will is expressed through law, democratic positivist judges are required to eschew independent assessment of what the law requires and act very much as if they are (merely) carrying out orders. For a critique of this model, see Scheppele (2002).

wake of World War II, an increased concern for human rights and a perceived need to build in checks on majority government led to the adoption of entrenched constitutions with extensive rights protection and the establishment of constitutional courts in many countries (Scheppele 2000; Stone Sweet 2000; Vallinder 1994; Cappelletti 1989; McWhinney 1986). The explicit duty of judges in these courts is to review, whether in the abstract or in situations of concrete case and controversy, the laws proposed and/or passed by parliament to ensure that they respect constitutional rules and standards (Stone Sweet 1999). The creation of these special courts has, in turn, affected the way that judges in other courts in these countries approach legal interpretation (Stone Sweet 2000). Moreover, the construction of the European Union, with its own founding documents (treaties) and a court whose rulings are supposed to be binding on the judiciaries of member states, has also disrupted the principal-agent relationship between national parliaments and their respective courts (Weiler 1999; Provine 1996). Citizens of the EU who feel that the standards established in the Union's founding documents (or, soon, in the Constitution for Europe) have been transgressed by national actors can appeal to the ECJ in Luxembourg. In addition, those whose countries (currently numbering 41) have ratified the European Convention for the Protection of Human Rights and Fundamental Freedoms (and its protocols) can appeal to the European Court on Human Rights (ECHR) in Strasbourg.[4] Member state judges, as well as other state actors, are to fall in line with the rulings of the ECJ, and, if they have formally incorporated the European human rights convention into national law, then should honour ECHR rulings as well.[5]

Willfully or not, then, judges in Europe are assuming an important position in the policy making process. Not only have judges at the transnational level played an active role in forging the contours of the new Europe (Nugent 1994; Dehousse 1998), but judges at the national ('member-state') level have also become involved in many fundamental political debates and contests (Stone Sweet 2000; Hirschl 2002). This involvement is usually explained and justified in conventional legalist terms: judges are sworn to apply the law, and, if they are to have any meaning, constitutions and treaties ratified by the people and/or their representatives must be understood to be as binding as any other law. In contrast to the past, however, judges are held out not merely as the 'mouthpieces of the law', but rather as guardians of the fundamental law to which the people have, directly or indirectly, committed.

---

[4] It should be noted that the ECHR previously functioned only part-time, ruling only on referrals from the European Human Rights *Commission*. However, as of 1999, this dual structure was abandoned and the ECHR became a full-time court.

[5] Britain's 'Human Rights Act' of 2000 incorporated the European Convention on Human Rights into British law and formally introduced judicial review of parliamentary acts for the first time. On the background and potential implications of this development, see Vick (2002).

To American ears, this reasoning sounds quite familiar. Such a 'liberal-legalist' conception of US constitutionalism is the dominant understanding among American theorists and (arguably) citizens, as well (Griffin 1996). As I will argue below, however, to the extent that the American constitutional model can be said to have succeeded,[6] it has done so not because judges have stood outside and above politics, defending rights against the machinations of self-interested majorities, but rather because they have been intimately enmeshed in the democratic political process.

## 2.   THE ROLE OF THE JUDICIARY AND THE LAW/POLITICS DISTINCTION IN THE AMERICAN DEMOCRATIC MODEL

In contrast to the traditional republican, solidaristic focus of European democracy, the democratic tradition in the United States has always been more liberal and individualist in emphasis. Cultural values of autonomy, self-reliance, and egalitarianism, and a historical demand for tolerance and pluralism, contribute to a propensity to privilege individual rights over community concerns (Merry 1990; Jacob 1996).[7] Indeed, the US Constitution was explicitly designed around a commitment to individual rights and limited government. The American founders were wary of concentrating power, even in the hands of the popular majority. They embraced the doctrine of the separation of powers developed by Montesquieu, but rather than advocate a complete functional separation, they argued for partial participation of each branch in the activity of the others. In other words, they sought to build in reciprocal institutional checks and balances, or mechanisms of power sharing, into the system (Bellamy 1996, 36–7).[8] They thus challenged the view, embodied in the European model of democracy that 'popular sovereignty issued in a monopoly of authority in which law meant no more than the commands of the majority' (Bellamy 1996, 37; Griffin 1996).

In this uniquely American schema, the judicial branch was accorded a significant role. In *Federalist* no. 78, for example, Alexander Hamilton specifically assigned the courts the task of keeping the legislature 'within the limits assigned to their authority'. In their role as 'an intermediate body

---

[6] How one gauges its success depends, of course, on what the criteria of evaluation are. For one recent assessment questioning the value of the American model in democratic terms, see Dahl 2001.

[7] Of course, the existence of these values does not imply their realisation in society. Discrimination, intolerance, elitism, and paternalism exist alongside and compete with these values, often affecting entire categories of people, and institutional change often lags behind attitudinal change. Nonetheless, these more noble values remain the yardstick against which social policies are generally measured, and around which political battles are constructed.

[8] See, for example, *Federalist*, nos. 10, 37, 47, 48 and 51, all written by James Madison.

between the people and the legislature', the courts were to be responsible
not only for preventing 'infractions of the Constitution', but also for 'miti-
gating the severity and confining the operation of [unjust and partial] laws'
which injure 'the private rights of particular classes of citizens' (Hamilton,
Jay and Madison 1937/1787, 506 and 509). Far from deferring to the legislature, then, judges in the American system were, from the start, to maintain a critical eye in their review and application of legislation, remaining
ever wary of implicit and explicit transgressions of individual rights upheld
in the constitution.

In the legal community, and among American liberals in general, many
interpret the framers' intentions as giving the Supreme Court ultimate
authority over constitutional interpretation, or a trumping position in the
political system. Indeed, this was the claim set forth in the famous US
Supreme Court case of 1803, *Marbury v Madison*, which established the
Court's judicial review power. Therein, Chief Justice John Marshall held
that the very logic of a written constitution required judicial supremacy.
Without it, he claimed, elected officials would be able to circumvent or
ignore the legal restraints that the constitution placed on them, and the
entire concept of limited government would thus lose meaning.[9] This view
has been reinforced in more recent Supreme Court decisions,[10] as well as
by constitutional theorists of many stripes who, in the face of concerns
about the 'counter-majoritarian difficulty', seek to justify judicial
supremacy by developing 'neutral' (ie, non-political) standards of constitutional interpretation.[11]

As Griffin (1996) and Peretti (1999) emphasise, the theoretical debate
over constitutional interpretation in the US has been driven by a perceived
need to maintain a strong distinction between law (what judges do) and
politics (what elected officials do). Judges (at least *federal* judges) are understood as the 'guardians' of constitutional rights, charged with defining the
limits of legitimate government authority (Dworkin 1978; Rawls 1996).
However, because they operate in a system (ostensibly) based on popular
sovereignty, their authority and legitimacy to defend rights 'against
the wayward effects of democracy' (Franck 1999, 276) depends on an
understanding of the constitution as a collection of transparent and
relatively unambiguous principles to which all reasonable citizens would

---

[9] See *Marbury v Madison,* 5 US (1 Cranch) 137 (1803).

[10] See, for example, *Cooper v Aaron,* 358 US 1 (1958), *US v Nixon,* 41 US 683 (1974), and
*City of Boerne v Flores,* 117 S Ct 2157 (1997).

[11] The term 'counter-majoritarian difficulty' was coined by Bickel (1986) to describe the challenge posed by the fact that unelected, tenured judges are empowered to nullify the decisions
of elected representatives. Ackerman (1984:1014) notes that the counter-majoritarian difficulty is 'the starting point for contemporary analysis of judicial review'. For a useful discussion of the variety of attempts at finding 'neutral principles' of interpretation, see Peretti
(1999).

(and, implicitly, do) consent to be bound. On this view, while politicians are self-interested, myopic, and often unscrupulous, judges, institutionally insulated from politics, are uniquely situated to hear and consider a variety of views, to reject expediency in favour of principle, and to decide impartially (Dworkin 1986; Eisgruber 2001). This view thus takes the traditional European 'democratic positivist' perspective and turns it on its head: law and politics remain strictly separated, but rather than judges, it is politicians who are suspect. Far from serving majority will, then, judges are instead to transcend and limit democratic politics.[12]

I contend, however, that this 'liberal'[13] view misunderstands the role of the judiciary in the US constitutional system. Law and politics (at least at the constitutional level) are not, nor were they meant to be, totally separate realms in the US case. It has been the duty of *everyone*, not just judges, to interpret and defend, through public debate and dialogue, the principles embodied in the American Constitution. Judges may have the power to challenge legislators, but the system contains mechanisms that encourage judicial engagement with and responsiveness to the legislature and the people at large, as well as on-going debate over the meaning of constitutional rights. Moreover, it is this overlap between 'law' and 'politics' in the American constitutional system that allows judges to play a supportive role in democracy. Indeed, a strict conceptual and institutional separation of law and politics — even in the name of liberal values — would be both illiberal and undemocratic, since it would remove (at least certain aspects of) justice from public debate and deliberation, thereby encouraging judicial elitism and discouraging citizen participation.

### 3. WHY, HOW AND WITH WHAT EFFECT LAW AND POLITICS OVERLAP IN THE AMERICAN CASE

Despite its persistence in the discourse of many legal actors and in the writings of constitutional theorists, the myth of 'legal neutrality' was in fact debunked long ago in the US. As legal realists, political jurisprudence theorists, and members of the critical legal studies movement have all argued, judges do not — and cannot — mechanically or objectively apply the law.

---

[12] This American 'liberal' suspicion of democratic politics is well described in Tushnet (1999) and Waldron (1999).

[13] I use the term 'liberal' here because this is, indubitably, how thinkers such as Dworkin, Franck, and Rawls (to name but a few) are labelled and self-identify. However, I place it in quotation marks because I also understand Madisonian thought to be deeply, and as I will elaborate below, more faithfully, liberal. For insightful discussions of liberalism, see Holmes (1989 and 1995), and Shklar (1989).

Law in any country, particularly constitutional law 'is not a brooding omnipresence in the sky'; rather, it is often vague, ambiguous, and sometimes even contradictory or antiquated (Murphy and Pritchett 1986, 2).[14] Thus, judges will always have to make choices in determining what the law is. In many of the cases before them, and certainly in the most socially and politically significant cases, judges ultimately must decide without clear, unequivocal support from legal texts, precedents, or universally-accepted moral principles; that is, they must exercise political judgement (Shklar 1986, 104; Dean 1967, 158). Judicial subjectivity is thus inevitable (Hirsch 1992, 89). A government of laws is still a government of men (humans), with all the risks that that entails.

The American founders seemed to have understood this well. They did not believe that judges should, or even could, have a supreme position in the political system, bearing ultimate authority over the definition of rights (Williams, this volume). The constitutional structure they created was designed around two clear beliefs: first, that 'parchment barriers' (eg, bills of rights) were not efficient mechanisms 'against the encroaching spirit of power'; and secondly, that the best way to avoid the abuse of power was to divide it (Hamilton, Jay, and Madison 1937/1787, 321–2, and 337). Thus, while the framers gave judges an important role in government, they did not give — and should not be understood as having given — them a superior position in the system. Rather, judicial review was part of a larger 'dynamic' system (Williams, this volume) that aimed at preventing the usurpation of sovereignty from the people as a whole, both by providing built-in checks on the power of the various departments of government and by providing multiple channels for citizens to make their views heard. As Richard Bellamy puts it, the special task of judges in the Madisonian constitutional schema was to act 'as defenders of, rather than proxies for, the 'will of the people', as declared in the Constitution ...' (Bellamy 1996, 40). In this system, 'oppression is guarded against not by virtue of abstract principles, such as rights, that might covertly embody the values and interests of hegemonic groups administering them [read judges], but through a political process which allows the people to voice their concerns for themselves' (Bellamy 1996, 43).

It makes sense, then, that in this system, judges were never considered as actors completely apart from politics. Although the framers believed that judicial independence was crucial to the success of the system, they also saw the need to ensure that judges were not insulated or removed from public debate and scrutiny. Thus, while they insisted on the need for secure judicial tenure to prevent direct control of the courts by the other

---

[14] Quote is from Oliver Wendell Holmes's dissent in *Southern Pacific Co. v Jensen*, 244 US 205 (1917), 222.

branches, they also built in a variety of mechanisms to increase the political representativeness and accountability of judges (Peretti 1999). The President and the Senate were to appoint judges jointly, the Congress was given the power to regulate the Supreme Court's appellate jurisdiction, juries were guaranteed for criminal trials, and the Senate retained the power to try impeachments. Emphasising this latter mechanism, Alexander Hamilton argued that there could

> never be the danger that the judges, by a series of deliberate usurpations on the authority of the legislature, would hazard the united resentment of the body entrusted with it, while this body was possessed of the means of punishing their presumption, by degrading them from their stations.
> (Hamilton, Jay, and Madison 1937/1787, 526–7)

In other words, because of the risk it would pose to the judges's own self-interest, Americans had no need to fear that judges would dismiss or attempt to supplant the views of elected representatives in the Senate.

Hamilton's prediction seems, for the most part, to have held true. Although public law theorists have spilled much ink debating the 'counter-majoritarian difficulty', several prominent contemporary analysts point out that, in fact, the broad political views of Court members are never too out-of-step with those of the nation's dominant political alliance (Dahl 1981; Friedman 1993; Peretti 1999). This is arguably less a result of the threat of impeachment than of the fact that the appointment process eliminates those candidates perceived to be out-of-touch with public understandings of constitutional values and principles.[15] As Herb Jacob explains,

> In the United States, judging is not a lifelong career. … Rather, it is a political position to which most incumbents bring a background of political activity and interest. Judges come to the bench in mid-career after significant political activity brings them to the attention of voters or appointing authorities.
> (Jacob 1996, 19)[16]

Because a new justice is added to the Supreme Court, on average, every 22 months, and because those nominated 'have engaged in public life and committed themselves publicly on the great questions of the day'

---

[15] Only thirteen federal judges have been impeached since 1803 and only seven of these were convicted and removed from their posts. At least one prominent observer claims that in all but three of the thirteen cases, partisan machinations were not the driving force behind the impeachment (Abraham 2001:26–9).

[16] Jacob cites a study showing that during the years 1963 to 1992, the percentage of federal appeals court judges having a record of party activism before their appointments ranged from 58 to 73, while the percentage of federal district court judges with such a record ranged between 49 and 61.

(Dahl 1981, 161–2), it is highly unlikely, despite the independence they enjoy,[17] that judges will become an out-of-control minority, imposing narrow and unpopular views on the American polity.[18]

The explicit 'politicization' of the American judiciary (in contrast to what might be called the 'bureaucratization' of justice in civil law systems), endows judges with both the capacity and the legitimacy to engage in policy-making behaviour. As Martin Shapiro puts it: 'The distinctive American mode of selecting judges from [a] broadly recruited, highly politicized, and overwhelmingly private practice bar' means that American judges 'bring the perspectives of the governed rather than those of the governors. Thus they have both the knowledge and the inclination to intervene in affairs of state to a far greater degree than do European judges' (M. Shapiro 1994, 102). Moreover, because the judicial selection process is 'controlled by elected officials, influenced by interest groups, and dominated by partisan and ideological considerations', judges can rightly (or should) regard themselves as representatives of the people (Peretti 1999:131; Eisgruber 2001).

This does not mean, however, that judges in the American system are leading protagonists of socio-political change. As several recent studies indicate, it has been mobilisation in civil society, accepted and facilitated but rarely instigated by judges, that has led to progress in the area of rights in the US (Rosenberg 1991; Epp 1998). Judges are simply one set of participants in the on-going debate over and reform of public policy around changing social conditions in America (Whittington 2001). Their role is politically provocative rather than peremptory (Macedo 1988, 227).

### 4.   ABSTRACTING FROM THE AMERICAN CASE: WHY DEMOCRACY REQUIRES A POROUS BOUNDARY BETWEEN LAW AND POLITICS

Europe's 'second democratic revolution',[19] with its emphasis on individual rights, seems to reflect a continental embrace of liberalism. Whereas liberalism

---

[17] Martin Shapiro (1997) explains that in the United States context, 'independence' most often means not independence from the three constitutional branches of government (ie, totally divorced from politics), but rather independence from the immediate control of either of the two major political parties (280). The key to this is long, staggered terms for appointed members of 'independent' agencies.

[18] There was, of course, the infamous crisis of the 1930s, in which President Franklin Roosevelt threatened to stack an intransigent Supreme Court to push forward New Deal legislation. However, Dahl (1981) notes that at this point there had been an unusually long lag between appointments, creating a somewhat anomalous situation for FDR and the Democrats. Moreover, one could argue that the system actually worked to correct itself as the framers intended, since in the end political pressure from the other branches (arguably) drove the Court to change its jurisprudential tune.

[19] Refer to page 122 above.

was long rejected by (progressive) European democrats as bourgeois ideology, propagated by property owners to secure their dominant position in society, many now recognise a supportive relationship, even a partial conceptual overlap, between liberalism and democracy (Bobbio 1987; Mouffe 1993; Habermas 1996; Touraine 1997). The link between the two ideals is a shared commitment to human autonomy and dignity, to equal self-determination, or to what Ian Shapiro has called the 'antihierarchical principle of non-domination' (I. Shapiro 1994). Prominent democratic theorists now agree that democracy is 'as much about opposition to the arbitrary [or unjust] exercise of power as it is about collective self-government'. Thus, 'there should always be opportunities for those affected by the operation of a collective practice both to participate in its governance and to oppose its results when they are so inclined' (I. Shapiro 1996, 224 and 260). This is particularly important given the cultural diversity that characterises modern societies. It is no longer possible to assert the existence, or even the possibility, of a harmonious collective will; rather, the permanence of conflicts and antagonisms must be accepted (Mouffe 1993; Holmes 1995; Touraine 1997).

This liberal desire to protect the inherent dignity of individual citizens, to demand that the government show equal concern and respect for *all* those whose lives it can affect, leads many to a focus on courts (Beatty 1994, 19–23; Dworkin 1996). As David Beatty puts it, 'For ordinary people, invoking the authority of law would be one of the most obvious ways of ensuring [that] the power of the [democratic] state would not be abused in the way which made colonial, fascistic, and communist governments so notorious in the past' (Beatty 1994, 3). Courts offer citizens an alternative channel in which to stake claims before the state, a channel in which they will be given the opportunity to air their particular views and grievances, and in which the institutional constraints and incentives, different from those at work in political parties and legislatures, may play in their favour. Because courts do not have the agenda-setting power that legislators do, they must address the issues brought before them.[20] Thus, courts have the unique role of 'thrusting one constituency's view to the fore, making it, for a short time, the focus of a discussion that many call dialogue' (Friedman 1993, 643).[21] As Stephen Macedo argues,

> The power of courts stands for the special form of respect we pay to those on the losing side of electoral struggles and legislative battles, and those who feel

---

[20] An obvious partial exception is the US Supreme Court's power of *certiorari*, but even with this relatively unique power, the Court's range of choice on what policies it can affect is still limited by what kinds of cases are appealed.

[21] Catalina Smulovitz contends that, as in Argentina after 1983, judicialization can become an alternative recourse for articulating and institutionalising political demands, demands which politicians can ignore or postpone indefinitely, but which courts, because of the rules that govern them, cannot (Smulovitz 1995). A similar argument is made by Giles and Lancaster (1989), and by Shapiro and Stone (1994).

victimized by officials executing the law. The courts embody (not alone, but most dramatically) a common determination to accompany the application of power with reasons, a regulative desire to govern ourselves reasonably.

(Macedo 1988, 225)

However, Europeans, like their American counterparts, should be wary not to carry their liberal idealism too far, depending on courts as 'forums of principle', where Herculean judges will fight to safeguard 'liberty and justice for all'.[22] The desire to move away from the 'democratic positivist' model, in which judges are servants to the sovereign (embodied in the parliament), does not have to and should not lead to a blind embrace of the 'liberal' model, in which judges embody or stand in for the sovereign. Indeed, such a move would subvert the ideals of the 'second democratic revolution'.

As noted above, the 'liberal' model of judging, like the traditional republican model common in Europe, is grounded in a strict law/politics distinction, meaning that law is considered to have an existence not only separate from but superior to political life (Shklar 1986, 8). Legal principles are considered transparent, or 'there', and judges are viewed as willing and able to apply them objectively. This means that judges can exempt themselves from the messy, subjective business of legislators, which focuses on the balancing of interests through negotiation and compromise (Shklar 1986, 12 and 38). If in the traditional or 'old' European model, judges are to act as Weber's passive administrator, 'execut[ing] conscientiously the order of the superior authorities, exactly as if the order agreed with [their] own conviction[s] ... [and] even if the order appears wrong to [them]' (Weber 1946, 95), in the 'liberal' model, judges are held out as philosophers, priests, or Platonic guardians of democracy, with insight into the universal and eternal principles that should guide the polity. Either way, judges can present law as an authoritative pronouncement, rather than a product of deliberation and compromise, subject to interpretation, critique, and even alteration. When law and politics are conceived as clearly distinct realms, legal interpretation becomes impenetrable and incontestable, and the office of judge becomes aloof and intractable. As Morton Horwitz has argued, 'Efforts to separate law and politics encourage the production of abstract jurisprudential debate divorced from more particular (and inevitably controversial) political and moral visions. ... By hiding behind unhistorical and abstract universalisms, [legalists] deny their own political and moral choices' (Horwitz 1992, 271–2).[23]

---

[22] The idea of courts as forums of principle and the reference to Herculean judges comes from Dworkin (1978 and 1986).
[23] Shklar (1986) offers a similar critique. See especially pp 38, 42–3, 74–5, and 104.

This is problematic for both liberalism and democracy. Liberalism is grounded in a belief in reason and choice, in an openness to critique, persuasion, and the re-assessment of goals.[24] Having grown, historically, out of a reaction to religious fundamentalism and political absolutism, it is suspicious of claims of uncomplicated and timeless truths. Liberalism is linked to democracy not simply because of its concern with fundamental human equality and dignity, but also because of this suspicion of paternalism.[25] As Robert Burt puts it, 'Unquestionable authority is at core an anti-democratic idea, no matter who purports to exercise that authority, no matter what its imagined scope' (Burt 1992, 374). A conception of law that allows judges to pose as final and (largely) unassailable authorities, and prevents (or at least discourages) public debate of the core assumptions and political premises that shape and inspire judicial interpretation (Schacter 1995, 656) thus subverts both liberalism and democracy.

To support liberal democracy, the judge should be conceived not as the guardian of a liberal code of rights, separate from and superior to politics, but as an important contributor to a polity-wide liberal *practice*, or 'a practice of the morality of citizenship', which 'shares responsibility for the past and responds sympathetically to the possibilities of the future' (Kahn 1993, 85). In other words, institutional mechanisms should encourage the judge to engage with the legislature and the citizenry, as an equal 'fellow in the community of ideas', such that she will 'try to answer their questions, weave [her] arguments into the fabric of their history' (Walzer 1981, 396). Not only might such an understanding discourage judicial elitism and dogmatism, but at the same time, it should help to 'engage the interpretive responsibilities of the other branches and the public' in the on-going debate over the meaning of constitutional rights (Macedo 1988, 227).

## 5.   CHALLENGES FOR CITIZENS OF A MADISONIAN REPUBLIC

The US constitutional system, although grounded in a liberal concern about rights, was designed not to degrade or strictly curb popular sovereignty, but rather to enhance it. Indeed, to function well, the system requires citizen participation. As Williams shows (this volume), none of the American founding fathers ever thought that government could be limited without vigilant citizens. The system they designed was one in which the meaning of limited government was 'dynamic', not 'pre-settled'. Such a regime does

---

[24] As Stephen Holmes (1995, 33) writes, 'Liberals believe that public disagreement is a creative force, producing more intelligent political decisions'.

[25] The idea that all citizens can make useful contributions to public debate is a fundamentally egalitarian idea (ibid).

not more than offer a framework for public debate and discussion about the meaning and content of rights, and it places a heavy burden on citizens to participate in that discussion, lest they find themselves subject to the tyranny of the minority.

If Europeans move towards a Madisonian model, then, they should be aware that, in ways, it demands *more* from citizens than a centralised system based in parliamentary sovereignty (Elkin 1996, 191). A Madisonian regime offers more channels for citizens to voice their opinions and influence government (ie, increases mechanisms of political representation). It is anti-majoritarian, or more consensual, by design. Therefore, it decreases the ability of political parties, once elected, to implement a platform (ie, reduces their efficiency).[26] In such a system, citizens cannot depend on parties alone to do the hard work of aggregating and voicing their views for them. They must find the motivation, energy, time, and (perhaps most challenging) the resources to organise with like-minded people to articulate their concerns in multiple channels.[27]

A call for greater participation may be a daunting challenge for citizens of the new Europe, given the relative weakness of European-wide political organisations and deliberative fora (Weiler 1999, 266). Yet without it, the broad realisation of rights is but a 'hollow hope' (Rosenberg 1991; Conant 2002). Neither judges nor any other authorities can be relied upon for the protection of rights and the public interest, 'unless an alert public is constantly on the watch and ready, individually and collectively, to insist upon the enforcement of the rights it recognizes as expressing the community's values, interests, and beliefs' (Friedrich 1974, 80). Actors in civil society must thus perform an 'educational' role, 'teach[ing] citizens how to relate to the legal system' and (I would add) aiding them financially to do so. At the same time, they must monitor the functioning of, and, where necessary, demand, push, promote, and monitor changes to, the judiciary and to the definition of rights and the public interest (Habermas 1996).

If Europeans want not just to imitate but to improve on the American experience, then, there are two important and inter-related lessons they can take from it. The first is to be especially attentive to cultivating judicial engagement with and responsiveness to diverse and complex public views, needs, and interests.[28] This is particularly important at the

---

[26] On this idea, see Shugart and Carey (1992).

[27] At the same time, it must be recognised that by dispersing power and throwing up multiple veto points to any given political decision, a Madisonian system reduces the likely effectiveness of *all* political action. Change in the system will — and can only be — moderate, and the prospect of slow and incremental change tends not to fuel interest and spark participation among most citizens.

[28] I should note that the importance of the 'democratic pedigree' (Eisgruber 2001) of judges is already acknowledged in the judicial appointment and tenure rules of the constitutional courts

Community level, where presently 'there appears to be little public scrutiny of appointments to the [ECJ] within member states and ... none within Community institutions' (Kenney 1999, 144).[29] The second lesson to take from the American case is the importance of building social and political networks and institutions (including public interest law organisations) that will facilitate communication among and organisation of citizens, such that *public* debate about collective values and goals can and will continue, even as old structures of representation and deliberation lose their previous relevance or are otherwise transformed. The nurturing of such networks and institutions — which might mobilise people in and around courts, among other arenas — will remain the key to making the new Europe a successful liberal *democracy*.[30]

## 6.   CONCLUSION

Until relatively recently, courts had only a marginal role to play in democratic politics in Europe. The pursuit of justice took place largely in the streets, through political parties, and in the legislature. However, as Europeans become increasingly liberal or individualist, challenging traditional rules regarding social and political behaviour and questioning existing hierarchies of power, they are turning to courts for enforcement of standards and rights embodied in national constitutions and international treaties. In so doing, they seem to be moving towards an American mode of politics, in which the liberal discourse of rights and limited government has always been central, and courts have always figured prominently. This is happening, moreover, at a moment when an entirely new political regime — the European Union — is being crafted. Because the new regime seems likely to be a federalised Madisonian-style republic, it seems both natural and prudent to reflect on the United States model, in both theory and practice, for potential lessons on what to imitate and what to avoid.

on the continent, and in the Labour government's recent proposals for judicial reform in the UK. However, the challenge persists at the level of the Community and (to varying degrees) in the ordinary courts of the continent, where judging is still part of the civil service.

[29] Mancini (2000) laments the ECJ's lack of links, whether direct or indirect, with the symbols of democratic government. Weiler decries the Court's 'scant regard for and weak sensibility to, the democratic processes by which the norms to which they demand supreme loyalty are enacted, and their veritable contempt for meaningful constitutional limits'. (Stith and Weiler 2002, 743). Stith agrees, stating that the EU risks 'rule by a deracinated judicial or quasi-judicial elite, cut off from both national traditions and from democratic majorities' (Stith and Weiler 2002, 746).

[30] See Conant (2002) for an analysis that demonstrates the importance of social and political mobilisation to the realisation and expansion of rights protection in four areas of European law.

In this chapter, I have sought to challenge the idea, widespread in liberal circles, that the courts have served, or were ever meant to serve, as the 'guardians' of rights in the US system. I have argued that this 'liberal' view depends on a strict distinction between law and politics, a distinction that is both false and, for a would-be liberal democracy, dangerous.

While the American founders thought it important to secure the independence of the judicial branch from direct political manipulation, and while they endorsed judicial review as a check on legislative tyranny, they also built in multiple mechanisms designed to keep judges generally representative of and responsible to the citizenry. Not only did they recognise that judges, as interpreters of law, were only human, subject to all the temptations of power to which politicians might be, but they also believed that the purpose of the Constitution was to protect not rights, per se, but popular sovereignty. Indeed, 'for Madison, a Bill of Rights was not addressed to the judiciary but the people as a whole'. A declaration of these fundamental principles would serve to provide 'the people rather than judges with "ground for an appeal to the sense of community" against the partial views of governments or majorities' (Bellamy 1996, 42, citing Madison).

Thus, judges in the American system have never been, and were never meant to be, detached from and 'above' politics. Rather, they are expected to have experience with ideological debate, negotiation, and deliberation. They are recruited in mid-career through an explicitly political process. Their stands on important public policy issues are subject to scrutiny, and, especially at the Supreme Court level, their decisions may become the focus of public debate. Drawing on empirical support from other political science studies, I hold that it is precisely this overlap between law and politics in the US system, and *not* an elevation of law *over* politics, that has allowed judges to play a significant and generally positive role in American democracy.

Moreover, I contend that a strict conceptual separation between law and politics would in fact work against the fundamentals of both liberalism and democracy. When judges are defined, in contrast to politicians, as 'neutral', 'objective', and 'aiming at justice', then they can remove themselves psychologically from the reach of ideological critique. Like technocrats, they can assert that they are simply applying 'neutral' or uncontroversial principles. They can claim that given their special training and unique experience in a 'politically antiseptic environment', they are able to reach superior decisions, decisions that are inescapable by virtue of their rational necessity (Shklar 1986, 97). They thus become aloof and dogmatic, and they work to frustrate or silence those outside the judiciary — that is, legislators or average citizens — who might disagree with them.

Although some self-styled 'liberals' might find the idea of aloof and dogmatically *liberal* judges attractive at first glance (who cares if they are elitist, if they are defending rights?), the fact is that such a desire is inconsistent with the underlying premises of liberalism and democracy alike. As argued above, one cannot be liberal or democratic if one claims, *a priori*, to have unquestionable authority on important political questions. Liberalism and democracy share a commitment to equal self-determination, which means that in a liberal democratic system, there must be a process by which the governed — *all* of the governed — are consulted, or at least given the opportunity to voice their support for or dissent from any given policy. In other words, liberal democratic government must involve public discussion or *deliberation*. In a system where, in the name of liberalism, law and politics are strictly separated, deliberation suffers. Judges portrayed as having superior insight into the meaning of liberal principles, or a monopoly on reason, will be less open and responsive to (ie, engaged with) arguments constructed outside the judiciary. At the same time, citizens will be less inclined to consider it their duty to deliberate about justice, or to demand that their legislators, as well as their judges, deliberate with the public interest in view.

The last thing that Europe needs today is more aloof experts and less public debate and deliberation. Many decisions that affect citizens of the European Union are made by independent agencies that lack the transparency and popular participation necessary for democratic legitimacy (Suleiman 2003; Shapiro 1997). The European political process is executive dominated, and 'in its present state, no one who votes in the European elections has a strong sense at all of affecting critical policy choices at the European level and certainly not of confirming or rejecting European governance' (Weiler 1999, 266). To avoid losing all input into the meaning of justice, and the allocational decisions that follow therefrom, European democrats thus need to construct and/or nurture institutional mechanisms that link judges, legislators, and citizens in the 'public moral enterprise' (Macedo 1988, 227) of deliberating about justice. Rather than accepting a strong law/politics distinction, they should seek ways of discouraging legal dogmatism and judicial elitism, and enabling vigorous public debate of law and justice.

This will require not only the reform of, in many cases, judicial institutions (eg, legal education, recruitment and appointment processes, and promotion rules), but also the strengthening of social and political networks and institutions (including transnational media, social movements, NGOs, political parties, and parliaments) at different levels of the European Union. Only thus might European citizens experience the on-going unification not as a purely liberal transition, but as a liberal *democratic* transition, in which public deliberation continues to be vital and popular sovereignty meaningful.

## 7.   REFERENCES

Abraham, Henry J. 2001, The Pillars and Politics of Judicial Independence in the United States. In *Judicial Independence in the Age of Democracy: Critical Perspectives from around the World,* edited by Peter H. Russell and David M. O'Brien, Charlottesville, VA: University Press of Virginia.

Ackerman, Bruce. 1984, 'The Storrs Lectures: Discovering the Constitution', *Yale Law Journal*, 93:1013–72.

Beatty, David. 1994, Human Rights and the Rule of Law. In *Human Rights and Judicial Review: A Comparative Perspective,* edited by David Beatty, Boston: Martinus Nijhoff.

Bellamy, Richard. 1996, The Political Form of the Constitution: the Separation of Powers, Rights and Representative Democracy. In *Constitutionalism in Transformation: European and Theoretical Perspectives*, edited by Richard Bellamy and Dario Castiglione, Oxford: Blackwell.

Bickel, Alexander. 1986, *The Least Dangerous Branch*, New Haven: Yale University Press. Original edition, 1962.

Bobbio, Norberto. 1987, *The Future of Democracy*, Minneapolis, University of Minnesota Press.

Burt, Robert. 1992, *The Constitution in Conflict*, Cambridge, MA: Harvard University Press.

Cappelletti, Mauro. 1989, *The Judicial Process in Comparative Perspective*, Oxford: Clarendon Press.

Conant, Lisa. 2002, *Justice Contained: Law and Politics in the European Union*, Ithacd: Cornell University Press.

Dahl, Robert. 1981, *Democracy in the United States: Promise and Performance, 4th edn*, Boston: Houghton Mifflin.

—— 2001, *How Democratic is the American Constitution?* New Haven: Yale University Press.

Damaska, Mirjan. 1986, *The Faces of Justice and State Authority*, New Haven: Yale University Press.

Dean, Howard. 1967, *The Judiciary and Democracy*, New York: Random House.

Dehousse, Renaud. 1998, *The European Court of Justice: The Politics of Judicial Integration*, New York: St. Martin's Press.

Dworkin, Ronald. 1978, *Taking Rights Seriously*, Cambridge, MA: Harvard University Press.

—— 1986, *A Matter of Principle*, Cambridge, MA: Harvard University Press.

—— 1996, *Freedom's Law*, Cambridge, MA: Harvard University Press.

Dyzenhaus, David. 1999, Recrafting the Rule of Law. In *Recrafting the Rule of Law: The Limits of Legal Order*, edited by David Dyzenhaus, Oxford: Hart Publishing.

Eisgruber, Christopher. 2001, *Constitutional Self-Government*, Cambridge, MA: Harvard University Press.

Elkin, Stephen L. 1996, Madison and After: the American Model of Political Constitution. In *Constitutionalism in Transformation: European and Theoretical Perspectives*, edited by Richard Bellamy and Dario Castiglione, Oxford: Blackwell.

Epp, Charles R. 1998, *The Rights Revolution*, Chicago: University of Chicago Press.

Favoreu, Louis. 1990, American and European Models of Constitutional Justice. In *Comparative and Private International Law: Essays in Honor of John Henry Merryman on his Seventieth Birthday*, edited by David S. Clark, Berlin: Duncker & Humbolt.

Friedman, Barry. 1993, 'Dialogue and Judicial Review', *Michigan Law Review*, 91 (Feb):577–682.

Franck, Thomas M. 1999, *The Empowered Self: Law and Society in the Age of Individualism*, Oxford: Oxford University Press.

Friedrich, Carl. 1974, *Limited Government: A Comparison*, Englewood Cliffs, NJ: Prentice-Hall.

Garapon, Antoine. 1999, 'La démocratie à l'épreuve de la justice'. *JUSTICES: Ce qui a changé dans la justice depuis 20 ans*, Paris: Éditions Dalloz.

Giles, Michael and Thomas Lancaster. 1989, 'Political Transition, Social Development, and Legal Mobilization in Spain', *American Political Science Review*, 83 (Sept):817–33.

Griffin, Stephen. 1996, *American Constitutionalism: From Theory to Politics*, Princeton: Princeton University Press.

Habermas, Jürgen. 1996, *Between Facts and Norms: Contributions to a Discourse Theory of Law and Democracy*, Cambridge, MA: MIT Press.

Hamilton, Alexander, John Jay, and James Madison. 1937/1787. *The Federalist: a commentary on the Constitution of the United States*, New Work: Modern Library.

Harlow, Carol. 2000, 'Disposing of Dicey: from Legal Autonomy to Constitutional Discourse?' *Political Studies*, 48:356–69.

Hirsch, H. N. 1992, *A Theory of Liberty: The Constitution and Minorities*, New York: Routledge.

Hirschl, Ran. 2002, 'Restituating the Judicialization of Politics: Bush v. Gore as a Global Trend', *The Canadian Journal of Law & Jurisprudence*, 15 (July): 191–218.

Holmes, Stephen. 1989, The Permanent Structure of Anti-Liberal Thought. In *Liberalism and the Moral Life*, edited by Nancy Rosenblum, Cambridge, MA: Harvard University Press.

—— 1995, *Passions and Constraint*, Chicago: University of Chicago Press.

Horwitz, Morton. 1992, *The Transformation of American Law, 1870–1960: The Crisis of Legal Orthodoxy*, New York: Oxford University Press.

Jacob, Herbert. 1996, Courts and Politics in the United States. In *Courts, Law, and Politics in Comparative Perspective*, by Herbert Jacob et al, New Haven: Yale University Press.

Kahn, Paul. 1993, Independence and Responsibility in Judicial Review. In *Transition to Democracy in Latin America: The Role of the Judiciary*, edited by Irwin P. Stotsky, Boulder: Westview Press.

Kenney, Sally J. 1999, The Judges of the Court of Justice of the European Communities. In *Constitutional Dialogues in Comparative Perspective*, edited by Sally J. Kenney, William M. Reisinger, and John C. Reitz, New York: St. Martin's Press.

Lijphart, Arend. 1977, *Democracy in Plural Societies*, New Haven: Yale University Press.

MacCormick, Neil. 1993, Constitutionalism and Democracy. In *Theories and Concepts of Politics,* edited by Richard Bellamy, New York: Manchester University Press.

Macedo, Stephen. 1988, 'Liberal Virtues, Constitutional Community', *The Review of Politics*, 50:215–40.

Mancini, G. F. 2000, *Democracy and Constitutionalism in the European Union: Collected Essays*, Oxford: Hart Publishing.

McWhinney, Edward. 1986, *Supreme Courts and Judicial Law-Making: Constitutional Tribunals and Constitutional Review*, Dordrecht, Netherlands: Nijhoff.

Merry, Sally Engle. 1990, *Getting Justice and Getting Even: Legal Consciousness among Working-Class Americans*, Chicago: University of Chicago Press.

Merryman, John Henry. 1985, *The Civil Law Tradition*, Stanford: Stanford University Press.

Montesquieu, Charles Baron de. 1989, Reprint. *The Spirit of the Laws*, New York: Cambridge University Press. Original edition, 1748.

Mouffe, Chantal. 1993, *The Return of the Political*, New York: Verso.

Murphy, Walter F. and C. Herman Pritchett. 1986, *Courts, Judges, and Politics: An Introduction to the Judicial Process*, 4th edn, New York: Random House.

Nugent, Neill. 1994, *The Government and Politics of the European Union* 3rd edn, Basingstoke: Macmillan.

Peretti, Terri Jennings. 1999, *In Defense of a Political Court*, Princeton: Princeton University Press.

Provine, Doris Marie. 1996, Courts in the Political Process in France. In *Courts, Law, and Politics in Comparative Perspective,* by Herbert Jacob et al, New Haven: Yale University Press.

Rawls, John. *Political Liberalism*, New York: Columbia University Press, 1996.

Rosenberg, Gerald N. 1991, *The Hollow Hope: Can Courts Bring About Social Change*, Chicago: University of Chicago Press.

Schacter, Jane S. 1995, 'Metademocracy: The Changing Structure of Legitimacy in Statutory Interpretation', *Harvard Law Review*, 108:593–663.

Scheppele, Kim Lane. 2000, Constitutional Interpretation after Regimes of Horror. University of Pennsylvania Law School, Public Law Working Paper No. 05, available on line at: http://ssrn.com/abstract=236219.

—— 2001, Democracy by Judiciary (Or Why Courts Can Sometimes Be More Democratic than Parliaments). Paper prepared for the conference on Constitutional Courts, Washington University, 1–3 November, available on line at: http://law.wustl.edu/igls/Conconfpapers/Scheppele.pdf.

—— 2002, Declarations of Independence: Judicial Reactions to Political Pressure. In *Judicial Independence at the Crossroads: An Interdisciplinary Approach,* edited by Stephen B. Burbank and Barry Friedman, Thousand Oaks, Cal: Sage Publications.

Shapiro, Ian. 1994, Introduction. In *Nomos XXXVI: The Rule of Law,* edited by Ian Shapiro, New York: New York University Press.

—— 1996, *Democracy's Place*, Ithaca: Cornell University Press.

Shapiro, Martin. 1994, 'The Juridicalization of Politics in the United States', *International Political Science Review*, 15:101–12.

—— 1997, 'The Problems of Independent Agencies in the United States and the European Union', *Journal of European Public Policy*, 4 (June):276–91.

—— and Alec Stone. 1994, 'The New Constitutional Politics of Europe', *Comparative Judicial Studies*, 26 (January):397–420.

Shklar, Judith. 1986, *Legalism: Law, Morals, and Political Trials*, Cambridge, MA: Harvard University Press.

—— 1989, The Liberalism of Fear. In *Liberalism and the Moral Life*, edited by Nancy Rosenblum, Cambridge, MA: Harvard University Press.

Shugart, Matthew Sobert and John M. Carey. *Presidents and Assemblies: Constitutional Design and Electoral Dynamics*, New York: Cambridge University Press.

Smulovitz, Catalina. 1995, Constitución y Poder Judicial en la Nueva Democracia Argentina. In *La Nueva Matriz Política Argentina*, Edited by Carlos H. Acuña, Buenos Aires: Nueva Visión.

Stith, Richard and J.H.H. Weiler. 2002, 'An Epistolary Exchange: Can Treaty Law Be Supreme, Directly Effective, and Autonomous — All at the Same Time?' *NYU Journal of International Law and Politics*, 34 (Summer): 729–747.

Stone Sweet, Alec. 1999, Constitutional Dialogues: Protecting Human Rights in France, Germany, Italy, and Spain. In *Constitutional Dialogues in Comparative Perspective*, edited by Sally J. Kenney, William M. Reisinger, and John C. Reitz, New York: St. Martin's Press.

—— 2000, *Governing with Judges*, New York: Oxford University Press.

Suleiman, Ezra N. 2003, Dilemmas of Democracy in the European Union. In *The Making and Unmaking of Democracy*, edited by Theodore K. Rabb and Ezra N Suleiman, New York: Routledge.

Toharia, José Juan. 2001, *Opinion Pública y Justicia*, Madrid: Consejo General del Poder Judicial.

Touraine, Alain. 1997, *What Is Democracy?* Boulder: Westview Press.

Tushnet, Mark. 1999, *Taking the Constitution Away from the Courts*, Princeton: Princeton University Press.

Vallinder Torbjörn. 1994, 'The Judicialization of Politics — A World-wide Phenomenon: Introduction', *International Political Science Review*, 15:91–9.

Vick, Douglas W. 2002, 'The Human Rights Act and the British Constitution', *Texas International Law Journal*, 37 (Spring):329–72.

Waldron, Jeremy. 1999, *Law and Disagreement*, New York: Oxford University Press.

Walzer, Michael. 1981, 'Philosophy and Democracy', *Political Theory*, 9:379–99.

Weber, Max. 1946, Politics as a Vocation. In *From Max Weber: Essays in Sociology*, edited by H.H. Gerth and C. Wright Mills, New York: Oxford University Press.

Weiler, J.H.H. 1999, *The Constitution of Europe*, Cambridge: Cambridge University Press.

Whittington, Keith. 2001, 'Presidential Challenges to Judicial Supremacy and the Politics of Constitutional Meaning', *Polity*, 33:3 (Spring): 365–395.

# 7

## Democracy Beyond Nation and Rule? Reflections on the Democratic Possibilities of Proceduralism

### WARREN BRECKMAN

S INCE THE EARLY 1980s, much of the debate within North American political philosophy has circled around the opposition between 'proceduralist' and 'republican' understandings of politics. In that debate, proceduralism is used not by its putative advocates, so much as by its opponents, most notably Michael Sandel, who first pitted these ideal types against each other in his book-length critique of the liberal philosopher John Rawls (Sandel 1982). In Sandel's most recent book, *Democracy's Discontent*, American history becomes an epic competition between these two principles. On the one hand, the republican conception views politics as a project of communal and individual formation, in which the civic virtues of individual citizens are both directed toward and fashioned by the collective's sense of shared goals. On the other hand, the liberal understanding insists that the state assume a neutral stance *vis-à-vis* contending conceptions of the good life and enshrine individual civil rights so as to enable individuals to pursue their own value choices unhindered by communal pressures. Sandel contends that in the last 50 years, the liberal vision has prevailed, thereby entrenching a 'procedural republic' that privileges fair procedures over particular ends, rights over values, individuals over communities, and judicial review over the decisions of legislative majorities. In short, Sandel argues, American citizenship and freedom are severely depleted by a political form that lacks the civic resources to sustain basic practices of democratic self-government, thereby imperiling the very liberties and rights it promises.

In Europe too a debate about proceduralism has emerged. In political theory, this has been due in some measure to the efforts of Jürgen Habermas to develop a discourse theory of democratic legitimation; but much more importantly, in the broader public sphere, it has been stimulated by the much-discussed 'crisis' of the nation-state. While Europeans also direct their concern toward the question of democracy, their discussion has quite a different accent. The American debate pits communities against the state, Tocqueville's town hall against Madison's capitol. In Europe, the enduring power of the French revolutionary conception of democracy — that the nation-state embodies the *pouvoir constituant* of the 'people', irrespective of whether the people is defined in civic or ethnic terms[1] — ensures that much discussion takes the nation-state as the proper departure point for any interrogation of democracy. In this view, the democratic nation-state faces challenges both from 'below', in the form of polities fragmented by both individualism and multiculturalism, and from 'above', in the form of global market forces and supranational organisations, most notably the European Union. The evolution of European Union institutions that create European law that binds member states and exposes the decisions of individual member states to judicial review by the European Court of Justice has prompted a discussion that has centred on the fate of national sovereignty. This is not an entirely alien concern to Americans, but it has remained largely muted due to both the history of American political culture and the relative invulnerability of American national sovereignty. The debate in Europe nonetheless resembles the American discourse in other ways, insofar as it centres on tensions between substantive notions of democracy and rights-based individualism, social interests and the free market, democratic will-formation and fair procedures, majority rule at the national level and bureaucratic administration and judicial review at the supranational level.

However, as one approaches the current debate over the prospects of democracy, it must be asked whether the concept of proceduralism really has much utility. Does the dichotomy drawn by Sandel between the republican-communitarian conception of democratic politics and the liberal conception of the 'procedural republic' have any substance? If we treat the communitarian republic and the procedural republic as 'normative models of democracy' (Habermas 1998, 239–52), do they serve to illuminate or obscure the problem of democracy? In what follows, I will argue that both sides of the dichotomy unduly restrict the understanding of democracy by neglecting the social experience of democracy. Thus, both sides constrain the discussion of democratic possibilities at the supranational level.

To substantiate this claim, I will begin by exploring the relationship between proceduralism and substantive choice within the polity. I will proceed to consider democracy as 'regime' or 'form of life', developing arguments found in the writings of Cornelius Castoriadis and Claude Lefort. The final section of the chapter will apply the insights gained through Lefort and Castoriadis to the question of proceduralism's relationship to democracy at both the nation-state and supranational levels. Before proceeding, it is

---

[1] For the most elaborate exploration of the familiar distinction between 'ethnic' and 'civic' nationalism, see Brubaker (1992).

important to be clear on the aims and limits of this chapter. I do not propose to evaluate empirically the question of proceduralism in the American or European contexts, nor do I intend to explore empirically the putative tension of the European tradition of 'substantive-solidaristic' national democracies and a European (procedural) federation of procedural republics. Rather, the chapter offers a theoretical evaluation of the utility of the dichotomy drawn between proceduralism and democracy. It aims at exploring alternative ways to conceptualise the basic questions intended by the dualism of proceduralism and substantive democracy.

## 1. PROCEDURALISM AND SUBSTANTIVE CHOICE

The claim of liberal theorists like John Rawls and Ronald Dworkin that their own thinking about political liberalism remains neutral toward competing comprehensive conceptions of the good fails to fully thematise the difficulties inherent in the concept of neutrality. If we consider Rawls, we see that in the interest of trying to secure the stability of a pluralistic constitutional regime, he attempts to distinguish between a strictly political conception of justice and comprehensive religious, moral or philosophical doctrines. Moreover, he repudiates communitarian attempts to describe the state as a 'community', because the unity of a community rests on a comprehensive conception of the good. In classic liberal fashion, he argues that the values of community should only be pursued in private forms of association. When states try to realise the values of community, they must rely on an unacceptable level of compulsion. Nonetheless, Rawls insists that

> in the well-ordered society of justice as fairness citizens share a common aim and one that has high priority: namely, the aim of political justice, that is, the aim of ensuring that political and social institutions are just, and of giving justice to persons generally, as what citizens need for themselves and want for one another. It is not true, then, that on a liberal view citizens have no fundamental common aims. Nor is it true that the aim of political justice is not an important part of their identity (using the term 'identity', as is now often done, to include the basic aims and projects by reference to which we characterize the kind of person we very much want to be). But this common aim of political justice must not be mistaken for (what I have called) a conception of the good.
> (Rawls 1999, 431–2)

This concession to common aims does not go far enough. In the case of a liberal like Rawls, the pursuit of political justice seems directly linked to a comprehensive view of what human beings are (autonomous and self-determining) and what they should be (*more* autonomous and self-determining). Of course, the whole point of Rawls's attempt to bracket out comprehensive views from his discussion of political liberalism is to address those people whose basic beliefs may conflict with liberalism, as in the case of people who view humans as the dependent creatures of a creator god or place religious law above the civil constitution. Yet, here, the separation of a political conception of justice from comprehensive doctrines seems particularly misleading. It is more convincing to argue that the ability of true believers to bracket their own general conception of truth or the good is already a fundamental transformation of the comprehensive conception itself. Historically, comprehensive views have been, as the phrase implies, totalising in their claims to righteousness and the imperative to organise spiritual, social and political life around their truth. By contrast, the willingness to privatise one's deepest religious or ethical convictions and the recognition of the value of pluralism and tolerance in the public sphere do not just stand alongside one's comprehensive view. Instead, those 'liberal' values must already have reached into the comprehensive doctrine itself, challenging its totalising impulse and relativising it in relation to competing general claims. Political justice is therefore not just a serious commitment within a carefully demarcated political domain; it belongs substantively to the comprehensive commitments of people who accept the liberal democratic order. This point is made forcefully whenever liberal societies encounter people whose comprehensive doctrines have not been transformed in this way, a lesson that the liberal democracies are presently learning anew.

The opening of comprehensive doctrines toward their own relativisation is itself a product of history. Just as the standpoint of liberal theory is not in fact neutral in any meaningful way, so too is the relationship of proceduralism to substantive values not one of neutrality. Both sides of the American debate distort the involvement of proceduralism in the historic struggle for democracy, as well as the historical imbrications of individualist rights and democratic will-formation. Blandine Kriegel has recently reminded us of these mutually implicating histories in her important reassessment of sixteenth and seventeenth century state theory. As she writes, the rule of law was at the core of the early modern struggle against feudalism. In the writings of natural-law philosophers and jurists like Thomas Hobbes, Charles Loyseau, and Jean Bodin, the demand for the right to personal security, the right to individual liberty, and due process sought to subdue feudalism's relations of personal power and deference. In place of feudalism's direct domination, which 'vassalized the individual, naturalized men, and privatized politics' (Kriegel 1995, 25), the theorists and jurists advocated impersonal rule, an alliance between ruler and ruled in the name of security, and the sovereignty of law.[2] Of course, the theorists discussed by Kriegel were not democratic, nor were civil rights on their agenda.

[2] Kriegel emphasises that even in absolutism, the sovereign is not the same as sovereignty (29). In arguing that the 'mortality of kings is outweighed by the immortality of the crown', Kriegel appears also to be gesturing toward the magisterial treatment of this issue by Ernst Kantorowicz (1957).

Moreover, the relationship of the actual states of early modern Europe to the principle of the rule of law was highly checkered, with England developing into a state under the rule of law, *ancien regime* France only approximating such a state, and the rule of law becoming more and more attenuated the further it stretched eastward (Kriegel 1995, 73–4). Distant as the early modern idea of rule of law was from modern democracy, Kriegel argues persuasively that 'it is, indeed, only in those states committed to rule of law that liberal democracy has taken root, for a people can choose its own destiny, enjoy political liberties and civil rights, only if it is composed of free beings' (Kriegel 1995, 50). A central contention of Kriegel is that the twentieth century's horror at the excesses of state power has frequently produced among political theorists a reflexive antistatism that obscures the role that the demand for rule of law played in the development of democratic politics.

The demand for the rule of law intrinsically linked the self-assertion of a new kind of political subject to the articulation of a newly constituted conception of a community of citizens. As such, proceduralism was historically a substantive choice about a shared good. This is perhaps an obvious point, but it is evidently easy to forget. American liberals downplay this historical dimension, perhaps because of a preference for *ahistorical* analytical modes of argument and their evident unease with the suggestion that the articulation of individual rights was the constituting claim of a community instead of the assertion of an existing individual subjectivity.[3] Communitarians seem equally reluctant to recognise this historical complexity, perhaps because, on the one hand, it obscures the attempt to distinguish between a regime devoted to the juridical protection of individual rights and substantive democratic republicanism, and on the other hand, this novel community of citizens constituted itself by a claim for autonomy that was as much a challenge to all earlier forms of community as it was their continuation. One of the merits of Jürgen Habermas's work, to which I will return later, is that in contrast to both sides of the American debate, Habermas recognises the historical role played by proceduralism in the establishment of democratic legitimation. His own attempt to reinvigorate democratic legitimation places great emphasis on defending and strengthening the procedures that stabilise discursive deliberation and political will-formation within complex and diverse polities and routinise the interactions between the public

---

[3] Although Rawls' definition of justice as fairness commits him to a form of redistributive politics that has provoked the ire of libertarians like Robert Nozick, democracy is clearly of secondary importance for Rawls. Rawls arrives at his conception of justice through a process of rational deduction that essentially adds-on the institution of majority rule. Majority rule 'is justified as the best available way of insuring just and effective legislation', but as it should function in the 'ideal procedure that forms a part of the theory of justice', majority rule would always hold a 'subordinate place as a procedural device' in relation to an already formed just constitution (Rawls 1971, 356–7).

sphere and the legislative and executive branches of the state. In brief, Habermas's argument for proceduralism rests on its contribution to the cultivation of a substantive conception of democratic citizenship.

Unless taken as the barest of legal fictions, proceduralism remains tied to substantive choices. This point comes out forcefully in J.H.H. Weiler's discussion of judicial protection of fundamental human rights by the European Court. Weiler argues that this judicial practice may operate as a 'source of both unity and disunity in the process of European integration'. As Weiler says, 'beyond a certain core, reflected in Europe by the European Convention on Human Rights, the definition of fundamental human rights often differs from polity to polity. These differences ... reflect fundamental societal choices and form an important part in the different identities of polities and societies' (Weiler 1999, 102). Hence, 'human rights are almost invariably the expression of a compromise between competing goods in the polity', most typically in liberal societies between the putative public concerns represented by governmental authority and individual interests in personal liberty. Weiler reasons that it is the balance between these competing interests that is 'fundamental' (Weiler 1999, 106), meaning that human rights represent 'both a source of, and index for, cross-national differentiation and not only cross-national assimilation' (Weiler 1999, 105). Richard Bellamy makes the point even stronger when he observes of the Charter of Fundamental Rights of the European Union that the Charter recognises the diversity of political and constitutional cultures in Europe, but then proceeds as if that diversity poses no problem to the articulation and implementation of a core set of fundamental rights. Bellamy argues persuasively that possibilities for reasonable disagreement over rights extend even to the most basic provisions, thus making the identification and articulation of basic rights a consummately political undertaking (Bellamy 2001, 58–9)

Proceduralism is not intrinsically democratic, but every conceivable form of democracy conformable to modern circumstances and expectations is procedural, though it is always also more. Undoubtedly, the substantive choices that have instituted forms of democratic decision-making and legal protections of individual rights may harden into legal formalisms; and delegated representatives and bureaucratic agents may grow distant from their source of legitimation. But those dangers should not be defined as democracy's slide from substantive commitments to proceduralism, as if procedure were little more than neutral technique. Rather, the danger lies in a democratic society's losing a vigorous relationship to its own choices and the procedures that encode them as institutionalised practices. In short, it is a problem of democracy losing its relation to its own deepest capacity, the ability to open and engage a debate over fundamental choices.

Of course, this capacity of political actors to make fundamental decisions about the institution of politics is most urgently at stake and most dramatically revealed in times of revolutionary upheaval.[4] In speaking of such times, Hannah Arendt has written of the 'vicious circle' present at the foundational moment of a new democratic order: 'those who get together to constitute a new government are themselves unconstitutional, that is, they have no authority to do what they have set out to achieve'. Arendt pointedly continues, 'The vicious circle in legislating is present not in ordinary lawmaking, but in laying down the fundamental law, the law of the land or the constitution which, from then on, is supposed to incarnate the 'higher law' from which all laws ultimately derive their authority' (Arendt 1982, 183–4). The tension between a 'vicious' foundational moment and 'ordinary lawmaking' transcendentally anchored by a constitution leads Arendt to distinguish between two types of modern revolution: permanent revolutions that continue to repeat the willful, violent act of foundation and conservative revolutions that bury the arbitrary moment of the founding in a language of legitimacy rooted in divinity, nature, or reason, or — as in the American case — all three. In Arendt's view, the Americans succeeded in ending the revolution, while the French were much less successful.[5]

Yet Arendt's antinomy of permanent and conservative revolutions raises a further question. Is constitutional government likely to succeed if it does not preserve possibilities for radical democracy like that which made revolution possible in the first place? Bruce Ackerman answers 'no' in *We the People*, but he argues contrary to Arendt that the framers of the American constitution successfully institutionalised the eighteenth century experience of public freedom in a dualism of constitutional and normal politics. In Ackerman's conception, as Andrew Arato comments in an essay on eastern European constitution-making, 'constitutional politics refers to movements of citizens, participating publicly through extraordinary but legal political forms, oriented primarily to making or revising constitutions, (Arato 1994, 166). Arato endorses Ackerman's distinction, as well as the normative demand for extraordinary 'democratic constitutionalism' as a dialectical complement to normal 'liberal constitutionalism'.[6] But he criticises Ackerman for relying too heavily on the eighteenth century American theory of popular sovereignty, 'according to which valid constitutions and constitutional revisions are acts of the sovereign people outside of all duly-constituted legislatures' (Arato 1994,166). Arato's misgivings about that 'mythical entity, the sovereign people', stem from his greater sensitivity to the European context, where the notion of the people as the *pouvoir constituant* has a much more troubling history than in North America.

---

[4] The inspiration for the problematic and the figures discussed in the next three paragraphs comes from an excellent article by William Scheuerman (1997).
[5] It is not surprising that it was a Frenchman, François Furet, and not an American who would argue that the compelling question for national politics remains 'how do revolutions end', or that other French people would feel provoked by Furet's declaration that the 'revolution is over' (1981).
[6] These are Arato's, not Ackerman's terms.

In pursuit of an alternative, Arato endorses Ulrich Preuss's argument that the Round Tables that played an important role in the central and east European revolts against Communism present at least the possibility of a different model of the founding agent. Echoing Hegel's preference for a body politic comprised of mediating corporate entities, Preuss notes that the Round Tables 'saw themselves as representing not a monolithic people in revolt against its masters but, rather, the multiplicity and diversity of all citizens' (Preuss 1995, 95).[7] Both Preuss and Arato acknowledge that this novel conception of the *pouvoir constituant* as an 'act of political self-organization of a civil society' (Preuss 1994, 148) has been largely eclipsed in the 1990s.[8] But whether one conceives the constituent power as the sovereign people, as Ackerman does, or as the negotiated power of groups within civil society, the important point for the present discussion follows. 'Although the constituent power is tamed insofar as it becomes subject to the rationalizing force of a procedural rule, it remains a potential power which may check the misuse of authority by the constituted powers' (Preuss 1994, 159). To that end, Preuss writes, 'what is important for the consideration of the relation between constitution and constituent power is the observation that a total and permanent exclusion of the unorganised constituent power of the people from the realm of politics tends to produce a formalism and rigidity of the constituted powers' (Preuss 1994, 160). Moving beyond Arendt's antinomy, Preuss concludes, 'The constituent power is simultaneously the creator of the constitution and a permanent threat to it. Yet, both functions are necessary for the vitality of the constitution' (Preuss 1994, 164).

## 2.   DEMOCRACY AS REGIME

The insistence upon the significance of unorganised popular action for the ongoing vitality of a democratic constitutional order implies a defense of the

---

[7] It is necessary to underscore the difference between Hegel and Preuss and Arato. Whereas they resist the classic definition of the democratic *pouvoir constituant* as the will of a homogeneous people because of their concern for pluralism, Hegel worries that an unmediated relationship between individuals and their collective power threatens anarchy: 'The aggregate of private persons is often spoken of as the 'people': but as such an aggregate it is vulgus, not *populus*.... That condition of the people is a condition of lawlessness, unethicality, brutishness: in it the people is only a shapeless, wild, blind force' (1991, 470).

[8] The Convention that submitted a draft Constitution for Europe to the European Council meeting in Thessaloniki in June 2003 does not alter the latter point. Despite efforts to reverse the lack of transparency and democratic involvement that had marked earlier intergovernmental conferences through broader consultation of other EU bodies and groups within civil society, the Convention remained dominated by national and European political elites. Indeed, in so far as the draft Constitution invokes a legitimating popular authority, it is the older notion of the *pouvoir constituant* that gets exercise.

right to civil disobedience. Crucial as this idea is, there is in fact a tautology in the very notion of such a right, as it legalises forms of action aimed at protest and change by securing the rights of free speech and assembly. If an act of civil disobedience is protected by the constitution, then it is not disobedient at all. It merely expresses a legal right or, it might be argued, even a civic duty. If an act of civil disobedience is judged to fall outside the scope of constitutional protection, then it is illegal, even if some such acts may be motivated by strongly defensible normative claims. In such cases, civil disobedience cannot be considered a right but a punishable offense, though other rights, such as a fair trial and the prohibition of certain forms of penalty, will determine the subsequent treatment of an offender. Ackerman clearly refers to the category of *legal* civil disobedience when he argues that American political culture has effectively incorporated 'constitutional' politics, that is, popular mobilisations, into the legal framework of the constitutional amendment process. Preuss too has in mind constitutionally protected forms of popular action, but he expresses a much greater awareness that the paradoxical *normalisation* of the non-normal contains risks that are not fully mastered. One might ask whether we have in fact progressed beyond Arendt's vicious circle or Carl Schmitt's belief that the violent willfulness of the foundational moment cannot be expunged by constitutionalism's appeal to norms, in which case, states of exception will always force a return to the arbitrariness of the founding instance (Schmitt 1985 and 1988). In trying to move further, it seems necessary to approach from a different angle the existential risk and the dialectical interplay between stability and the capacity for invention acknowledged by Preuss.

In this section, I want to consider two theorists who place risk, indeterminacy, and the tension between stability and radical invention or creation at the core of their theories of democracy. By pushing these themes to their most radical conclusions, Cornelius Castoriadis provides a point of entry into a deeper reflection on the questions posed in this chapter. From Castoriadis, I will proceed to argue that Claude Lefort's discussion of the symbolic dimension of democracy offers a more viable way to assess proceduralism against a deepened appreciation of the social preconditions of democracy.

Castoriadis's theory of the imaginary institution of society rests on the claim that all human societies are constituted by the interplay between the radical capacity to create new worlds of meaning and the institution of meaning in laws, social significations, practices, and works.[9] Most societies have occulted this self-creation by 'imputing it to an extrasocial source — in any case, one that is external to the effective activity of the effectively existing collectivity: the ancestors, the heroes, the gods, God, the laws of history or those of the market' (Castoriadis 1997c, 4). In contrast to such

---

[9] See the distinction that Castoriadis draws in *The Imaginary Institution of Society* between the 'instituted imaginary' and the 'instituting imaginary' (Castoriadis 1987, 108).

'heteronomous societies', a rupture in the closure of meaning marks democracy, ancient and modern. Despite salient differences between the ancient *poleis* and the modern polity, their common feature is the emergence of both philosophy (or reflection) and politics, both oriented toward a mutually implicating questioning of the already instituted forms of human society and belief.[10] Castoriadis thus arrives at a distinction relevant to our discussion between '*le* politique' and '*la* politique'. 'Le politique' refers to the 'dimension of the institution of society pertaining to *explicit power*, that is to the existence of *instances capable of formulating explicitly sanctionable injunctions*. This dimension is to be called the dimension of '*the political*'. It matters little, at this level, whether the instances in question are embodied by the whole tribe, by the elders, by the warriors, by a chief, by the *demos*, by a bureaucratic apparatus, etc'. (Castoriadis 1991, 156). By contrast, he writes

> ... politics (la politique) properly conceived, can be defined as the explicit collective activity which aims at being lucid (reflective and deliberate) and whose object is the institution of society as such. It is, therefore, *a coming into light*, though certainly partial, of the instituting [activity itself]; a dramatic, though by no means exclusive illustration of this is presented by the moments of revolution. The creation of politics takes place when the established institution of society is put into question as such and in its various aspects and dimensions (which rapidly leads to the discovery and the explicit elaboration, but also *a new and different articulation*, of solidarity), that is to say, when *another relation*, previously unknown, is created between the instituting and the instituted.
>
> (Castoriadis 1991, 160)[11]

Although actually existing societies may leave many things outside this questioning, as is the case in both the democratic Greek *poleis* and the modern liberal democracies, 'true politics' is 'from the start potentially radical as well as global' (Castoriadis 1991, 160). No institution, no hierarchy of preestablished difference, no foundation is exempt once explicit and unlimited interrogation emerges as an effective and actual social and individual practice.

Politics (*la* politique) is the essential activity of what Castoriadis calls the project of collective and individual autonomy: '*auto-nomos*, ... to make one's laws, knowing that one is doing so'. Here, Castoriadis makes an important distinction between his conception of autonomy and one of the dominant modern understandings of autonomy, that articulated by Kant: 'Autonomy does not consist in acting according to a law discovered in an immutable Reason and given once and for all. It is the unlimited

---

[10] See 'The Greek and the Modern Political Imaginary' (1997b, 84–107).
[11] Translation slightly amended. See Castoriadis (1988, 93).

self-questioning about the law and its foundations as well as the capacity, in light of this interrogation, *to make, to do* and *to institute* (therefore also, *to say*). Autonomy is the reflective activity of a reason creating itself in an endless movement, both as individual and social reason' (Castoriadis 1991, 164). The project of autonomy is inseparable from democracy. In its moment of birth and in its subsequent manifestations, democracy '*is not* the reign of law or of right, nor that of the 'rights of man', nor even the equality of citizens as such, but rather the ... questioning of the law in and through the actual activity of the community' (Castoriadis 1991, 164).

In an article responding to criticism by Habermas, Castoriadis extends this distinction between rule of law and type of activity into a distinction between democracy as 'procedure' and democracy as 'regime'.[12] He writes:

> We thus define politics as explicit and lucid activity that concerns the instauration of desirable institutions and democracy as the regime of explicit and lucid self-institution, as far as is possible, of the social institutions that depend on explicit collective activity. It is hardly necessary to add that this self-institution is a movement that does not stop, that it does not aim at a 'perfect society' ... but, rather, at a society that is as free and as just as possible.
> (Castoriadis 1997c, 5)

As such, democracy must be seen as a 'project', neither an unattainable ideal nor an achieved reality; and 'it is our free and historical recognition of the validity of [the project of autonomy], and the effectiveness of its partial realization up to now, that binds us to these claims ... ' (Castoriadis 1991, 32). The absence of any stronger defense of the normative value of autonomy beyond a will that is simultaneously a self-commitment and a self-limitation, points to a further dimension of democracy as regime: democracy is the 'tragic regime' because it is that form of social life that renounces extra-social support from gods or transcendent ideas and accepts its own responsibility and historical risk.

Judged by Castoriadis's stringent radical standard, 'rules like those (imperfectly) expressed by the 'rights of man', *nullem crimen poena sine lege*, due process of law, the plea of illegality or unconstitutionality, are an essential minimum' to maintaining the gains of democratic revolutions. Crucial as these historically emergent rules are, however, democracy cannot be defined in legalistic terms, because democracy as regime will push beyond the instituted rules at any given juncture; the kind of distinction that Ackerman wishes to draw between 'normal' and 'constitutional' politics thus yields to a more fluid notion of politics as an activity of elucidation

---

[12] Habermas's critique of Castoriadis is found in *The Philosophical Discourse of Modernity*, 327–35.

and invention. Hence, for example, Castoriadis argues that insofar as rights are to be criticised, critique should not aim at 'their allegedly 'formal' character (as is done by the Marxists) but, rather, at their *partial* character' (1997a, 408). Moreover, from the standpoint of a radical democrat for whom 'representation is a principle alien to democracy', amounting to an expropriation of political authority, activity, and initiative from the body of citizens (Castoriadis 1997a, 276), the modern liberal republic is also at best a partial realisation of democracy.

Whatever one thinks of the utopian (or dystopian) aspects of direct democracy, Castoriadis raises a point worth holding onto in the context of present debates about the European Union and democracy. Supranational European institutions are often accused of suffering a 'democratic deficit', an accusation that arises from a comparison with the liberal democratic forms of the member nation-states. To organise a discussion around this comparison, however, operates with the tacit assumptions that the substance of democracy is fixed once and for all and that the institutions of the existing national liberal democracies have already succeeded in embodying this substance.

Castoriadis's theory of democracy has the important effect of underscoring the volatility of democracy in relationship to the various discourses that attempt to ground it, whether one speaks of sanction in terms of the 'need for gods' (Arendt 1982, 184), the inviolability of individual right, or the objective reason of the constitution. Of course, each of these forms has functioned significantly at various times and in various places in the institution of the democratic imaginary, but democracy as that regime in which all questions may be asked supercedes each of these foundational logics. This volatility would seem to throw Castoriadis back upon Carl Schmitt's existentialist notion that the authentic collectivity must be brought face-to-face with its moment of founding, with some sort of primordial decision that brought the community into being. But that is not the case. Interminable questioning actually distances the autonomous society from its 'origins', from the kinds of foundation myths that seek to transfix social meaning. *Contra* Schmitt, the ability to put society and oneself into question is not won through some sort of privileged access to the primordial moment of indeterminacy. Rather, democracy is itself historical in the strong sense, in that it is the reflective activity of a reason creating itself in an unceasing movement. Or, in other words, 'once formed, the reflective instance plays an active and not predetermined role in the deployment and the formation of meaning, whatever its source (be it the radical creative imagination of the singular being or the reception of a socially created meaning)' (Castoriadis 1991, 165). Castoriadis incorporates an element of precisely that decisionism that has gained so much notoriety since Schmitt made it the centrepiece of his critique of the *Rechtsstaat*. But decision is not equivalent to irrationalism or a return to the 'vicious circle' of foundational politics. Although the guarantees of democracy are unavoidably 'contingent' and 'relative', their effectiveness depends on an unceasing deployment of collective activity aimed at explicit and lucid self-institution.

Understood as a project, this vision of democracy is neither utopian nor actual; it contains elements of a convincing phenomenological description of modern democracy, a sober assessment of the partial gains of the modern democratic process, and a strident normative demand for direct democracy. However, as a paradigm for political organisation in any foreseeable future, it makes demands on citizens that even Castoriadis admits are unlikely to be met. Large-scale democratic participation on the level of normal politics is virtually inconceivable in modern societies. Not only does the complexity of governance and state administration demand specialists and delegation, but relative affluence, consumerism, television, and leisure have produced a prevailing trend toward a passive, privatised citizenry. Moreover, in imagining 'a state of affairs in which man as a social being is able and willing to regard the institutions that rule his life as his own collective creations, and hence is able and willing to transform them each time he has the need or the desire' (Castoriadis 1988, 31), Castoriadis starts to sound a bit too weightless despite his emphasis on 'history' as event and advent. As one critic writes, 'Castoriadis lacks a textured way of conceiving and believing in the regularities of the human domain' (Khilnani 1989, 416). Claude Lefort, who was the co-founder with Castoriadis of the radical left-libertarian group Socialisme ou Barbarie in 1949 and a close collaborator until their split in the late 1950s, advances a more defensible theory of democracy that takes up many of the themes encountered in Castoriadis but tempers them with a more nuanced appreciation of the constraints that operate on really existing historical democracy.

Indeed, Lefort's work is best seen not as an attempt to provide liberal democracy with new or renewed normative foundations, but rather as an attempt to identify the social preconditions of democratic pluralism (Harrison 1995, 106). Lefort's emphasis on the social experience of democracy, on democracy as a 'form of society', leads him also to define democracy as a *'politeia'* or 'regime'. He insists 'the word is worth retaining only if we give it all the resonance it has when used in the expression "the *ancien regime*"'. Used in that sense, regime combines on the one hand the idea of a 'type of constitution', understood not in its juridical acceptation but in the sense of 'form of government' and 'structure of power', and on the other hand a 'style of existence or mode of life'. 'The expressions 'style of existence' or 'mode of life' should, for their part, evoke everything that is implied by an expression such as 'the American way of life', namely, those mores and beliefs that testify to the existence of a set of implicit norms determining notions of just and unjust, good and evil, desirable and undesirable, noble and ignoble' (Lefort 1988, 2–3).

For Lefort, the investigation of differences between regimes or forms of society 'prohibits the designation of politics (la politique) as a particular sector of social life' (Lefort 1986a, 8).[13] That is, Lefort does not view the political as a historical development imposed on a pre-existing social order, but as a formative principle of the social experience itself. Hence, Lefort's investigation implies ' the notion of a principle or an ensemble of generative principles of the relations that people maintain with each other and with the world' (Lefort 1986a, 8). The search for the generative principle of modern democracy leads Lefort back to a basic position advanced by Tocqueville. In Tocqueville, Lefort finds the argument that democracy is not simply a form of government, but is a form of society, as well as the further claim that what is most important about democracy is not what it 'does' but what it 'causes to be done', namely its power to arouse 'constant agitation in people' (Lefort 1986a, 201). The core of democracy lies not in a particular set of institutions acting in a certain way, but in the open, indeterminate, and unmasterable process that democracy generates. Lefort traces this power of democracy historically to a 'symbolic mutation' in the order of power, wherein power undergoes a radical 'disincorporation' during the early modern revolutionary struggle against Absolutism. Earlier social forms were dominated by symbolic logics of embodiment or incorporation. In the *ancien régime*, the monarch incorporated sovereign power, knowledge, and law; and in the unity of the king's body was incorporated the body politic. The radicalism of modern democracy lies in the novel disincorporation or disembodiment of power in the name of an egalitarian perception of social relations. The centre of modern democratic power is, in Lefort's phrase, a 'lieu vide', an 'empty place'. Democratic power may be contested, but no one can appropriate or incarnate it, nor can such power be 'represented'. One consequence of this view is to challenge accounts of modern democracy that focus on the embodiment of democratic sovereignty in the people or some other form of *pouvoir constituant*.[14]

With the disembodiment of power goes a dispersal of power, knowledge, and law; law, knowledge, and power enter into contestatory relations. A single logic or representation cannot master them, and they are always in *excess* in relation to each other. A double phenomenon marks the political originality of democracy. First, power, law, and knowledge are constantly and interminably in search of a foundation, a situation that invites us to

---

[13] Lefort also uses the distinction between 'la politique' and 'le politique'. See 'Permanence du théologico-politique?' (1986a, 256) where he associates 'le politique' with the 'generative principles' of a form of society.

[14] Lefort writes of the institution of universal suffrage, at the 'very moment when popular sovereignty is assumed to manifest itself, when the people is assumed to actualize itself by expressing its will, ... social interdependence breaks down and ... the citizen is abstracted from all the networks in which his social life develops and becomes a mere statistic' (1988, 18–19). Superficially, this resembles Hegel's criticism of universal suffrage (Hegel 1991, 350–1), but unlike Hegel, Lefort does not contrast the insubstantiality of the 'people' to something more real or substantial.

'replace the notion of a regime governed by laws, of a legitimate power, by the notion of a regime founded upon the legitimacy of a debate as to what is legitimate — a debate which is necessarily without any guarantor and without any end' (Lefort 1986a, 39). Insofar as legitimacy is as much a restriction on the exercise of power as it is an authorisation of power, it belongs to the specific nature of democracy that any form of limitation (and empowerment) must be determined through debate itself. Secondly, democracy in its liberal form institutes an original form of society in which social division is not occluded, as it was, for example, in Soviet Russia or Nazi Germany. Rather, social division is the essence of its political logic. Once the markers of certainty that situated people in relation to each other have been lost, the conflict of opinion and the debate over rights become interminable.

## 3. PROCEDURALISM AND DEMOCRACY

From this excursus into the thought of Castoriadis and Lefort, what lessons might we draw for the discussion of the relationship between democracy and proceduralism?

First of all, Lefort's insight into the historical originality of democracy strongly challenge a proceduralist conception, because it suggests that rights and the procedures by which they are to be protected cannot be known except through the debates by which their meaning is put up for question. Take John Rawls's position by contrast. Rawls writes, 'A liberal conception meets the urgent political requirement to fix, once and for all, the content of basic rights and liberties. ... Doing this takes those guarantees off the political agenda' (Rawls 1999, 442). In seeking to remove rights from politics, Rawls mistakes the nature of rights. For in searching for a system of rights that belong once and for all to citizens, Rawls neglects the fact that as soon as nobody is able to occupy the position, at a distance from all others, from which he would have the authority to grant or ratify rights, it becomes impossible to detach the statement of right from the utterance of right: 'Rights are not simply the object of a declaration, it is their essence to be declared' (Lefort 1986b, 257). And in being formulated, rights-language invites the demand for the reformulation of rights. Following a basic insight from Hannah Arendt, Lefort argues that what was fundamental to the great eighteenth-century declarations of rights was their enunciation of *the right to have rights*. This opened a dynamic that surpasses any specific formulation of rights, whether one speaks of the 'bourgeois' rights denounced by Karl Marx in the early nineteenth century or Rawls's search for 'the most extensive total system of equal basic liberties compatible with a similar system of liberty for all'. (Rawls 1971, 250). In short, there is no way to remove rights from politics, understood precisely as the relation of human speech to the generative principle of this particular form of society.

Lefort's views also challenge the conception of proceduralist democracy proposed by Habermas. It is important to distinguish clearly Habermas's use of proceduralism from the meaning assigned to proceduralism in the American debate. At stake in the latter discussion are the procedures that protect rights and liberties from encroachments by other individuals, communities, or the state. For Habermas, who rejects the ontological individualism implied by liberalism in favor of a theory of communicative intersubjectivity, proceduralism refers to the means whereby communicative interaction may be stabilised and routinised. Habermas's concern is to establish boundaries of legitimate action as well as regularised conduits of communication, whereby individuals, publics, and governments within complex pluralistic polities may interact, exchange information and opinion, and contribute to the formation of a democratic will. In short, for Habermas, proceduralism is best understood as a vital part of democratic legitimation, and less as a defensive strategy against democracy. Undoubtedly, Habermas's project bears some resemblance to Lefort and Castoriadis. Castoriadis and Lefort's repudiation of foundational philosophical argument leads them both to a great emphasis on civic discourse. This is obviously central for Lefort's theory of rights. Likewise, for Castoriadis, the absence of an extrasocial foundation for democratic society places it 'under the obligation of *logon didonai* — of giving account and reason for whatever we say and do publicly' (Castoriadis 1991, 29–30). So, he argues, the value of autonomy cannot be 'grounded' or 'proven'; at most, autonomy can be 'reasonably argued for and argued about' once it has emerged (Castoriadis 1991, 172). This postfoundationalist recognition of the discursive and agonistic dimensions of civic life leads him to accentuate the terms of ancient Greek democracy: *paideia*, or education in the practices of citizenship, and *phronesis*, or prudential wisdom.

Castoriadis and Lefort's arguments also imply a move beyond liberal individualism in that they both emphasise the role of social and linguistic forces in the formation of the individual subject. In this sense, their critiques of the philosophy of the subject are not too remote from Habermas's own efforts to move from 'subject-centered' to 'communicative reason' (Habermas 1987, 294–326).[15] A significant difference from Habermas immediately presents itself, however. Habermas's search for the linguistic pre-conditions of consensus renounces metaphysics, but in fact he aspires

---

[15] It must be noted, however, that Castoriadis frequently criticises Habermas's 'intersubjective' model from the standpoint of Castoriadis's psychoanalytically informed understanding of the relationship between psyche and society as well as his commitment to a specific theory of mental representation that gives primacy to pictorial, over linguistic representation.

to foundational validity for certain forms of speech and action understood now as procedures. Hence, Habermas writes,

> According to this proceduralist view, practical reason withdraws from universal human rights or from the concrete ethical life of a specific community into the rules of discourse and forms of argumentation that derive their normative content from the validity-basis of action oriented to reaching understanding, and ultimately from the structure of linguistic communication.
>
> (Habermas 1998, 246)

As this passage suggests, Habermas attempts to ground the framing rules of democratic discourse through a kind of quasi-transcendental argument about the structure of communication.[16] Habermas starts out from the premise that no procedure emerges except from within a debate about procedure, but he then attempts to remove procedures from their embeddedness in politics.

It goes without saying that societies create more or less stable institutions that embody values and regulate social interactions. Any theory that emphasises the indeterminacy of democracy has the further obligation to explain the stability that does emerge and the self-limitations that democratic societies create for themselves. This issue cannot detain us here, despite its importance, though I hope enough has been said to indicate the ways in which neither Castoriadis nor Lefort are celebrants of radical indeterminacy *à la* Jean-Luc Nancy or Gilles Deleuze.[17] Castoriadis rejects 'mere indetermination', arguing instead of democratic society's capacity to create 'other *determinations*, new laws, new domains of lawfulness' (Castoriadis 1997a, 308). Lefort emphasises the stabilising effects of a historically emergent democratic *mise en scène* (Lefort 1986a, 20). Nonetheless, their understanding of democracy does suggest a forceful critique of the kind of political positivism that underpins proceduralist views. From the vantage point offered by Castoriadis and Lefort, it can be said that a proceduralist understanding of politics errs most fundamentally in its attempt to fix the meaning of democracy and rights within a specific set of positive institutions.

This is a critique that differs significantly from that of communitarians who would argue that proceduralism's flaw lies in its elevation of individual rights over substantive communities and judicial review over majoritarian decisions. Indeed, it is an argument that applies forcefully to communitarian arguments as well. No set of communal values can act as the bedrock of a democracy because once all grounds for political authority are open

[16] On the question of whether Habermas's theory is a transcendental theory, see further Ingram (1994, 226–7).
[17] The shortcomings of Nancy's notion of political indeterminacy are explored in Norris (2000, esp 284–5).

to interrogation, a community exposes its own traditions and substantive commitments to questioning. Castoriadis makes the argument against positivism in a position that stands at the farthest reaches of modernity's demystification of its institutions, such that institutions become nothing more than the human imagination that makes and remakes them. Lefort challenges positivism by shifting his inquiry to the level of the social experience of democracy. The specificity of modern democracy, in his view, is that the disappearance of the body of the king and the disembodiment of the social that follows from it opens the political scene for a permanent demanding, a permanent displacement of these demands from one focal point to another, a transformative action exercised transversally on individuals and institutions, a permanent tension between laws as forces of social conservation and demands for rights as the speech acts of a society that constitutes itself in the search for itself.

As a symbolic matrix of social relations, democracy is always in excess of the institutions through which it manifests itself. In a passage that warrants quotation at length, Lefort explores this relationship:

> [Rights] do not exist in the same way as positive institutions, whose actual elements can be listed, even though it is certainly true that they animate institutions. Their effectiveness stems from the allegiance that is given them, and this allegiance is bound up with a way of being in society, which cannot be measured by the mere preservation of acquired benefits. In short, rights cannot be dissociated from the awareness of rights. ... But it is no less true that awareness of rights is all the more widespread when they are declared, when power is said to guarantee them, when liberties are made visible by laws. Thus the awareness of right and its institutionalization are ambiguously related. On the one hand, this institutionalization involves, with the development of a body of law and a caste of specialists, the possibility of a concealment of the mechanisms indispensable to the effective exercise of rights by the interested parties; on the other hand, it provides the necessary support for an awareness of rights.
> (Lefort 1986b, 260)

Lefort's warnings against trying to capture the inventions of democracy within a particular set of positive institutions or treating power as a positive fact were first directed against Stalinism, of which he was an early and influential French critic. Stalinism attempted to cover over social division through the figure of the 'People-as-One' and the embodiment of all power in the omnipotent leader. The same temptation is, of course, present in ethnic or racial nationalism. In fact, Lefort views these examples as extreme expressions of a temptation that belongs intrinsically to democracy, namely, the desire to reverse the 'indetermination that was born from the loss of the substance of the body politic' (Lefort 1986b, 306). Hence, it is also latent in the civic idea of the nation-state formed by the constituent power of the people. Lefort's insight may even be extended to current discussions of the

European integration process. It has become a commonplace to note that there is no European *demos* (Bellamy 2001, 60). For some Eurosceptics like the German political philosopher Hermann Lübbe, this rules out the possibility of a 'United States of Europe' because 'a European people has no political existence and, while there is no reason to think that an experience of mutual belonging among Europeans analogous to that which unites a people is inconceivable, at the present time there are no foreseeable circumstances under which a legitimacy-founding European will could take shape' (Lübbe quoted in Habermas 1998, 152). On the other hand, if we accept J.H.H. Weiler's argument, then with or without a European *pouvoir constituant*, the phase of European unification opened by Maastricht has in fact already recapitulated the logic of identity whereby indeterminacy is occluded. For at least in rhetoric, 'Maastricht appropriates the deepest symbols of statehood: European citizenship, defense, foreign policy — the rhetoric of a superstate. We all know that these are the emptiest and weakest provisions of the Treaty, but they undermine the ethics of supranationalism'. Weiler contends that Maastricht swung the European integration process toward the ideal of 'unity', whereby the 'exclusivist ethos of statal authority' and the exclusivist idea of the 'people' begin to reemerge at the European level (Weiler 1999, 258).[18] Certainly the draft Constitution for Europe submitted to the European Council meeting in Thessaloniki on 18 July 2003 does not deviate from that trend. The Constitutional Convention gestured toward the pluralistic model of political foundation represented by the eastern European Round Tables insofar as the Convention made efforts to reverse the lack of transparency and democratic input that had typified earlier intergovernmental conferences through broader consultation of other EU bodies and groups within civil society. But in essence, the Constitutional convention sought its legitimation in the old notion of the *pouvoir constituant*, this time reconfigured as the 'peoples of Europe' 'united' in their 'diversity'. Of course, this language might have been a calculation based on a sober awareness of the utility and virtual necessity of invoking the *fiction* of a European *demos* as the source of foundational legitimacy, as well as recognition of the paradox that the *demos* that is called upon to accept the constitution is constituted legally by that constitution (Weiler 2002, 567). Underscoring the rhetorical function of this appeal to the 'peoples of Europe' is the fact noted by Castiglione and Bellamy in their contribution to this volume that the draft Constitution is really a treaty subject to agreement by the member states in an intergovernmental conference rather than a constitutional document in the strict sense. Although here, one must also note that the emergence by early August 2003 of calls

---

[18] The paradoxical relationship between growing internationalism *within* Europe and a strengthening of 'Eurocentrism, a sort of higher xenophobia' is a recurring theme in the essays collected in Cesarani and Fulbrook (1996).

for national referenda on the draft Constitution suggests that diverse forces in European politics might mobilise the logic of the *pouvoir constituant* in ways that were not desired by the national and European élites who steered the constitutional Convention.[19]

The phase of unification opened by Maastricht and continued by the recent Convention has stifled, at least for now, the competition between the ideal of unity and that of 'community', by which Weiler means an arrangement 'premised on limiting, or sharing, sovereignty in a select albeit growing number of fields, on recognizing, and even celebrating, the reality of *interdependence* ... ' (Weiler 1999, 92). This idea of community, Weiler asserts, is the 'unique contribution of the European Community to the civilization of international relations'. It civilises intra-European 'statal intercourse', deriving as it does 'from that very tension among the state actors and between each state actor and the community. It also derives from each state actor's need to reconcile the reflexes and ethos of the 'sovereign' national state with new modes of discourse and a new discipline of solidarity' (Weiler 1999, 93).

Weiler's lament for the eclipse of this community idea echoes the efforts of numerous political theorists across a broad political spectrum to imagine what Jean Bethke Elshtain calls a 'politics without strong sovereignty' (Elshtain 1991, 1376). This is the burden too of Sandel's recent work, where he argues for a 'dispersal of sovereignty' to a 'multiplicity of communities and political bodies — some more, some less extensive than nations — among which sovereignty is diffused' (Sandel 1996, 345). It is also a basic impulse of Habermas's discourse theory of democracy, which rejects both the republican-communitarian and liberal-proceduralist perspectives, both of which insist that 'state and society must be conceived in terms of a whole and its parts, where the whole is constituted either by a sovereign citizenry or by a constitution' (Habermas 1998, 251). In opposition, Habermas proposes the 'image of a *decentered* society', the abandonment of a singular logic of power, and the adoption of a relational model wherein 'sovereignty need neither be concentrated in the people in a concretistic manner nor banished into the anonymous agencies established by the constitution' (Habermas 1998, 251). Inspired by Habermas, Andrew Arato and Jean Cohen likewise call for a politics of civil society that must involve a 'self-limiting' process of democratisation, a process that resists temptations to construct politics in terms of strong, monopolistic sovereign power, whether construed as nation-statism or supranational union (Arato and Cohen 1992).

---

[19] However the debate over the draft Constitution plays out, the level of involvement of the 'peoples of Europe' can hardly go anywhere but up. The online news service *EUobserver* reported on 25 July 2003 that of 25,000 Europeans polled immediately after the submission of the draft Constitution at Thessaloniki, 55% did not even know that there had been a constitutional convention.

From a poststructuralist perspective, Chantal Mouffe evokes the ideal of 'post-modern' pluralism:

> Our understanding of radical democracy ... postulates the very impossibility of a final realization of democracy. It affirms that the unresolvable tension between the principles of equality and liberty is the very condition for the preservation of the indeterminacy and undecidability which is constitutive of modern democracy. Moreover, it constitutes the principal guarantee against any attempt to realize a final closure that would result in the elimination and the negation of democracy.
>
> (Mouffe 1992, 13)

Such pluralism, in the words of Kirstie McClure, demands a critique of 'unitary, monolithic or totalizing conceptions of the political domain', as well as resistance to 'constructions of political identity and subjectivity that take state institutions as the principal sites, and state power as the primary object, of political struggle' (McClure 1992, 115, 120).

Lefort contributes significantly to this critique of unitary notions of politics, sovereignty, and power by providing a compelling description of the symbolic function of democratic power and by shifting our attention to the social experience of democracy. Through signifying the 'empty place' of democratic power and the disembodiment of the social, Lefort suggests ways to understand the historical process whereby modern civil society has detached itself from the state and attained by this action an abundant, pluralistic, and self-questioning experience of itself. The excess of democratic society in relationship to its institutions urges us toward a more acutely historical understanding of that relationship. It replaces the punctuated rhythm suggested by Ackerman's suggestion of alteration between 'constitutional' and 'normal' politics with an appreciation for the ongoing constitution of political subjectivity and citizenship as well as innovation within institutions by reminding us that democratic invention belongs not only to founding acts but to political practices embedded in everyday life. It challenges us to look beyond specific institutions toward the conditions whereby the originary social division opened by democracy may continue to develop.

If no particular institution can embody democracy, it also means that no particular form monopolises democracy. Lefort's perspective suggests that democracy understood as 'regime' or form of society has no intrinsic or necessary relationship to a specific set of institutions cast at a specific level of community or polity. This should be an important theoretical point to remember for both Eurosceptics who lament the demise of the nation-state and Europhiles who dream of reconstituting the paradigm of nation-state democracy at the European level. Lefort's description of the symbolic dimension of democratic power and the mobility unleashed by the right to have rights lends substantial weight to an important point made by Andrew Arato about the normative 'need to combine different forms and types of democracy'. If it is impossible to fully embody the elements of democratic society in the empirical institutions of public life, then it is important to acknowledge that all types of democratic institutions involve forms of exclusion, limits on discussion, sources of asymmetry among participants. However, writes Arato, 'the forms that non-democracy takes within various types of democracy are significantly different. Thus in principle, other things being equal, it is highly desirable to combine different types of democratic institutions and processes (direct and representative, centralistic and federal, civil and political) in a given constitutional framework' (Arato 1994, 171–2).

Measured against this call for a multiplication of types of democracy, the present situation in the European Union is ambiguous. The EU has responded to the legitimacy gap revealed by the struggles to ratify the Treaty on European Union in 1992–93 by accentuating the importance and desirability of enhanced democratic processes, a shift that may be measured not only in rhetoric but perhaps in a moderate trend toward a heightened role of the European Parliament in the EU's decision-making structure (Eriksen and Fossum 2002, 412). Nonetheless, among European populations, the EU continues to suffer a 'legitimacy deficit' (Bellamy and Castiglione, see chapter two this volume) that reflects the persistent distance of the EU from the kinds of liberal democratic institutions that continue to enjoy quite high levels of popular legitimacy within the member states. At the same time, however, numerous observers have emphasised that the EU's institutions are in fact producing a *sui generis* political form characterised by Bellamy and Castiglione as 'a polycentric 'polity' possessing a multilevel governance 'regime' (Bellamy and Castiglione, see chapter two this volume) or, as Andrew Moravcsik writes: 'The EU is not a system of parliamentary sovereignty but one of separation of powers. Power is divided vertically among the Commission, Council, Parliament and Court, and horizontally among local, national and transnational levels — requiring concurrent majorities for action' (Moravcsik 2002, 610). This institutional pluralism has evolved not as the result of a blueprint or the unfolding realisation of the foundational moment, but through a contingent process of compromise among different levels and parties. From this vantage point, the effort to create a European constitution provokes a complicated response. On the one hand, one can readily understand Habermas's insistence that Europe needs a constitution in order to ensure the transparency, coherence, and intelligibility needed if a political system is to generate enhanced opportunities for democratic participation (Habermas 2001). On the other hand, there are well-founded concerns that a formal definition of competencies will freeze a set of relations that are but the latest products of an ongoing negotiation. Weiler worries that a formal constitution will 'chill' the 'constitutional dialogue' that has developed among different decision-making entities and enabled a reasonably flexible articulation of the EU's institutional structure (Weiler 2002, 576). In similar spirit, Richard Kuper rejects the idea of a 'founding moment' and urges his readers to embrace 'a view of an on-going, shifting process, hopefully of constructive learning and experimentation. One needs to conceptualize it precisely as constitution *building*, as an *on-going constitutionalizing process*, in which, *as a goal*, the EU can come to be perceived as a community created by its citizens' (Kuper 2000, 165).

A formal constitution risks the creation of a split between a *fundamentalist* constitutional camp whose appeal to the higher legality of the constitution would aim at the depoliticisation of conflicts and those who struggle to keep the constitutionalising process within the domain of politics, a tension that is familiar to any observer of American politics. If the constitutionalising process is to remain political *and* contribute to the development of democracy at the European level, then it must go hand-in-hand with the process of developing an 'active European citizenry' (Kuper 2000, 172), a 'trans-national European subject of politics' (Bellamy 2001, 64). Here again the present situation is ambiguous. The absence of a European public sphere, lamented in the early 1990s by commentators like Dieter Grimm (Grimm 1992), has been offset to some extent by the emergence of European public interest organisations as well as forums and proposals aimed at promoting the development of a European public (Bellamy 2001, 63). The EU has enhanced its openness to interest groups that have organised themselves at a trans-national level, but it bears noting that the relationship between civil society organisations and EU institutions has a tendency toward the integration of contention. This is seen, for example, in non-occupational interest groups, such as ecologists, which upon reaching Brussels are, according to Tarrow and Imig, 'likely to take advantage of the lobbying opportunities that the European Union makes available rather than to take to the streets' (Imig and Tarrow 2001, 38). Perhaps the most striking example of this integrative effect is in trade union organisation at the European level; with the union organisations slow to move outside their traditional national frameworks, advocates of the Europeanisation of trade unionism came to rely heavily on incentives and resources from EU institutions. 'The result', write Martin and Ross, 'was that European trade unionism found itself restructured along lines that were only partly its doing and not always clearly to its advantage. ... The [European Trade Union Confederation], in other words, has developed from the top down rather than as a mass organization built from below' (Martin and Ross 2001, 74–5). For most forms of contentious politics, domestic political issues remain the dominant focal point and the nation-state the dominant space. Indeed, as Imig and Tarrow have found in a careful study of European contentious politics from 1984 to 1997, even the overwhelming majority of protests against EU policies attacked domestic rather than European targets and occurred within the domestic rather than the transnational political sphere (Imig and Tarrow 2001, 35–6). Still, Imig and Tarrow discern a tendency toward transnational co-operation among domestic actors, as well as collective European protests, although they do resist the conclusion that a new era of transnational social movements has arrived as a popular response to Europe's democratic deficit. 'Rather than seeing an immediate and direct displacement of contentious politics from the national to the supranational levels', they write, 'we are more likely to see a range of social movement approaches to the European level of governance' (Imig and Tarrow 2001, 47). In this sense, popular political contention may be emerging as a mirror of the polycentric and multilevel governance regime of the EU. There are encouraging signs of the development of new democratic practices at the supranational level, but it remains to be seen just how far Europe will develop as a space for the non-institutionalised public acts and everyday political practices that are vital to democracy as a social form.

## 4.   CONCLUSION

The perspective advanced in this chapter suggests a necessarily paradoxical conclusion, that democracy is both more deeply rooted and more fragile than is indicated by the normative accounts offered by either republican-communitarians or liberal-proceduralists. It is more deeply rooted because democracy is linked to a metaphysical event, a tear in the tissue of human belief and symbolic order. No positive description can fully account for the depth of that tear or for the generative forces of the world brought into being by the collapse of certainties. By the same token, democracy is more fragile, because it stands only in relation to itself. It is not the necessary outcome of an historical process nor does it rest on a transcendental foundation, but depends on the power of speech and the will to exercise, contest and claim rights. The democratic gains in the EU over the last decade are real enough that at least for now the dire prognoses of a democratic deficit in the EU have lost much of their purchase; nonetheless, the gains have been sufficiently hesitant and the process of integration is still subject to so many different forces and alternative directions that European democrats must remain vigilant and active.

Yet to measure the deficit of the European Union against the alleged democratic plenitude of the nation-state, or to rest a critique on a dubious dichotomy between democracy and proceduralism, would be an error. Rather, what seems at issue is a more fundamental crisis of 'democracy'. Society's openness to further democratic invention, to further specifications of autonomy, seems to be on the wane in the face of political apathy and privatisation. Exhorting people to connect with their communities, as Sandel does, or trying to make democratic legitimacy less dependent upon the specific civic virtues of citizens, as Habermas does, seem inadequate. There seems to be a crisis in the very value of autonomy itself, exposed but not caused by the collapse of the metanarratives of emancipation that have animated two centuries of democratic struggle. Castoriadis, the radical champion of democratic autonomy, deserves the last word:

> Autonomy is an objective that we want [*voulons*] for itself — but also for something else. Without that, we fall back into Kantian formalism, as well as into its impasses. We will [*voulons*] the autonomy of society — as well as of individuals — both for itself and in order to *make/do* [*faire*] things. To make/do *what?* This is perhaps the most weighty interrogation to which the contemporary situation gives rise: this *what* is related to *contents*, to substantive values — and this is what appears to be in crisis in the society in which we live. We are not seeing — or are seeing very little of — the emergence of new contents for people's lives, new orientations that would be synchronous with the tendency — which, itself, actually appears in many sectors of society — toward an autonomy, a liberation *vis-à-vis* inherited rules. Nevertheless, we may think that, without the emergence of such new contents, these tendencies will be able neither to expand nor to deepen and to become universalized.
>
> (Castoriadis 1997a, 315)

Indeed.

## 5.  REFERENCES

Ackerman, Bruce. 1991, *We the People 1. Foundations*, Cambridge, MA: Harvard University Press.

Arato, Andrew and Jean L. Cohen. 1992, *Civil Societies and Political Theory*, Cambridge, MA: MIT Press.

Arato, Andrew. 1994, Dilemmas Arising from the Power to Create Constitutions in Eastern Europe. In *Constitutionalism, Identity, Difference, and Legitimacy. Theoretical Perspectives*, edited by Michel Rosenfeld, Durham: Duke University Press.

Arendt, Hannah. 1982, Reprint. *On Revolution*, New York: Penguin Books Ltd. Original Edition, 1963.

Bellamy, Richard. 2001, The 'Right to Have Rights': Citizenship Practice and the Political Constitution of the EU. In *Citizenship and Governance in the European Union*, edited by Richard Bellamy and Alex Warleigh, London: Continuum.

Brubaker, Rogers. 1992, *Citizenship and Nationhood in France and Germany*, Cambridge, MA: Harvard University Press.

Castoriadis, Cornelius. 1987, *The Imaginary Institution of Society*, translated by Kathleen Blamey, Cambridge, MA: MIT Press.

—— 1988, 'Pouvoir, politique, autonomie', *Revue de Metaphysique et de morale*, 93; 81–104.

—— 1991, *Philosophy, Politics, Autonomy. Essays in Political Philosophy*, edited by David Ames Curtis, Oxford: Oxford University Press.

—— 1997a, *The Castoriadis Reader*, edited by David Ames Curtis, Oxford: Blackwell.

—— 1997b, *World in Fragments. Writings on Politics, Society, Psychoanalysis, and the Imagination*, edited and translated by David Ames Curtis, Stanford: Stanford University Press.

—— 1997c, 'Democracy as Procedure and Democracy as Regime', *Constellations*, 4, 1–18.

Cesarini, David and Mary Fulbrook, (ed), 1996, *Citizenship, Nationality and Migration in Europe*, New York: Routledge.

Deleuze, Gilles and Felix Guattari. 1983, *Anti-Oedipus: Capitalism and Schizophrenia*, translated by Robert Hurley, Mark Seem, and Helen R. Lane, Minneapolis: University of Minnesota Press.

Elshtain, Jean Bethke. 1991, 'Sovereign God, Sovereign State, Sovereign Self', *Notre Dame Law Review*, 66; 1355–84.

Eriksen, Erik Oddvar and John Erik Fossum. 2002, 'Democracy through Strong Publics in the European Union? *Journal of Common Market Studies*, 40, 401–22.

Furet, François. 1981, *Interpreting the French Revolution*, translated by Elborg Forster, Cambridge: Cambridge University Press.

Grimm, Dieter. 1992, 'Der Mangel an europäischer Demokratie', *Der Spiegel* 43, 57–9.

Habermas, Jürgen. 1987, *The Philosophical Discourse of Modernity. Twelve Lectures*, translated by Frederick G. Lawrence. Cambridge: MIT Press.

—— 1998, *The Inclusion of the Other. Studies in Political Theory*, edited by Ciaran Cronin and Pablo De Greiff, Cambridge, MA: MIT Press.

—— 2001, 'Why Europe needs a Constitution', *New Left Review*, 11, 5–26.

Harrison, Paul. 1995, The Turn to Political Liberalism in Contemporary French Thought. In *Forms of Commitment: Intellectuals in Contemporary France*, edited by Brian Nelson, Melbourne: Monash University Press.

Hegel, G.W.F. 1991, *Elements of the Philosophy of Right*, edited by Allen W. Wood and translated by T.M. Knox, New York: Cambridge University Press.

Imig, Doug and Sidney Tarrow. 2001, Mapping the Europeanization of Contention: Evidence from a Quantitative Data Analysis. In *Contentious Europeans. Protest and Politics in an Emerging Polity*, edited by Doug Imig and Sidney Tarrow, New York: Rowman & Littlefield.

Ingram, David. 1994, Foucault and Habermas on the Subject of Reason. In *The Cambridge Companion to Foucault*, edited by Gary Gutting, New York: Cambridge University Press.

Kantorowicz, Ernst. 1957, *The King's Two Bodies. A Study in Medieval Political Theology*, Princeton: Princeton University Press.

Khilnani, Sunil. 1989, Castoriadis and Modern Political Theory. In *Autonomie et autotransformation de la société*, edited by Giovanni Busino, et. al, Genève: Libraire Droz.

Kriegel, Blandine. 1995, *The State and the Rule of Law*, translated by Marc A. LePain and Jeffrey C. Cohen, Princeton: Princeton University Press.

Kuper, Richard. 2000, Democratization: A Constitutionalizing Process. In *Democratizing the European Union. Issues for the Twenty-First Century*, edited by Catherine Hoskyns and Michael Newman, Manchester: Manchester University Press.

Lefort, Claude. 1986a, *Essais sur le politique. XIXᵉ–XXᵉ siècles*, Paris: Seuil.

—— 1986b, *The Political Forms of Modern Society. Bureaucracy, Democracy, Totalitarianism*, edited by John B. Thompson, Cambridge, MA: MIT Press.

—— 1988, *Democracy and Political Theory*, translated by David Macey, Minneapolis: University of Minnesota Press.

Martin, Andrew and George Ross. 2001, Trade Union Organizing at the European Level: The Dilemma of Borrowed Resources. In *Contentious Europeans. Protest and Politics in an Emerging Polity*, edited by Doug Imig and Sidney Tarrow, New York: Rowman & Littlefield.

McClure, Kirstie. 1992, On the Subject of Rights: Pluralism, Plurality and Political Identity. In *Dimensions of Radical Democracy. Pluralism, Citizenship, Community*, edited by Chantal Mouffe, London: Verso.

Moravcsik, Andrew. 2002, 'In Defence of the "Democratic Deficit": Reassessing Legitimacy in the European Union', *Journal of Common Market Studies*, 40, 603–24.

Mouffe, Chantal. 1992, Democratic Politics Today. In *Dimensions of Radical Democracy. Pluralism, Citizenship, Community*, edited by Chantal Mouffe, London: Verso.

Nancy, Jean-Luc. 1991, *The Inoperative Community*, edited by Peter Connor and translated by Peter Connor, Lisa Garbus, Michael Holland, and Simona Sawhney, Minneapolis: University of Minnesota Press, 1991.

Norris, Andrew. 2000, 'Jean-Luc Nancy and the Myth of the Common', *Constellations*, 7, 272–95.

Poltier, Hugues. 1993, La pensée du politique de Claude Lefort, un pensée de la liberté. In *La démocratie à l'oeuvre. Autour de Claude Lefort*, edited by Claude Habib and Claude Mouchard, Paris: Editions Esprit.

Preuss, Ulrich K. 1994, Constitutional Powermaking of the New Polity: Some Deliberations on the Relations Between Constituent Power and the Constitution. In *Constitutionalism, Identity, Difference, and Legitimacy. Theoretical Perspectives*, edited by Michel Rosenfeld, Durham: Duke University Press.

—— 1995, *Constitutional Revolution: The Link between Constitutionalism and Progress*, translated by Deborah Lucas Schneider, Atlantic Highlands: Humanities Press.

Rawls, John. 1971, *A Theory of Justice*, Cambridge, MA: Harvard University Press.

—— 1999, *Collected Papers*, edited by Samuel Freeman, Cambridge, MA: Harvard University Press.

—— 1982, *Liberalism and the Limits of Justice*, Cambridge: Cambridge University Press.

Sandel, Michael, 1996, *Democracy's Discontent. America in Search of a Public Philosophy*, Cambridge, MA: Harvard University Press.

Scheuerman, William. 1997, 'The Rule of Law at Century's End', *Political Theory*, 25, 740–60.

Schmitt, Carl. 1985, *The Crisis of Parliamentary Democracy*, translated by Ellen Kennedy. Cambridge, MA: MIT Press.

—— 1988, *Political Theology. Four Chapters on the Concept of Sovereignty*, translated by George Schwab, Cambridge, MA: MIT Press.

Weiler, J.H.H. 1999, *The Constitution of Europe. 'Do the New Clothes Have an Emperor?' and Other Essays on European Integration*, Cambridge: Cambridge University Press.

—— 2002, 'A Constitution for Europe? Some Hard Choices', *Journal of Common Market Studies*, 40, 563–80.